DEFENCE AGAINST DISASTER

DEFENCE AGAINST DISASTER

IN ACCURATELY DETERMINING
THE POSITIONS OF THE COMPANIONS
AFTER THE DEATH OF THE PROPHET

BY
QADI ABU BAKR IBN AL-'ARABI

WITH COMMENTARY BY
MUHIBB AD-DIN AL-KHATIB

TRANSLATED BY
AISHA ABDURRAHMAN BEWLEY

Classical and Contemporary Books on Islam and Sufism

Copyright © Aisha Bewley

2nd edition 2020 CE/1441 AH

3rd edition 2026 CE/1447 AH with the Introduction of Shaykh Dr. Abdalqadir as-Sufi

DEFENCE AGAINST DISASTER

IN ACCURATELY DETERMINING THE POSITIONS OF THE COMPANIONS AFTER THE DEATH OF THE PROPHET

Published by: Diwan Press Ltd.
311 Allerton Road
Bradford
BD15 7HA
UK

Website: www.diwanpress.com
E-mail: info@diwanpress.com

All rights reserved. No part of this publication may be reproduced, stored in any retrieval system or transmitted in any form or by any means, electronic, mechanical, photocopying, recording or otherwise without the prior permission of the publishers.

Translated by: Aisha Bewley

A catalogue record of this book is available from the British Library.

ISBN-13: 978-1-908892-21-8 (casebound)
ISBN-13: 978-1-908892-22-5 (paperback)
ISBN-13: 978-1-908892-23-2 (ebook)

Contents

INTRODUCTION BY SHAYKH DR. ABDALQADIR AS-SUFI	I
FOREWORD	XI
QADI ABU BAKR IBN AL-'ARABI	XIX
His early life	xix
His journey from Seville	xx
His ship sinks	xxi
Passing through Egypt	xxiii
His arrival in Jerusalem and eastern Jordan	xxiv
His visit to Damascus	xxv
His arrival in Baghdad and devoting himself to the quest of knowledge	xxvi
Meeting Abu Hamid al-Ghazali	xxix
Hajj and return to Baghdad	xxxi
His return by way of Damascus, Palestine and Alexandria	xxxi
His arrival in Seville	xxxii
DEFENCE AGAINST DISASTER	1
THE BACK-BREAKING DISASTER	3
Defence	10
DEFAMATION OF 'UTHMAN	35
Defence	36

DISASTER – THE BATTLE OF THE CAMEL	139
Defence	143
DISASTER – THE BATTLE OF SIFFIN	157
Defence	159
DISASTER – THE ARBITRATION	170
Defence	175
DISASTER – CLAIMS MADE ABOUT 'ALI IBN ABI TALIB ﷺ	181
Defence	185
DEFAMATION OF AL-HASAN AND MU'AWIYA, AL-HUSAYN AND YAZID	199
Defence	200
DISASTERS AND DEFAMATIONS – SUMMARY	264
Defence	266
REFERENCES	273

INTRODUCTION
BY SHAYKH DR. ABDALQADIR AS-SUFI

SEVERAL YEARS ago during the Visit in Madinah I visited the quarter of the bookshops. While browsing, I suddenly became aware of a group of young men who were grabbing copies of one edition with such speed and excitement that I saw it disappearing before my eyes. So intrigued was I that I took a copy myself and bought it at the same time. For I quickly realised that the work which had caused such a commotion was not only an Islamic classic but an important work by one of the Imams of the Muslims and one of the leaders among the masters of the School of the People of Madinah, Qadi Abu Bakr ibn al-'Arabi of Seville. Not only that but the work could be considered the definitive statement on the distressing issue of the great primal fitna at the time of the Kaliphate. The clarity of the notes in the Arabic edition seemed almost as important as the text itself. Since the notes were necessary for the clarification of this work, which was written in 536 Hijra, I decided to unify the two parts of the book into one continuous text, differentiating Qadi Abu Bakr's statements from his modern editor's comments by the simple expedient of a distinguishing typeface, while leaving the enumeration of the notes to allow easy access.

Qadi Abu Bakr was born in Seville, Andalucia in 468 Hijra. He travelled extensively in the Muslim world, and studied in Baghdad. Although one of the leaders of the fuqaha' of the Murabitun and a supporter of Yusuf ibn Tashfin, he met Abu Hamid al-Ghazali both in Baghdad and in the Syrian deserts. On his return from the Hajj he settled in Seville. Great Islamic scholars studied under him including Shaykh al-Islam, Qadi 'Iyad ibn Musa, the author of *Ash-Shifa'*. At one point in his work as Qadi he led the community in working to restore the safety of the wall around Seville. As a result of this he created enemies who stirred people up against him with slander until he was besieged in his own house in the same way as Amir al-Mu'minin 'Uthman ibn 'Affan had been when the rebels attacked his house.

His most famous book is his *Ahkam al-Qur'an* which remains one of the great source-books on the legal judgments of the Qur'an. Another work, *'An-Nasikh wa'l-Mansukh fi'l-Qur'an'*, is considered the most correct on the subject. The Qadi was buried in Fes in 543 Hijra, may Allah have mercy on him. The title of the present book in Arabic is *al-'Awasim min al-Qawasim* which means 'The defences or protections from disasters', however the singular is more appropriate in the English language, and the book itself is that defence.

The significance of the events laid out in this great text are of enormous importance to all the Muslims, not only because of the nature of the crisis, and of the elevated spiritual status of the people involved, but because of the historical resonance of these events. The innovation of the Shi'a politique, coming as it does after the age of the Khulafa al-Rashidun is nevertheless inextricably bound up with the end of rule from Madinah. It is a doctrine which structurally seems to evolve through three phases. One, the claim that the fourth Kaliph, 'Ali should have been the immediate successor in power and not the fourth in line. Two, the claim of injustice in the events that led to Mu'awiya assuming power. Three, the emergence of a series of martyred descendants whose twelfth member went into miraculous suspended existence in the Unseen with a promise to appear at the end of time. That twelve generations should fail to assume the power they claimed was theirs suggests their lives were based on unsound foundations.

As the descendant of a leading Jacobite warrior who died at Culloden in the attempt to restore Charles Stuart to the Scottish throne, I can directly intuit the danger of living in the darkness of a lost leader. After the defeat of Bonny Prince Charlie, the Jacobites, knowing they had irrevocably lost, began to dream of his return. The people sang, "Will ye no' come back again". There is a world of lamentation for dead martyrs, for a lost way of life, and for a lost leader, and it can quickly be given metaphysical status. In politics the crucial issue is the taking of power and the wielding of power. It is on that basis that the just or the unjust society is achieved. The moment a people turn to lamentation, denounce the rulers as unjust and evil, and await a miraculous delivery by an absent leader, a tragic, psychological dislocation has taken place. If the people of power are evil that becomes your licence to claim that you are good. The act of denouncing others, far from being a path to social renewal, is a path to psychological breakdown. More profoundly, it is a failure to recognise and accept the Decree of Allah, glory be to Him. For the establishment of the just in power and the sweeping away of injustice itself cannot be established once your reason for living is your lament at the presence of injustice and your tear-filled cry that the good leader has still to come. All this implies that the religion is not complete, and ironically, will only be completed at the end of time, when in fact, that surely is too late for things to be put right. The message of this great book seems to be that of course things came about as they had to come about, and in it there was a great glory for the protagonists, and at the heart of the affair, there is no one worth waiting for. There is no need to live in hope of one who will come. It is the utmost ignorance to imagine it. He already came. He was the first of the sons of Adam, and he said that without boasting. And Allah, The Exalted, has told us: *"Certainly, there has come from among you, a Messenger. He is concerned about you, and with the Believers he is gentle and compassionate."* Who could ask for anything more?

Shaykh Dr. Abdalqadir as-Sufi
Achnagairn,
Scotland

Foreword

In the name of Allah, the All-Merciful, the Most Merciful

PRAISE BELONGS to Allah who has blessed humanity with the message of Islam and may Allah bless the highest man, the most perfect teacher, Muhammad ibn 'Abdullah, whom He chose from His creation. He elevated the station of those who undertook to implement His message into actuality and those who were in the company of the Prophet ﷺ and were excellent caliphs for his Community. Those who continued their work after them will cling to their sunna and pursue their goals until the Day of Rising.

The Muslim world, to which we are proud to be affiliated and for whose happiness we live, was mostly conquered in the first Islamic state which came after the Rightly-Guided Caliphs. Most of these people followed the guidance of Islam through the Umayyad caliphs, governors and generals, thus completing what was begun by Abu Bakr and 'Umar, the first two caliphs and Companions of the Messenger of Allah ﷺ. May Allah be pleased with them and give them the best repayment from us, Islam and all its people.

The spread of Islam and various nations embracing it is a point of pride in history and something about which subsequent generations have boasted until the present. This fills the hearts of the Muslims with joy and they pray to Allah to bless those who were the impetus behind this great blessing. Some people, however, were grieved by it and their hearts were filled with malice towards those who worked for it and they make it their habit to blame them for every shortcoming.

We might excuse those who have not tasted the sweetness of Islam since there is a great divide between them and the people, their noble goals and the course of life which they followed. Thus they glance at Islamic history and form a picture in their minds which is not a true one. However, I do admit, and there is no point in denying it, that among those who call themselves Muslims are some who even hate the first caliph after the Messenger of Allah ﷺ and call all his good deeds evil deeds. A man who saw the justice of 'Umar with his own eyes and saw his asceticism with regards to the goods of this world and his fairness to all people could not overcome the malice he bore for Islam which moved him to attack 'Umar with a knife even though he had done him no injury. The people who have attacked 'Umar with a knife include those who write books right up until today which tarnish the good actions of this paragon of justice, humanity and good. In the time of 'Uthman some of them were aggrieved by the goodness of that caliph whose heart was formed with the mercy of Allah. They fabricated and attributed wrong actions to him and continued to repeat them in their hearts until they believed them and became experts in disseminating these lies. Then they made his blood, which was sacrosanct, lawful in a sacred month in the vicinity of the father of his two wives: Muhammad ﷺ.

Humanity still witnesses miracles from the men of Islam in their spreading Islam, bringing nations into Islam and expanding its horizons so that the words of the *adhan* are heard from the mountains of China and the lands of India to the plains of the Mediterranean in the west and the valleys and mountains of Europe. Even the enemies of Islam can do no more than call it a miracle. All of that took place in the time of the Umayyads. If a tenth of the good that issued from this dynasty had issued from the Magians and pagans or even a hundredth part

Foreword

of the justice, manly virtue, generosity, courage, altruism, eloquence and nobility they demonstrated, those Magians and pagans would have raised banners of praise and esteem in the world. True history does not want anyone to raise the banner of praise and esteem, but rather wants to mention the good qualities of its men and to fear Allah in mentioning their evil qualities. So they should not go to excess in that nor be deceived by lies.

We, as Muslims, do not believe that anyone after the Messenger of Allah ﷺ was infallible. Whoever lays claim to infallibility for anyone after the Messenger of Allah ﷺ is a liar. Man is man. What comes from man comes from him, and that is both true and good and false and evil. Truth and good in a man may dominate and so he is considered to be one of the people of truth and good, but this does not keep him from making mistakes. He may be a man who is mired deep in falsehood and evil and is counted one of the people of falsehood and evil, but this does not prevent him from doing the odd good action at certain times.

When someone speaks about the people of truth and good and is aware of errors on their part, he must not behave badly towards those who were dominated by good and truth. None of this should be denied simply on account of those errors. When someone speaks about the people of falsehood and evil and knows of right actions on their part, people still must not imagine that they are among the right-acting because of some rare righteous actions.

The events of the first century of Islam are considered to be among the miracles of history. Neither the Romans nor the Greeks before them, nor any of the nations of the world after them have achieved the deeds of the first century of Islam.

Abu Bakr and 'Umar and the rest of the four Rightly-Guided Caliphs and their brothers were among the ten men who were promised the Garden and among the Companions of the Messenger of Allah ﷺ,

those who clung to the Prophet ﷺ, saw him and enjoyed his company, both those who supported him before the Conquest and fought and those who supported him after the Conquest and fought: all of these individuals are like radiant suns who rose in the sky of mankind once and humanity cannot hope that suns like them will appear in their sky ever again.

When Muslims resolved to return to the natural state of Islam and to take on their proper behaviour anew, Allah created another generation who lived for the truth and good and fought against falsehood and evil so that mankind would recognise its true path to happiness. These luminaries among the Companions of the Messenger of Allah ﷺ are clearly distinct in their types of virtues, although all of them possessed the highest degree of virtues.

When the best of the Muslims who are interested in Islamic history begin by distinguishing the basis from what has been interpolated into the lives of those great and excellent men, they are astonished at what the fellows of Abu Lu'lu'a and the students of 'Abdullah ibn Saba' have forged, as well as the Zoroastrians who were unable to resist Islam in the noble fight. They claimed that Islam was a lie and entered its citadel with their armies by stealth and fought them with the weapon of dissimulation (*taqiyya*) after they had altered its meaning and made it into hypocrisy.

They interpolated into Islam things which are not part of Islam, and they added to the lives of its people things which were untrue and came from the traits of their own people. In this way they changed the greatest and most perfect of Allah's messages to a path of lethargy, inactivity and passivity when, by right, they ought to have fought Islam and the Muslims properly but could not do so due to the vitality of Islam. This is the vitality to which we hope to return and isolate from unexpected events. We have dedicated ourselves to the biographies of its

Foreword

men and travelled the path of the sincere in order to bring Muslims back to the original true picture which actually existed, not in the manner which those who hate the Companions and Tabi'un want to present it to people.

These facts were already written down by Imam Ibn al-'Arabi and the original sources on which we relied. We wanted the opposite of what is desired by those researchers who repeat the fictions which time has effaced. The Companions possessed the highest character and truest sincerity to Allah and were too removed from the infamies of this world to disagree for the sake of worldly matters. However, in their time there were foul hands that worked to bring about and spread disagreement, similar to those foul hands which came later and depicted events in an untrue manner. The Companions of the Messenger of Allah ﷺ are our models in our deen and they are the bearers of the Divine Book and the Sunna of Muhammad ﷺ to those who took their trusts from them until it reached us.

Part of the duty, made incumbent on those like us by virtue of receiving trusts, is to remove all the unjust and hostile lies which have been foisted onto the lives of those first bearers, so that their form can be shown to people – and that form will be the pure and truthful one of what they were really like. They were an excellent model and people will be put at rest regarding the blessing which Allah brought people by them. The Muslim Shari'a considers an attack on them to be an attack on the deen that they transmitted. To sully their biography is to sully the trust which they bore and to cast doubt upon the entire foundation on which the Shari'a is based in this noble natural religion. The initial result of that is the deprivation of the young men of that generation and every generation after them of the righteous model with which Allah blessed the Muslims so that they could imitate it and continue to bear the trusts of Islam after them. That is only achieved through learning about their good deeds, recognising their noble qualities and perceiving that those who sullied those good deeds and depicted those traits in other than their proper form, wanted to injure Islam itself by injuring its first people. It now time for us to call attention to that heedlessness and recognise the true value of our forebears so that we can travel on with guidance and light from their sound lives and pure secret.

This book was written by one of the great Muslim Imams in order to throw light on the qualities of perfection which the Companions of the Messenger of Allah ﷺ had and to show the falsity of the lies told about them and their helpers among the Tabi'un. In spite of its small size, it puts matters straight because it is one of the clarion calls of the truth which should awaken Muslim youth to this deception which the enemies of the Companions foisted on them. They can use it as a model to protect them against that type of deception.

Those of them who have been successfully guided to the best have devoted themselves to studying the true history of Islam and discovering the noble qualities of its men. They know that Allah repaid them for those qualities with the miracles that were carried out by them and their helpers in carrying out the greatest transformation known in human history. If the Companions and Tabi'un had been how their enemies and opponents depicted them, it is utterly illogical that those conquests could have been carried out by them and that nations would have answered their call by entering into the deen of Allah in droves.

Qadi Abu Bakr ibn al-'Arabi, the author of *Defence against Disaster*, is one of the Imams of the Muslims. The *fuqaha'* of the school of Imam Malik consider him to be one of their Imams whose judgments are followed. He was one of the shaykhs of Qadi 'Iyad, the author of the *Shifa'*, and one of the shaykhs of Ibn Rushd, the faqih and scholar who was the grandfather of the philosopher, Abu al-Walid. His students included

Foreword

thousands of people of this calibre as you will see in his biography which follows this foreword. *Defence against Disaster* is one of his best books. He wrote it in 536 AH when he had reached his full maturity and the cities were full of his books and students who, in their own time, became Imams who were followed.

This book is in two medium sized parts. The study of the Companions which we offer our reader is one of the studies of the second part (from page 98 to 193 in the edition published by Al-Jaza'iriyya al-Islamiyya in Constantine, Algeria, in 1347). The Shaykh of the scholars of Algeria, Professor 'Abd al-Hamid ibn Badis, was involved with that edition. Unfortunately, a copyist who was not very good wrote out the primary source on which that edition is based. Thus there are mistakes and errors of dictation we would like to restore to the original. It appears that in the handwritten text on which the Algerian edition was based, the binder transposed some pages and put them out of order and we have restored them according to what is indicated by the continuity of the text and the order of the questions covered. We tried our best to fulfil the trust in presenting the book, and comments have been footnoted in every section to make the subject clearer. These are taken from the most reliable sources and the source Islamic books. Every text is made clear with clarity and trustworthiness.

I hope that Allah will reward Imam Ibn al-'Arabi for his defence of the Companions of the Messenger of Allah ﷺ who bore the greatest of Allah's messages from him and who were his truest helpers in conveying the message both during his life and after Allah took the Prophet ﷺ to Himself. Indeed, they are the reason for our being Muslims and they have the reward of our association with this noble original religion in which there is no fault. However, we are unable to take on all its proper behaviour in ourselves and to make its *sunnas* universal in our homes, society, markets, courts and centres of government. Perhaps Allah will make some of those who read this work better than us in action and sounder than us in knowledge. The end of the goal is Allah.

Muhibb ad-Din al-Khatib
Editor of the Arabic edition and commentator

Qadi Abu Bakr ibn al-'Arabi (468 – 543 AH)
Author of the Defence against Disaster

His early life

He is Muhammad ibn 'Abdullah ibn Muhammad ibn 'Abdullah ibn al-'Arabi al-Mu'afiri. He was born in Seville, one of the great capitals of Andalusia, on Thursday, 22nd Sha'ban 468 AH in one of the greatest houses of its king, al-Mu'tamid ibn 'Abbad. His father was 'Abdullah ibn Muhammad ibn al-'Arabi, one of the notable scholars and important men of the state. His maternal uncle, Abu al-Qasim al-Hasan ibn Abi Hafs al-Huzani, also enjoyed high standing in Andalusian society. However, these two houses were on opposite sides politically. Ibn al-'Arabi's father was one of the supporters of the government who enjoyed position and influence with the authorities. His uncle was one of the people of energy and ambition who participated in the plots against al-Mu'tamid because the King had killed his father, Hafs al-Huzani. Ibn al-'Arabi's uncle was in communication with Yusuf ibn Tashfin, the ruler of the Maghrib, inciting him against Ibn 'Abbad until Ibn 'Abbad's kingdom was lost and destroyed according to what ash-Shihab al-Maqarri states in *Nafh at-Tib*. Ibn Tashfin arrested al-Mu'tamid and imprisoned him in Aghmat where he remained a prisoner until he died in Shawwal, 448 AH. This reversal was a disaster for his government, especially the people in the capital and even more so for his retinue and helpers.

Ibn al-'Arabi grew up in this fine noble environment. He learned his initial culture and educational methods from these two men who assisted in this through his tutor, 'Abdullah as-Saraqusti. These three men were facilitated in their task of forming manly virtue in him by his distinguished gifts of intelligence, great perceptiveness and gentle character which enabled this excellent youth to enjoy all that prepared him for his early maturity. He said about himself:

> "I was well-versed in the Qur'an when I was nine. Then I spent three years acquiring accuracy in the Qur'an, and learning Arabic and mathematics. When I was sixteen, I had studied ten of the Qur'anic readings (*qira'at*) with all the rules of *idhhar*, *idgham*, etc. (rules for pronunciation in recitation). I was well-trained in unusual words (*gharib*), poetry and language."

His Journey from Seville

In 485 AH, when he was seventeen, Allah decreed that the 'Abbadid government fall. So on Sunday, the beginning of Rabi' al-Awwal, he and his father left Seville and made for North Africa. They first stopped at a port that had been built a few years before on the Algerian coast. It was the port of Bougie (Bejaia) whose location was discovered by Muhammad ibn al-Ba'ba', one of the men of Tamim ibn al-Mu'izz ibn Badis who agreed to its construction in 457 AH with an-Nasir ibn 'Alnas, the nephew of Tamim, his rival. The two of them turned this port into the crossroads of the Mediterranean for Andalusia, Morocco, Algeria and Tunisia.

Ibn al-'Arabi and his father landed at Bougie and remained there for a time in which Ibn al-'Arabi studied with its great scholar, Abu 'Abdullah al-Kila'i. Then they embarked again and went eastwards to the port of al-Mahdia. There he studied with the scholar, Abu al-Hasan 'Ali ibn Muhammad ibn Thabit al-Haddad al-Khawlani al-Muqri'. Ibn al-'Arabi said, "I read to him his book called *al-Ishara* along with its commentary as well as other books of his. That was in al-Mahdia in the months of 485." In al-Mahdia, he also studied with Imam Abu 'Abdullah Muhammad ibn 'Ali al-Maziri at-Tamimi. (453-536)

HIS SHIP SINKS

When they left al-Mahdia for the coasts of Egypt, disaster visited them anew when the sea turned rough. They found themselves in a situation which is described by the words of Ibn al-'Arabi himself when he wrote his *tafsir, Qanun at-Ta'wil*. He said:

"Allah already knew that the sea would be hard on us and that our ship would sink. We left the sea like a corpse emerging from the grave and, to make a long story short, we reached the houses of the Banu Ka'b ibn Sulaym nearly dead from hunger and having only the ugliest garments. The sea had cast up skins used for transporting oil which had been ripped open by the rocks and which we used as cloaks, so that our hair and skin were covered in grease and oil. At first our appearance caused people to shy away from us. Their governor was kind to us so we sought refuge with him and he received us. Allah fed us and gave us something to drink and a comfortable place to rest. He did this by means of a weak and indigent boy with some very superficial knowledge.

"When we stopped at his door, we found him playing chess. I approached him in those rags and his guards let me do so because I was so young. I stood there watching the progress of the game since, being still a youth, I was not averse to spending some time in frivolous pursuits. Also having the bravado of youth, I did not hesitate to say to those watching the game, 'The governor is in a better position than his companion.' They started to look at me with more respect, since I clearly knew the game, and told the governor what I had said and invited me to draw near. He asked me, 'Do I have a move I should consider?' I said, 'I have thought it over and it will soon be clear to you too. Move that piece there.' He did it and his companion moved in reply. I told him to move another, and the movements continued until the governor defeated his companion. They said, 'You must be older than you look.'

"During the chess, the governor's nephew chanted a poem:

How sweet is the passion which, in separation,
    does not doubt it will reach its lord.
It is Time which should be the focus of our hopes and fears.

"He said, 'May Allah curse Abu at-Tayyib! Did he doubt the Lord?'

"I said to him immediately, 'It is not as your companion thinks, governor. By 'lord', the poet meant a companion. The sweetest passion of the lover is that yearning for the beloved which does not doubt its eventual consummation. He fears Time because it is Time alone which allows him to fulfill his hopes or cuts him off from achieving his goal. It is as the poet says:

"If there were no separation in the course of love, where would the sweetness of messages and letters be?"

"'We add to those desires which end in accomplishment or failure.' This explanation moved the governor to rise to his feet out of respect for me and he asked me my age and who I was. This gave me the opportunity to tell him everything that had occurred and I informed him that my father was also present. He called for him and the three of us went to the governor's private quarters, where he gave me his own robe to wear and expressed his great sorrow at the situation in which we found ourselves. He made us comfortable and ordered all kinds of food and drink to be brought for us.

"I utilised a small amount of a sort of learning, which is in fact closer to ignorance than knowledge, and accompanied it with a minimum amount of *adab* and yet it was enough to rescue us from death. This incident made us all the more determined to pursue our quest for the benefits of true knowledge. We continued until we reached the houses of Egypt."

When we discuss the books of Ibn al-'Arabi, you will see that he wrote a large book called *Tartib ar-Rihla li at-targhib fi al-Milla* (The order of the journey to awaken desire for the Religion). It is unfortunate that this book is considered to be lost, but those bits we have read of it in the examples which are quoted in collections by scholars indicate that it was one of the rare treasures which describe many of the states of Muslim society and the civilisation of its inhabitants in the second half of the fifth century AH. He mentioned personal information about the major scholars and judges according to what this intelligent, accurate travelling scholar who was eager for all areas of knowledge had learned. If we had the book of his journey, we would have found it very useful for writing his biography, especially in the nine years (485-493 AH) which he spent outside Andalusia between the fall of the 'Abbadid government and the time when he returned to his homeland.

Passing through Egypt

There is no doubt that Ibn al-'Arabi and his father did enjoy the hospitality of the ruler of the tribe of Banu Ka'b ibn Sulaym for a long time. They then set out for Egypt. At the time they arrived in Egypt at the end of 485 AH, the ruler was the Fatimid, al-Mustansir Abu Tamim, the grandson of al-Hakam. There were very few Sunni scholars to be seen until Ibn al-'Arabi went to the smaller Qirafa near the grave of Imam Muhammad ibn Idris ash-Shafi'i to meet his shaykh, Qadi Abu al-Hasan 'Ali ibn al-Hasan ibn al-Hasan ibn Muhammad al-Khil'i al-Mawsuli al-Misri ash-Shafi'i (405-492). The biography of this scholar is found in *Wafiyat al-A'yan, Tabaqat ash-Shafi'iyya* by Ibn as-Subki (3:296) and in *Shadharat adh-Dhahab* by Ibn al-'Imad al-Hanbali (3:398). The men he met in Egypt and studied with included Abu al-Hasan ibn Sharaf, Mahdi al-Waddaq and Abu al-Hasan ibn Dawud al-Farisi.

HIS ARRIVAL IN JERUSALEM AND EASTERN JORDAN

Ibn al-'Arabi continued his journey with his father to Jerusalem. Imam Abu Bakr Muhammad ibn al-Walid at-Tartushi al-Fihri (451-520 AH), one of the great Andalusian Maliki scholars, was there. Like Ibn al-'Arabi, he had left Andalusia to go to the east and had gone to Iraq and come from there to Damascus and Jerusalem. Ibn al-'Arabi met him there and benefited greatly from him before at-Tartushi went to Alexandria. According to what the author of the *Nafh at-Tib* quoted (341:1), Ibn al-'Arabi said: "With our Shaykh, Abu Bakr al-Fihri at-Tartushi, I studied the *hadith*: 'Beyond you are days in which one who works will have the reward of fifty of you because you find helpers in good while they will not find helpers in it.' We discussed how the reward could come from the Community many times over that of the Companions although they founded Islam and supported the *deen* and established the minaret. They attacked cities and protected the heartland and made the religion accessible. The Prophet ﷺ said in the *Sahih*, 'If one of you were to spend the amount of Uhud in gold every day, it would not reach the *mudd* or even half the *mudd* of one of them.' We discussed it and found something to clarify it in the commentary on the *Sahih*. In a nutshell, it is that the Companions did many actions which no one can do as well nor that anyone can endure. There are other actions that are branches of the *deen* in which people can be equal if they have sincerity and are free of the taints of innovations and showing off to others. Commanding the correct and forbidding the objectionable is an immense subject that exists both at the beginning and the end of the *deen* and Islam. So when someone undertakes it when surrounded by terrors and sells himself by calling people to it, he will receive a reward many times over what someone has who is firm in it and has many to help him call to Allah."

He also met Ibn al-Kaziruni in Jerusalem. He said that he had retired to the al-Aqsa Mosque and that later he spent three years with him. He used to recite in 'Isa's Cradle [in the Aqsa Mosque] and he could be heard on the Mount [of Olives]. When he was heard reciting, no one could do anything but listen to his recitation.

Ibn al-'Arabi visited the territories of Palestine and eastern Jordan. The author of *Nafh at-Tib* (1:340), quotes him, "I witnessd the Table at the Mount of Olives repeatedly and ate there night and day. I remembered Allah there secretly and openly. It was a hard rock unaffected by axes. People used to say that the rock had been transformed, and that which I thought was rock originally, and cut from the earth was a place for the Table which descended from heaven and all around it was rock like it. What was around it was surrounded by castles carved in that hard stone. The doors of the houses were made of it and their seats were cut from it. I used to retire there to study." (I think that he is talking about the valley of Musa and the castle of Sil' which the Romans called Petra. See our essay on this.)

His visit to Damascus

Then Ibn al-'Arabi continued on his journey to Syria. He stayed in Damascus and studied with its scholars, including the Shafi'i Shaykh, Abu al-Fath Nasr ibn Ibrahim al-Muqaddasi (409-490). He has a biography under *nun* in the *History of Damascus* by Ibn 'Asakir and *Tabaqat of the Shafi'is* (4:27) and *Shadharat adh-Dhahab* (3:395-396). He studied with Abu Muhammad Hibatullah ibn Ahmad al-Akfati al-Ansari ad-Dimashqi (444-524) whose biography is under *ha'* in the *History of Damascus* and *Shadharat adh-Dhahab* (4:73). He also studied with Abu al-Fadl Ahmad ibn 'Ali ibn al-Furat, who died in 494 AH and was one of the Shi'ite scholars. He met some of the Syrian scholars: Abu Sa'id ar-Ruhawi, Abu al-Qasim ibn Abi al-Hasan al-Muqaddasi and Abu Sa'id az-Zanjani.

One of the wonders which he mentioned about the culture of Damascus and its high standard of luxury, security and ease in his time was what the author of *Nafh at-Tib* quoted from him, (1:338) when he was invited to dine in the house of one of the great men. He saw a river flowing to the place where they were sitting and then going out on the other side. He said, "I did not understand what this meant until the tables came on the river towards us and the servants took them and set them before us. When we had finished, the servants threw the vessels and what was on them into the returning stream and the water took them to the women's quarters without the servants coming near. So I learned the secret, and this was extraordinary."

HIS ARRIVAL IN BAGHDAD AND DEVOTING HIMSELF TO THE QUEST OF KNOWLEDGE

Then he set out with his father from Damascus making for the capital of the 'Abbasid caliphate in Baghdad. The Caliph in the first two years of this journey had been al-Muqtadi bi'llah. He was a good man in the *deen*, strong-minded, a man of knowledge and zeal of the noble 'Abbasids. In his reign, there had been many good works and excellent matters. One of his good deeds was to ban singers and sinners and to command that the honour and security of people be respected. The centres of the caliphate were splendid and full of honour.

After him, allegiance was given to al-Mustazhir billah Ahmad. He was a man of culture and refinement and great knowledge of literature and far-reaching official acts. However, his reign was full of unrest. It was in that atmosphere that Ibn al-'Arabi began to study knowledge with their people so that he became proficient in the sciences of the *Sunna*, the biographies of transmitters, the roots of the *deen*, the bases of *fiqh* and knowledge of Arabic and literature. Among those he studied under were: Abu al-Husayn al-Mubarak ibn 'Abd al-Jabbar as-Sayrafi known as Ibn at-Tayyuri (411-500 AH), the widely-versed and sound *hadith* scholar, Abu al-Hasan 'Ali ibn al-Husayn ibn 'Ali ibn Ayyub al-Bazzar (410-492 AH), Abu al-Mu'ali Thabit ibn Bandar al-Baqqal al-Muqri' (d. 498), Qadi Abu al-Barakat Talha ibn Ahmad ibn Talha al-'Aquli al-Hanbali (432-512 AH), and Fakhr ad-din Abu Bakr Muhammad ibn Ahmad ibn al-Husayn ibn 'Umar ash-Shashi ash-Shafi'i (429-507 AH). This later was a scrupulous man in the *deen*, and he was the leader of the Shafi'is in Baghdad.

Ibn al-'Arabi mentioned the good qualities of the Imam of the Shafi'is and said that one of them was that he heard him supporting the school of Abu Hanifa in a debate session. He said, "Linguistically, if it is *la taqarrabu*, it means do not doubt the action. If it is *la taqrubu*, it is do not go near the place." This is one of the proofs of the soundness of his knowledge and its extensiveness. A scholar is not mature until he is above the rivalry of the *madhhabs* and inclines to the truth and good wherever they live. When someone seeks after truth, he pursues it and inclines to it and goes to it in every situation. As for rivalry of the parties and schools and structures of the Path and the weakness of the arguments for that, all that comes from small-mindedness, fraudulent knowledge and being constantly involved with what is false.

Those with whom Ibn al-'Arabi studied in Baghdad include Abu 'Amir Muhammad ibn Sa'dun ibn Marja al-Mayruqi al-'Abdari (d. 524 AH). He was one of the *fuqaha'* of the Zahiri school. Qadi Ibn al-'Arabi said, "He was the noblest of those I met." He also studied with Abu al-Husayn Ahmad ibn 'Abd al-Qadir al-Yusufi (411-492 AH), the Shaykh of Baghdad in literature, Abu Zakariyya Yahya ibn 'Ali at-Tabrizi (421-502 AH), Abu Muhammad Ja'far ibn Ahmad ibn Husayn as-Sarraj al-Hanbali (416-500 AH), the author of *Masari' al-'Ushshaq*, Abu Bakr Muhammad ibn Tarkhan at-Turki ash-Shafi'i (446-513 AH), the student of the Shafi'i Imam, Abu Ishaq ash-Shirazi, author of *at-Tanbih* and *al-Muhadhdhab*, and the *Musnad* scholar of Iraq, Abu al-Fawaris Tarad ibn Muhammad ibn 'Ali al-'Abbasi az-Zaynabi (398-491 AH) who has the highest position with the Caliph.

He used to frequent the gatherings of general knowledge which were held in the house of the Caliph's wazir, 'Amid ad-Dawla Abu Mansur Muhammad ibn Fakhr ad-Dawla Muhammad ibn Muhammad ibn Juhayr (d. 493 AH) who was called "the just wazir". Ibn al-'Arabi said, "I was in the wazir's gathering when the reciter recited, '*Their greeting on the day that they meet is 'Peace.'* I was in the second row of the circle behind Abu al-Wafa' ibn 'Uqayl, the Hanbali Imam in Madina as-Salam (431-513 AH). Even though he was a Hanbali Imam, he was a Mu'tazili in *usul*. When I heard the *ayat*, I said to my companion on my left, 'This *ayat* indicates that Allah will be seen in the Next world. The Arabs only say, "I met so-and-so," when they have seen him.' Abu al-Wafa' quickly turned around to me and said, 'The school of the Mu'tazila is helped in their position that Allah will not be seen in the Next World because Allah says, *"He has punished them by putting hypocrisy in their hearts until the day they meet Him* (9:77)," and you know that the hypocrites will not see Allah in the Next World.'" Ibn al-'Arabi said, "We explained the meaning of the *ayat* in *Kitab al-Mushkilayn*."

One of Ibn al-'Arabi's biographers, Ibn Sa'id, said that Ibn al-'Arabi studied with Ibn al-Anmati in Alexandria. Many scholars accept that Ibn al-Anmati was in Egypt and Iraq in the time of al-Muzani, the student of ash-Shafi'i, in the third century to the end of the seventh century. But I have not found any of them who was in Alexandria in the time of Ibn al-'Arabi. The scholar of the Banu al-Anmati who was contemporary with Ibn al-'Arabi was Abu al-Bakarat 'Abd al-Wahhab ibn al-Mubarak ibn Ahmad al-Anmati al-Hanbali (462-538 AH), one of the great shaykhs of Abu al-Faraj ibn al-Jawzi. He may be the one with whom Ibn al-'Arabi studied in Baghdad. It is unclear in among his Maghribi biographers and they suppose that he was from the Egyptian Banu al-Anmati.

Also in Baghdad, Ibn al-'Arabi met Muhammad ibn 'Abdullah ibn Tumart al-Masmudi (d. 524 AH) who afterwards claimed to be the Mahdi and to be descended from 'Ali. He initiated 'Abd al-Mu'min ibn 'Ali (490-558 AH), the founder of the Muwahhid state. Ibn al-'Arabi's biographers say that he accompanied Ibn Tumart to the east and Ibn Tumart recommended him to 'Abd al-Mu'min. This must have been a long time after they had both returned to the Maghrib. We have no doubts about the fact that he did not make use of it and that it had no effect on the course of his life. Perhaps that was part of Allah's blessing to him. At the end of Ibn al-'Arabi's life, he was maltreated when he came from Andalusia to Marrakesh, the centre of the Sultanate of 'Abd al-Mu'min, as we will see later.

Meeting Abu Hamid al-Ghazali

Ibn al-'Arabi met Abu Hamid Muhammad al-Ghazali (450-505 AH) in Baghdad and later in the Syrian deserts. It is clear to me that when Ibn al-'Arabi arrived in Baghdad at the beginning of his journey, al-Ghazali was teaching in the Nizamiyya Madrasa and Ibn al-'Arabi was content to listen to him with the other people in his public gatherings.

Then al-Ghazali went on *hajj* and travelled to Damascus in 488 in an ascetic state during which he wrote his book, *al-Ihya'*. Then he returned to Baghdad and lived in the *ribat* of Abu Sa'd opposite the Nizamiyya. It was at that time that Ibn al-'Arabi met him and stayed with him. After Ibn al-'Arabi went on *hajj*, as we will mention, and returned from Iraq to Syria on his way home, he met al-Ghazali in the Syria deserts while he was in his final stage. We have found some texts in which Ibn al-'Arabi describes his connection to al-Ghazali.

The first text is quoted by al-Maqarri in the *Nafh at-Tib* (1:338) and in *Azhar ar-Riyad* (3:91) from *Qanun at-Ta'wil* by Ibn al-'Arabi: "Danishmand (i.e. al-Ghazali) came to us and stayed at the *ribat* of Ibn Sa'd opposite the Nizamiyya Madrasa, turning aside from this world and devoting himself to Allah. We went to him and told him what we hoped for. I told him, 'You are the object of our quest and our Imam from whom we seek guidance.' So had a meeting of gnosis and saw things from him which cannot be described."

The second text is quoted in the *Nafh at-Tib* (1:343) where Ibn al-'Arabi says, "An hermaphrodite who had a beard and breasts and who had a slave-girl used to study with us in the *ribat* of Abu Sa'd with Imam Danishmand. Allah has the best knowledge of him. Even though I was in his company a long time, modesty kept me from questioning him."

The third text is found in *Shadharat adh-Dhahab* (4:13), and Shaykh 'Ala' ad-din 'Ali ibn as-Sayrafi mentioned in his book, *Zad as-Salikin*, that Qadi Abu Bakr ibn al-'Arabi said: "I saw al-Ghazali in the desert. He had a staff in his hand and was wearing a patched cloak and had a coffee pot on his shoulder! I had seen him in Baghdad where four hundred turbaned men from the great and most excellent men attended his lessons and took knowledge from him. I approached him and greeted him. I said to him, 'Imam! Is not teaching knowledge in Baghdad better than this?' He looked askance at me and said, 'When the moon of happiness rose on the horizon of the will and I inclined to the sun of arrival.'"

One of the shaykhs of Ibn al-'Arabi in Baghdad was another Danishmand whom they called, "the Elder Danishmand." He was Isma'il at-Tusi. They called al-Ghazali "the younger Danishmand". Al-Maqarri quoted this in *Azhar ar-Riyad* (3:91) from Abu 'Abdullah Muhammad ibn Ghazi, one of the scholars of the Maghrib. In Persian, "*danishmand*" means scholar.

HAJJ AND RETURN TO BAGHDAD

Ibn al-'Arabi left Baghdad with his father to go to Makka and Madina on the *Hajj* in 489. He went to Makka and studied with its *mufti* and *hadith* scholar, Abu 'Abdullah al-Husayn ibn 'Ali ibn al-Husayn at-Tabari ash-Shafi'i (418-498 AH). Ibn 'Arabi said this about Makka: "While I was in Makka in 489 I spent a lot of time looking for Zamzam water. Whenever I drank it, I intended knowledge and belief. By His blessings, Allah opened to the amount of knowledge that He gave me and I forgot to drink it for action. I ask Allah for preservation and success by His mercy."

Ibn al-'Arabi returned to Baghdad with his father, and spent about two years there in the company of al-Ghazali who was in his middle phase between outward appearance and his final state of retreat and travel.

HIS RETURN BY WAY OF DAMASCUS, PALESTINE AND ALEXANDRIA

In 492 AH, Ibn al-'Arabi's father was suffering because of his advanced age and they both left Baghdad and made for Syria and Palestine, Ibn al-'Arabi renewed his contacts with those he knew in Damascus and Jerusalem and many Syrian cities. He studied with the shaykhs of this land and met other ones. Then he went to Alexandria and his father died in the beginning of 493 AH and was buried in the Alexandrian port. Imam Abu Bakr at-Tartushi was living in Alexandria at that time and his students and *murid*s from the people of the *Sunna* had settled there and multiplied so that there were hundreds of them who were resolved to revive the path of the people of the *Sunna* after they had become weak and negligent under the rule of the 'Ubaydids. The activities of at-Tartushi worried the 'Ubaydid governors in Cairo. Their leader from 487 AH had been al-Musta'ali Ahmad ibn al-Mustansir Abi Tamim Mu'izz. They had come to lose their ascendancy in Syria because the Turks had occupied some of the Frankish territory. Al-Musta'ali had no influence with his wazir, al-Afdal. Al-Afdal began to persecute at-Tartusi later because he had so many followers, but this is not the place to mention it. When Ibn al-'Arabi's father died in Alexandria, he travelled from there to return home in 493. Ibn 'Asakir said that Ibn al-'Arabi began to write his book, *'Arida al-Ahudhi* when he travelled westwards from Alexandria. It was the first of his books.

His arrival in Seville

When Ibn al-'Arabi reached his home, Seville, it was still being ruled by Yusuf ibn Tashfin who remained in that position until his death in 500 AH. When this exile arrived bringing the knowledge of the east to the scholars and men of culture and literature in Seville and the neighbouring capitals of Andalusia, he received an unparalleled welcome. Students and intelligent men of Andalusia flocked to him from every region. He moved to a mosque and held study circles in the mosques. A group of the great scholars of Islam studied under him, including the Shaykh of the Maghrib, Qadi 'Iyad ibn Musa al-Yahsubi, the author of *ash-Shifa'* and *Mashriq al-Anwar*, his son Qadi Muhammad ibn 'Iyad, the historian Abu al-Qasim Khalaf ibn 'Abd al-Malik ibn Bashkuwal, Imam Abu 'Abdullah Muhammad ibn Ahmad ibn Mujahid al-Ishbili, Abu Ja'far ibn al-Badhish, Abu 'Abdullah Muhammad ibn 'Abdullah ibn Khalil al-

Qadi Abu Bakr the author of Defence Against Disaster

Qaysi, Abu al-Hasan ibn an-Ni'ma, Abu Bakr Muhammad ibn Khayr al-Umawi al-Ishbili, Abu al-Qasim 'Abd ar-Rahman ibn Muhammad ibn Habish, Imam 'Abd ar-Rahman ibn 'Abdullah as-Suhayl, the *sira* commentator, Abu al-'Abbas Ahmad ibn 'Abd ar-Rahman as-Saqr al-Ansari, Abu al-Hasan 'Ali ibn 'Atiq al-Qurtubi, Abu al-Qasim Ahmad ibn Muhammad ibn Khalad al-Haqfi, Abu Muhammad 'Abd al-Haqq ibn 'Abd ar-Rahman al-Azdi al-Kharrat, Abu Bakr Muhammad ibn Muhammad al-Lakhmi al-Balanqi, Abu 'Abdullah ibn al-Ghasil al-Gharnati, Abu al-Hasan 'Abd ar-Rahman ibn Ahmad ibn Baqi, Abu al-'Abbas Ahmad ibn Abi al-Walid ibn Rushd, Abu Muhammad 'Abdullah ibn Ahmad ibn Sa'id al-'Abdari, the commentator on *Sahih Muslim*, Abu al-Mahasin Yusuf ibn 'Abdullah ibn 'Iyad, Abu al-Hajjaj Yusuf ibn Ibrahim al-'Abdari, Qadi Ahmad ibn 'Abd ar-Rahman ibn Mada' al-Lakhmi, and Abu Ishaq Ibrahim ibn Yusuf ibn Qarqul, the commentator of *Mashariq al-Anwar*.

A scholar is unrivalled when he has such noble people whose names Ibn al-'Arabi's biographers mentioned and those they did not mention because they were so numerous or because they were among his later students when this Imam was an old man. One of those who related his book, *Defence against Disaster*, was Salih ibn 'Abd al-Malik ibn Sa'id who mentioned at the beginning of the book that he read it to Ibn al-'Arabi. We have said that after Ibn al-'Arabi returned from the east to Andalusia, he became a focus from which knowledge issued to all his contemporaries who were able to learn. He was the teacher of the generation who lived with him in that area.

His biographers said that Ibn al-'Arabi gave *fatwa* and taught for forty years. Before he was made Qadi, he had authority from the official authorities that he could take the position of consultation for the qadiship. It was a very high position which issues what the Egyptians now call ordinances. One of the examples of the ordinances of this position is seen on the margin of page 89 in the book, *Ghabir al-Andalus wa hadiruha* by Prof. Muhammad Kurd 'Ali, and the margin 1:162 of *Shajarat an-Nur az-Zakiyya*. A scholar in Andalusia could not give *fatwa* unless he knew the *Muwatta'* and *al-Mudawwana* by heart or 10,000 *hadith*s. He was distinguished by wearing a certain sort of tall hat (*qalansuwa*).

While the circle of Ibn al-'Arabi produced the scholars of the generation, the kingdom of 'Ali ibn Yusuf ibn Yashfin was expanding because of the territory of the Taifa kingdoms which he annexed and what he recovered or conquered from the Spaniards. The governor over eastern and southern Andalusia for 'Ali ibn Yusuf ibn Tashfin was his brother, Tamim ibn Yusuf. In 513AH, the Spaniards began to attack Muslim territory. 'Ali ibn Yusuf ibn Tashfin crossed over from the Maghrib to Andalusia and fought them and defeated them. He returned in 515 AH and the situation remained like that until Tamim ibn Yusuf died in 520 AH. Then 'Ali ibn Yusuf ibn Tashfin put his son, Tashfin ibn 'Ali, in charge of Andalusia. In this time, Ibn al-'Arabi had reached the peak of his scholarly position because of his great books which had appeared and his students and *murids* had spread throughout the regions of Andalusia. In Rajab 528 AH he was summoned to become Qadi in Seville. Those who had related from him like Qadi 'Iyad, Ibn Bashkuwal, Ibn Sa'id and all the historians of Andalusia agreed that he was a model of justice, uprightness, and well suited to carry out the duties of the Qadi. Qadi 'Iyad said, "Allah has given benefit to the people of Seville by him through his sharpness, severity and effective judgments. He came down heavily on those who were unjust, while he was kind to the poor. He carried out the duty of the qadiship and continued to write books even though he had little time, so that his student, Imam Abu 'Abdullah al-Isbilli, had to cut off his studies. He was asked about that and said, "He used to teach and I found him at the door waiting to ride to the Sultan."

Qadi Abu Bakr the author of Defence Against Disaster

The position which Ibn al-'Arabi reached in knowledge, in his might and mastery over the hearts, before he became Qadi made official scholars, who pursued superficial knowledge to gain this world, envy and hate him. When his position was higher because he was qadi, he continued as a *mujahid* in the way of justice, putting things right, commanding the correct and forbidding the reprehensible. All of that is part of the path of Allah which combines all the proper deportment of good character, good behaviour, leniency, tolerance, generosity, good relations, and firm love. That increased the rancour of his enviers and the malice of the petty against him, especially the people of injustice, wrong and usurpation against whom he was severe in judgment and in punishment of them on behalf those who were wronged. They were joined by the people of impudence and licentiousness with whom Ibn al-'Arabi dealt when he commanded the correct and forbade the reprehensible. The impudent were mostly to be found in Seville at that time which is shown by the conversations about Seville and Cordoba which took place in the assembly of Mansur ibn 'Abd al-Mu'min between Abu al-Walid ibn Rushd and Abu Bakr ibn Zuhr. Ibn Rushd said to Ibn Zuhr, "I do not know what you are saying, except that when a scholar dies in Seville and his books are to be sold, they are carried to Cordoba to be sold. When an entertainer dies in Cordoba and what he left is to be sold, it is carried to Seville."

While he was Qadi, Ibn al-'Arabi felt that the walls of Seville would not sustain an attack if disaster befell the land. He resolved to restore them and fill up the gaps in them. This took place at a time when the government was diverted from this type of thing or there were not enough funds available for it. Ibn al-'Arabi spent all the funds under his control and his personal money to achieve this general religious duty. He invited the community to spend on it and it was begun in the first days of the months of Dhu al-Hijja. Ibn al-'Arabi was the first to think of using the skins of the animals slaughtered for the general good. He encouraged people to fold the skins of slaughtered animals in four to build this wall. He was successful in that, but nonetheless his enemies and haters stirred up the common people against him by foul means until he was besieged in his house one day, as the Amir al-Mu'minin 'Uthman ibn 'Affan had been when the rebels attacked him in his house. There is no doubt that this event took place at the end of his term as Qadi. He referred to this in his book, *Defence against Disaster*, which he wrote in 536 AH. Thus this event took place after 530 and before 536 AH. He described this in the book:

> "I judged between people, made them perform the prayer and commanded the good and forbade the bad so that there would not be anything objectionable in the land. I made strong speeches against the people who usurp other's property and took a severe stand against licentiousness. They got together and conspired and rebelled against me. I surrendered my business to Allah and commanded all of those around me not to defend my house. I went out on the roof alone and they did me mischief. If it had not been for a good decree written for me, I would have been murdered in the house. Three things moved me to that: (1) the advice of the Prophet ﷺ: 'Refrain from fighting in civil unrest;' (2) imitating 'Uthman; and (3) the defamation from which the Messenger of Allah ﷺ fled, which was confirmed by revelation when the Messenger of Allah ﷺ prevented 'Umar from killing Ibn Salul when the Prophet ﷺ returned from the raid on the Banu al-Mustaliq."

Ibn al-'Arabi suffered a misfortune in this rebellion and all his books were looted. He retired or was dismissed from the office of qadi and so he moved immediately to Cordoba where he had students and *murid*s. By this journey, the number of his intelligent students and *murid*s increased.

Part of the wisdom of Allah in this event was that Ibn al-'Arabi was able to devote himself to knowledge and continued to write his great books. We can now indicate his legacy in knowledge. A list of some of his books follows:

1. *Anwar al-fajr fi tafsir al-Qur'an* (The Lights of dawn in the explanation of the Qur'an). He wrote this over twenty years and it reached 80,000 sheets (or 160,000 pages). Yusuf al-Hizam al-Maghribi saw it in the eighth century in the library of Sultan Abi 'Inan Faris in Marrakech. It was in eighty volumes. His biographers say that it had ninety volumes. People consulted this *tafsir* in his books.

2. *Qanun at-ta'wil fi tafsir al-Qur'an* (The law of Qur'anic interpretation). A large book which was extant and widespread until the eleventh century. Al-Maqarri quotes from it in *Nafh at-Tib*, and we have quoted some of it here.

3. *Ahkam al-Qur'an* (Judgments of the Qur'an). A previous book published by the Sultan of Morocco, Moulay 'Abd al-Hafiz

4. *An-Nasikh wa al-mansukh fi al-Qur'an*

5. *Kitab al-mushkilayn, Muskhil al-Kitab wa Mushkil as-Sunna*

6. *Kitab an-niran*, on the two *Sahih* collections

7. *Al-Qabas*, a commentary of the *Muwatta'* of Malik ibn Anas, which was one of his last books. His *tafsir*, *Anwar al-Fajr*, is mentioned in it.

8. *Tartib al-Masalik*, on the commentary of the *Muwatta'*

9. *'Arida al-ahwadhi*, a commentary on at-Tirmidhi. It was one of his first books. Ibn 'Asakir says that he began the book when he was returning to the Maghrib from his great journey. We came across a manuscript of it in the library of the University of Islamic Guidance which was brought from Morocco by our friend, Muhammad al-Khidr Husayn.

10. Commentary on the *hadith* of Jabir on Intercession

11. The *Hadith* of the Lie

12. *Al-'Asawim min al-qawasim* (Defence against Disaster)

13. Commentary on the *hadith* of Umm Zar'
14. Discussion on the weakness in the *hadith* of glories and veils
15. *As-Saba'iyat*
16. *Al-Musalsat*
17. *Al-Amad al-aqsa bi-Asma' Allah al-Husana wa as-sifatihi al-'ulya*
18. *Tafsil at-tafsil*
19. *At-Tawassut fi ma'rifa sihha al-i'tiqad*
20. *Al-Mahsul fi 'ilm al-usul*
21. *Al-Insaf* in twenty volumes
22. Commentary on the rare words of the *Risala* of Ibn Abi Zayd al-Qayrawani
23. *Kitab sitr al-'awra*
24. *Al-Khalafiyat*
25. *Maraqi az-zulaf*
26. *Siraj al-muridin*
27. *Nawahi ad-dawahi*
28. *Al-'Aql al-akbar li'l-qalb al-asghar*
29. *Al-Kafi fi an la dalil 'ala an-nafi*
30. *Sarah al-muhatadin*
31. *Tabyin as-Sahih*
32. *Malja' al-mutafaqqihin*
33. *A'yan al-a'yan*
34. *Takhlis at-takhlis*
35. *Tartib ar-rihla*

While Ibn al-'Arabi was occupied with teaching and writing in the last ten years of his life, men of literature used to visit him, and he debated literature and poetry with them with talent and great clarity. There is not enough space here to describe his literary station and we must content ourselves with quoting the following example. The man of letters, Ibn Sara ash-Shantarini was present when Qadi Abu Bakr had a fire with ashes in it in front of him. He said to Ibn Sara, "Say something about this." He said:

> "The forelocks of the fire have become white after they were black, and are veiled from us by the garment of ash."

Ibn al-'Arabi said, "Good," and said:

> "It has become white just as we have. Our youth is gone,
> and it is as if we were returning."

Before mentioning his death, we will conclude this biography with a section in which he is described by the Andalusian wazir, Abu Nasr al-Fath ibn Khaqan al-Qaysi in his book, *al-Matmah*. He described the *faqih*, Abu Bakr ibn al-'Arabi:

> The pure star of the distinguished men of pure garments, radiant among the intelligent, who makes one forget acuteness of despair and leaves behind imitation for analogy, who took the wholesome root from the source and became an effective arrow in the hand of Islam. Andalusia was refreshed by him after its sciences had dried up and he spread his luxuriant shadow across it. He robed it in the splendour of his high nobility and let it drink of the full bloom of his outpourings.
>
> His father, Abu Muhammad, was like a full moon in the horizon of Seville and a leader in the assembly of its king. Mu'tamid ibn 'Abbad chose him as a trustee for Ibn Abi Dawud and gave him noble appointments and high ranks. When the Hums [rulers of Seville) family were ravaged and displaced and thrown out of it and cut off, he travelled to the east and there he fell into a fearful and disquieting position. He travelled within it and brandished the flame of hope in receiving and initiating renown. He did not seek to pursue a school and he was not like someone who relied on someone to spend on him and give to him. So he returned to transmission and listening and

how greatly he benefitted from accomplishing those desires! At that time Abu Bakr was a twig in the earth of cleverness which had not yet spread out. He was a flower in the meadows of youth which had not dried. He kept constantly to the gatherings of knowledge, going to and fro. He continued to push forward in it until his gatherings were firm in it. He was serious in his quest.

His father was overcome by fever and was entombed there [in the east]. Abu Bakr remained alone and devoted to the quest until he became unique in knowledge, but we did not find him avoiding leadership. He returned to Andalusia and landed there and people looked to it and listened to his sons. What excellent esteem he received! What might he was given! What a height he rose to and ascended to! It is enough for you that someone boasts of imitating him.

In the final years of Ibn al-'Arabi, 'Ali ibn Yusuf ibn Tashfin, the ruler of the Maghrib and Andalusia, died. His son, Tashfin, who had been his father's governor of Andalusia, succeeded him in 537 AH. In his reign, the position of the Muwahhids who had been initiated by Ibn Tumart, became strong. His task had been taken over by his protégé, 'Abd al-Mu'min ibn 'Ali. 'Abd al-Mu'min defeated al-Mu'izz Tashfin and exiled him to Oran in western Algeria. Then he killed him in Oran in Ramadan 539 AH. His brother, Ishaq ibn 'Ali ibn Yusuf ibn Tashfin, was besieged in Marrakech in 540 AH for nine months, defeated and the city taken in 541. Thus ended the state of the Murabitun or Mulaththama (veiled ones) after a reign of one hundred and forty-one years. Thus Ibn al-'Arabi witnessed the fall of the 'Abbadid through Yusuf ibn Tashfin in his youth, and then he witnessed the fall of the state of the Banu Tashfin to 'Abd al-Mu'min ibn 'Ali, the Muwahhid, at the end of his old age.

Qadi Abu Bakr the author of Defence Against Disaster

After that, the delegations of the cities of Andalusia began to visit Marrakech to ask 'Abd al-Mu'min to take their lands from the rest of the Murabitun. The delegation of Seville came in 542 AH under their leader and the leader of the scholars, Imam Abu Bakr ibn al-'Arabi. For some obscure reason which we still do not understand, 'Abd al-Mu'min detained this delegation in Marrakech for about a year and then they were released. He died on the way back from Marrakech at place called Aghlan, a day's journey west of Fes. His corpse was carried to Fes on the second day after he died, and his friend 'Abd al-Hakam ibn Hajjaj prayed over him. He was buried on Sunday, 7 Rabi' al-Awwal, 543 AH, outside the Bab al-Mahruq in the upper part of Fes in the graveyard of al-Qa'id al-Muzaffar. May Allah have mercy on him and elevate his station in the Eternal Abode.

DEFENCE AGAINST DISASTER

IN ACCURATELY DETERMINING
THE POSITIONS OF THE COMPANIONS
AFTER THE DEATH OF THE PROPHET
BY QADI ABU BAKR IBN AL-'ARABI
WITH COMMENTARY BY
MUHIBB AD-DIN AL-KHATIB

*In the name of Allah, the Merciful, the Compassionate
And may Allah bless Muhammad and his family.*

SALIH IBN 'Abd al-Malik ibn Sa'id said that he read this to Imam Muhammad Abu Bakr ibn al-'Arabi, may Allah be pleased with him:

Praise be to Allah, Lord of the worlds.

> Imam Ibn al-'Arabi began the first section of his book, *Defence against Disaster*, with this praise and this exact supplication. We have used it to begin this section from the second part.[1] We decided to make this section, which is devoted to the accurate assessment of the status of the Companions, may Allah be pleased with them, after the death of the Prophet ﷺ, a book on its own, as we indicated in the preface of this book.

O Allah! Bless Muhammad and the family of Muhammad as You

blessed Ibrahim and the family of Ibrahim! Grant *baraka* to Muhammad and the family of Muhammad as You granted *baraka* to Ibrahim and the family of Ibrahim. You are the Praiseworthy, Glorious.

O Allah, we ask You to grant us benefit, just as we ask You to repel affliction from us. We ask You for protection and we ask You to give us mercy.

O our Lord, do not lead our hearts astray after You have guided us. Make the actions You have taught us easy for us to perform. Grant us thankfulness for what You have given us. Make a path clear to us that will lead us to You. Open a door between us and You by which we can come to You. You possess the keys of the heavens and the earth. You have power over all things.

The Back-Breaking Disaster

ALLAH TOOK His Prophet ﷺ back to Himself, having perfected the *deen* for him and us and completed His blessings on him as Allah says: *"Today I have perfected your deen for you and completed My blessing upon you and am pleased with Islam as a deen for you."*²

> Nothing in this world is perfected but that imperfection then comes to it, since perfection is only that which is meant for Allah alone: righteous actions and the Next World, which is the perfect Abode of Allah.

Anas said, "We had not shaken the earth of the grave of the Messenger of Allah ﷺ from our hands before we doubted our own hearts."

> The Algerian edition has "our selves". "Our hearts" is related in the *hadith* in several variants. Ibn Kathir indicated this in *al-Bidaya wa an-Nihaya*.³ One of them is reported by Ahmad ibn Hanbal from Anas: "On the day when the Messenger of Allah ﷺ came to Madina, all of it was illuminated. On the day he died, all of it was darkened." He said, "We had not shaken the earth of the grave of the Messenger of Allah ﷺ from our hands before we began to doubt our own hearts." At-Tirmidhi and Ibn Majah related this. At-Tirmidhi said, "This is a *hadith* which is *sahih gharib*." Ibn Kathir said, "Its *isnad* is sound according to the preconditions of the *Sahih* collections.

The situation became unsettled and then Allah restored Islam by the oath of allegiance given to Abu Bakr. The death of the Prophet ﷺ was the Back-breaking Disaster and the Terrible Calamity.

'Ali kept himself out of sight in his home with Fatima.

> Because Fatima was angry with Abu Bakr when he insisted on acting by the words of the Messenger of Allah ﷺ: "We do not leave any legal inheritance. All we leave is *sadaqa*." The details of this will be dealt with later. Fatima lived for six months after the Prophet's death secluded in her house and 'Ali remained with her.

Ibn Kathir said in *al-Bidaya wa an-Nihaya*:[4] "When she became ill, Abu Bakr as-Siddiq went to her to try to make amends with her and she accepted his overture." Al-Bayhaqi related that by means of Isma'il ibn Abi Khalid from ash-Sha'bi. Then he said that is a good *mursal hadith* with a sound *isnad*. Al-Bukhari reported the *hadith* of 'Urwa via 'A'isha: "When Fatima died, her husband 'Ali buried her at night without informing Abu Bakr about it and prayed over her. During Fatima's lifetime, 'Ali had a good standing among the people. When she died, eminent people expressed disapproval to 'Ali and so he made peace with Abu Bakr and gave him his allegiance..." This was the second allegiance which 'Ali gave after his first *bay'a* in the hall of the Banu Sa'ida. Ibn Kathir adds in *al-Bidaya wa an-Nihaya*[5] that 'Ali did not cease to perform his prayers behind Abu Bakr. He went out with Abu Bakr when he marched out to Dhu al-Qassa and unsheathed his sword to fight the apostates in the Ridda War.

It is possible that when he said that 'Ali kept out of sight the author meant what he and az-Zubayr did just before people were meeting in the hall of the Banu Sa'ida. 'Umar ibn al-Khattab indicated that in the great speech which he made in Madina at the end of Dhu al-Hijja after the last *hajj* which he performed.[6]

In fact, there is confusion in the *riwayats* about the position of 'Ali ibn Abi Talib during the caliphate of Abu Bakr as-Siddiq. Many intrigues played their part. Lies and fabrications have been woven around this whose

The Back-Breaking Disaster

intention is to unsettle confidence in Islam in general and the Companions in particular. They display fear and enthusiasm concerning positions and property, even when this is in opposition to the Shari'a. In what follows, we will present the soundest of the *riwayats* regarding 'Ali's position. Then we also mention some of the *riwayats* which say that he refused to take the oath of allegiance until Fatima, the daughter of the Messenger of Allah ﷺ, had died. We will make the forgeries and lies clear.

Muhammad 'Izza Daruza said in *The Arab Race*:[7] "At-Tabari related from 'Abdullah ibn Sa'id az-Zuhri from his uncle, Ya'qub from Sa'id ibn 'Umar from al-Walid ibn 'Abdullah from al-Walid ibn Jami' az-Zuhri that 'Amr ibn Harith asked Sa'id ibn Zayd, 'When was Abu Bakr given the oath of allegiance? Were you present at the death of the Prophet ﷺ?' He replied, 'Yes. On the day that the Messenger of Allah ﷺ died, they did not want even part of the day to pass without meeting together.' 'Amr asked, 'Did anyone oppose him (Abu Bakr)?' He replied, 'No, except for those who were apostates or who would have apostatised if Allah had not delivered them from the Ansar.' He asked, 'Did any of the Muhajirun abstain?' He answered, 'No, they followed in giving him allegiance without being summoned to do so.'"

It is evident that what the speaker meant by saying what he did about the Ansar was the position taken by Sa'd ibn 'Ubada and his helpers on the 'Day of the Verandah' and their striving for leadership. Allah saved them and made them back down and follow Abu Bakr rather than bring about division, opposition and contention. This demonstrates the strong desire of the Companions of the Messenger of Allah ﷺ, both the Muhajirun and the Ansar, to be very quick in settling the problem of leadership. It also shows that the Hashimites, who were among the Muhajirun, followed in giving the oath of allegiance to Abu Bakr and that none of them abstained from it.

At-Tabari related the tradition of 'Ali giving his allegiance to Abu Bakr immediately and openly when it is related with his *isnads* from Habib ibn

Abi Thabit that 'Ali was in his house when the news came to him that Abu Bakr was sitting taking the oath of allegiance. He went out in his unbuttoned shirt, without a cloak, in haste, not wanting to delay giving him allegiance. Then he sat with him, sent for his outer garment to be brought to him, put it on and stayed in the assembly.[8]

In any case, what is agreed upon, in the Shi'ite accounts and elsewhere, is that 'Ali and the Banu Hashim immediately offered their allegiance to Abu Bakr or, as at-Tabari related from one Shi'ite account, after some hesitation, and they gave him their assistance. This indicates a decisive proof that there was neither a clear will nor implicit bequest from the Prophet ﷺ that authority should go to 'Ali after him.

At-Tabari related the same as that with other *isnad*s in his report that 'Ali and the Banu Hashim refused to pay homage to Abu Bakr as long as Fatima was alive because Fatima and al-'Abbas had come to Abu Bakr asking for their inheritance from the Messenger of Allah ﷺ, which consisted of his land at Fadak and his share of Khaybar, but Abu Bakr told them, "I heard the Messenger of Allah ﷺ say, 'We do not leave any legal inheritance. What we leave is *sadaqa*.' Muhammad's family will have provision from this money. By Allah, I will not leave anything that I saw the Messenger of Allah ﷺ do. I will do the same." Fatima left him and did not speak to him until she died six months after the death of the Prophet ﷺ. 'Ali saw the eminent people turning away from him, and neither he nor any of the Banu Hashim had offered their allegiance to Abu Bakr. The story is a long one, but in the end 'Ali gave his homage to Abu Bakr, i.e. after the death of Fatima.

It is to be noted that the text of the report of at-Tabari makes the question of the inheritance the reason for 'Ali and the Banu Hashim refusing to give their allegiance to Abu Bakr. Their seeking this legacy from Abu Bakr means that they must have first recognised that he was the Caliph. This involves a contradiction which makes the story break down. If it has any basis at all, it is only possible after they had given their allegiance to Abu

Bakr. They tried to get what they considered to be their inheritance from the Prophet ﷺ. Abu Bakr told them the *hadith* of the Prophet ﷺ that he had heard and the business stopped at this point. Anything beyond that is an addition and one of their intrigues because it is not possible that 'Ali, Fatima and the Banu Hashim did not confirm Abu Bakr in the *hadith* that he related because they did not argue and persist after they had heard it.

It is strange that the enemies of Islam attack Abu Bakr, may Allah be pleased with him, for denying Fatima her inheritance from Fadak and her share of Khaybar while when 'Ali himself became Caliph, he did not give any of her heirs nor any of the Banu Hashim what the Messenger of Allah ﷺ had left, precisely because of the *hadith*, "We do not leave inheritance." When Abu Bakr forbade it, he also denied his daughter 'A'isha this inheritance.

There are other mixed and false reports about 'Ali and the Banu Hashim rejecting the oath of allegiance to Abu Bakr. We have ignored them since they are discredited. There are many which confirm that 'Ali hastened to offer his allegiance to Abu Bakr and to help him in the affairs of the caliphate. He, of all people, knew best how excellent Abu Bakr was.

As for 'Uthman, he was silent. As for 'Umar, he spoke foolishly, saying, "The Messenger of Allah ﷺ has not died! Allah has allotted a time for him as He did for Musa!...

> This is an allusion to the words of Allah in *Surat al-Baqara*,[9] "When We allotted to Musa forty nights." Allah says, "We set aside thirty nights for Musa and then completed them with ten, so the appointed time of his Lord was forty nights in all."[10]

"...The Messenger of Allah ﷺ will return and cut off the hands and feet of some people!"

The *Musnad* of Ibn Hanbal[11] has the *hadith* of Anas ibn Malik about the day of the death of the Prophet ﷺ: "Then the curtain was let down and he died on that day. 'Umar stood up and said, 'The Messenger of Allah ﷺ has not died, but his Lord has sent for him as He sent for Musa. He remained away from his people for forty days. I expect the Messenger of Allah ﷺ to live until he cuts off the hands and tongues of some men among the hypocrites who claim that the Messenger of Allah ﷺ has died!'"

In the 'Virtues of the Companions' in *Sahih Bukhari*[12] it is reported that 'A'isha said: "'Umar got up saying, 'By Allah, the Messenger of Allah ﷺ has not died! By Allah, I can only assume that Allah will bring him to life and he will cut off the hands and feet of some men!'"

Ibn Kathir quoted in *al-Bidaya wa an-Nihaya*[13] what al-Bayhaqi related from Ibn Lahi'a from Abu al-Aswad from 'Urwa ibn az-Zubayr. He said: "'Umar ibn al-Khattab stood up and addressed the people and threatened those who said, 'He has died' with death and having their hands cut off. He said, 'The Messenger of Allah ﷺ has fainted. When he comes to, he will have people killed and their hands cut off.'" *Al-Bidaya wa an-Nihaya* contains an excerpt from a *hadith* of 'A'isha[14] where she mentions the time when the Messenger of Allah ﷺ died: "'Umar and al-Mughira ibn Shu'ba came and asked permission to enter. She gave them permission. Then they got up. When he was near the door, al-Mughira said, "Umar, the Messenger of Allah ﷺ is dead.' 'Umar said, 'You lie! You are a man with whom sedition has been mixed. The Messenger of Allah will not die until Allah has eradicated the hypocrites!'"

The meaning of the verb *ahjara* is to talk irrationally, to mix words and to talk a lot. It arose from the panic which 'Umar felt because of this terrible event. He almost could not believe it.

Al-'Abbas and 'Ali were concerned with their position during the illness of the Prophet ﷺ. Al-'Abbas said to 'Ali, "I can recognise imminent death in the faces of the Banu 'Abd al-Muttalib. Let us ask the Messenger of Allah ﷺ. Then we will know if this business is ours or not."

The Back-Breaking Disaster

'Ali answered, "By Allah, if we ask the Messenger of Allah ﷺ and he denies it to us, the people will never give it to us after him. By Allah, I will not ask the Messenger of Allah ﷺ for it."[15]

Al-'Abbas and 'Ali were concerned about their inheritance of the property the Prophet left from Tabuk, the Banu an-Nadir and Khaybar."

Details of this will come in the discussion about the hadith of 'We do not leave legal inheritance. What we leave is *sadaqa*.'

The Ansar were in a state of great agitation, not knowing whether to seek authority for themselves or share it with the Muhajirun.

A meeting took place in the hall of the Banu Sa'ida. Sa'd ibn 'Ubada was among them. They thought that the leadership should be given to them because it was their land and they were the Ansar (Helpers) of Allah and the squadron of Islam. Quraysh were a troop who had emigrated little by little. Authority should not be denied to the Ansar. One of their speakers (al-Hubab ibn al-Mundhir) said, "I am the rubbing-post and the fruitful propped-up palm. Let there be a ruler from us and a ruler from you." In contrast to that, a man of the Ansar, Bashir ibn Sa'id al-Makhzumi, the father of an-Nu'man ibn Bashir, went before 'Umar in offering allegiance to Abu Bakr. Before that, there were two righteous men in the hall, 'Uwaym ibn Sa'ida al-Awsi and Ma'n ibn 'Adi, the ally of the Ansar. They did not like this contention on the part of the Ansar. They left, thinking that the Muhajirun would finish the business without turning to anyone. But the wisdom of Abu Bakr and the light of faith which filled his heart was a match for the situation and he was more than adequate in dealing with the community at the time of its greatest calamity.

Those who had gone out on the expedition with Usama ibn Zayd stopped at al-Jurf.

There were seven hundred in this army. The commander was Usama ibn Zayd. The Messenger of Allah ﷺ had ordered them to travel to the area of al-Balqa' (east Jordan) where Zayd ibn Haritha, Ja'far ibn Abi Talib and Ibn Rawaha had been killed. When the Prophet ﷺ died, many of the Companions, including 'Umar, suggested that Abu Bakr should not send this army out because of the disturbance which had arisen among the people, especially among the tribes. In *al-Bidaya wa an-Nihaya*[16] Ibn Kathir quoted the *hadith* which al-Qasim and 'Amra reported from 'A'isha. She said: "When the Messenger of Allah ﷺ died, the Arabs apostatised and drank in hypocrisy. By Allah, something happened to me and if it had come down on the firm mountains, they would have broken. The Companions of Muhammad ﷺ became like agitated goats put out to grass on a stormy night in the wilderness. By Allah, they did not disagree about a single dot without my father nullifying their prattle, their doubts and their conclusions."

DEFENCE

Allah helped Islam and the people and caused their grief to pass just as clouds pass. The promise of Allah was fulfilled when Allah took the Messenger of Allah ﷺ to Himself...

Allah takes people to Himself when they die.

...and established His *deen* in its full perfection. Islam was afflicted by the calamity which befell it, and Allah helped it through Abu Bakr as-Siddiq, may Allah be pleased with him.

Allah helped both Islam and the people by Abu Bakr.

When the Prophet ﷺ died, Abu Bakr was away at his property at as-Sunh.

In *al-Bidaya wa an-Nihaya*,[17] Ibn Kathir reports that Abu Bakr led the Muslims in the morning prayer. The Messenger of Allah ﷺ had fainted due

The Back-Breaking Disaster

to the pain caused by his illness shortly before this, but during the prayer the curtain of the room was raised and he looked at the Muslims who were lined up for the prayer behind Abu Bakr. He liked that and smiled until the people were so moved that they almost left the prayer because of their joy at seeing him. Abu Bakr wanted to go back into the rows. The Messenger of Allah ﷺ indicated to them to continue as they were and the curtain came down again. When Abu Bakr finished the prayer, he came to the Prophet and said to 'A'isha, "I cannot see the Messenger of Allah ﷺ without feeling his pain." That day was the turn of Bint Kharija, one of Abu Bakr's two wives, who lived in Sunh in the eastern part of Madina. He rode to his house there on his horse. The Prophet ﷺ died during the heat of the mid-morning. Salim ibn 'Ubayd went after Abu Bakr and informed him that the Prophet ﷺ had died, and Abu Bakr came as soon as he heard. He did what the author mentioned. Sunh consisted of some houses of the Banu al-Harith ibn al-Khazraj in the upper part of Madina about one mile from the Prophet's mosque.

He came to the room of his daughter 'A'isha, in which the Prophet ﷺ had died and uncovered his face. He bent over him and kissed him. He said, "May my father and mother be your ransom, Messenger of Allah! You were good in life and in death! By Allah, Allah will not give you two deaths. As for the death which Allah has written for you, you have come to it."

Then he went out to the mosque where the people were gathered and 'Umar had already begun to speak foolishly as has already been stated. Abu Bakr ascended the *minbar*. He praised Allah and then said: "O people! Whoever worships Muhammad, he is dead. Whoever worships Allah, Allah is the Living who does not die." Then he recited, *"Muhammad is only a Messenger. Messengers have passed away before him. If he dies or is killed, will you turn back on your heels? Whoever turns back on his heels, he will not harm Allah in any way. Allah will repay the thankful."*[18] People began to recite this in the streets of Madina as if it had only been revealed on that day.

> Al-Bukhari related this in the Book of the Virtues of the Companions in the *Sahih*[19] from the *hadith* of 'A'isha. In *al-Bidaya wa an-Nihaya*,[20] Ibn Kathir has the *hadith* of Abu Salama ibn 'Abd ar-Rahman ibn 'Awf az-Zuhri, one of the eminent men of the Muslims, from his father, one of the ten men who was promised the Garden, from 'A'isha, *Umm al-Mu'minin*, in whose room these events took place and in the mosque of the Prophet ﷺ onto which her room looked. All the volumes of the *Sunan* record this great stand by Abu Bakr with the soundest *hadiths* whose wordings are similar.

The Ansar gathered together in the hall of the Banu Sa'ida to consult each other. They did not know what to do. The Muhajirun heard about the meeting and said, "We will send for them to come to us." Abu Bakr said, "Rather we should go to them." Some of the Muhajirun went to them. They included Abu Bakr, 'Umar and Abu 'Ubayda. They consulted one another. One of the Ansar said, "We will have a leader and you will have a leader."

> The man who said that was one of the public speakers of the Ansar, al-Hubab ibn al-Mundhir.

Abu Bakr said many correct things. He spoke at length and went straight to the point. He said, "We are the rulers and you are the helpers (*wazirs*). The Messenger of Allah ﷺ said, 'The rulers are from Quraysh,'...

> This *hadith* is in the *Musnad* of at-Tayalasi, from Abu Barza and from Anas.[21] It is in the Book of Judgments in *Sahih Bukhari*[22] where Mu'awiya reports that he heard the Messenger of Allah ﷺ say, "This command is in the hands of Quraysh. No one will attack them in it without Allah throwing him down on his face, as long as they establish the *deen*." Ibn

The Back-Breaking Disaster

'Umar reports that the Messenger of Allah ﷺ said, "This business will remain in Quraysh as long as two of them remain." In the *Musnad* of Imam Ahmad ibn Hanbal[23] Anas ibn Malik states, "The Messenger of Allah ﷺ stood at the door of the house while we were inside it and said, 'The Imams are from Quraysh. They have a right over you... etc.'" Ibn Hanbal also related this in the *Musnad*[24] from Anas. He said, "We were in the room belonging to a man of the Ansar. The Prophet ﷺ came and stood there. He leaned on the doorpost and said, 'The rulers are from Quraysh. They have a right over you and you have the like of that, etc.'" Ibn Hanbal related it like that[25] from Abu Barza directly (*marfu'*) to the Prophet ﷺ. He said, "The Imams are from Quraysh, who when they are asked for mercy, show mercy, when they make a contract, they fulfil it, and when they judge, they are just. If any of them do not do that, the curse of Allah, the angels and all mankind is upon them."

"...and he said: 'I urge you to treat the Ansar well. You should accept their good and overlook their evil.'

We find in the Book of the Virtues of the Ansar in *Sahih Bukhari*[26] the *hadith* reported by Hisham ibn Zayd ibn Anas who heard Anas ibn Malik say: "Abu Bakr and al-'Abbas passed by one of the assemblies of the Ansar who were weeping. (It is evident that this was during the final illness of the Prophet ﷺ.) He asked, 'Why are you weeping?' They replied, 'We were remembering the assembly of the Prophet ﷺ.' He came to the Prophet ﷺ, and told him that. He said that the Prophet went out with a bandage on his head and ascended the *minbar*, which he never again ascended after that day. He praised and glorified Allah. Then he said, 'Treat the Ansar well. They are my close Companions to whom I have entrusted secrets. They have discharged what they had to do and what they are owed remains. Accept the good among them and overlook the bad.'" Then after that in *Sahih Bukhari*, we find the *hadith* 'Ikrima reported from Ibn 'Abbas and the *hadith* Qatada reported from Anas with the same meaning. Close to it is what is in *Sahih Muslim* from Abu Sa'id al-Khudri and in the *Sunan* of at-Tirmidhi from Ibn 'Abbas.

"Allah called us 'truthful' and He called you 'successful'.

> We find in *Sura* 59:8-9: *"It is for the poor Muhajirun who were driven from their homes and wealth, desiring the favour and pleasure of Allah, and supporting Allah and His Messenger. Such people are truly sincere. Those who were already settled in the abode and in faith before they came love those who have made hijra to them and do not find in their hearts any need for what they have been given and prefer them to themselves even if they themselves are needy. It is the people who are safe-guarded from the avarice of their own selves who are successful."*

"He commanded you to be with us wherever we are when He said, *'O you who believe, fear Allah and be with the truthful.'*[27]" He said other cogent things and produced strong evidence in support of them. The Ansar acknowledged what he said and submitted to it and gave their allegiance to Abu Bakr as-Siddiq, may Allah be pleased with him.

> We find in *al-Bidaya wa an-Nihaya*[28] that Ibn Kathir quoted the *hadith* Ibn Hanbal has from Hamid ibn 'Abd ar-Rahman ibn 'Awf az-Zuhri (the nephew of the Amir al-Mu'minin 'Uthman) from Abu Bakr's speech in the hall of the Banu Sa'ida. Part of it is: "You know that the Messenger of Allah ﷺ said, 'If people were to travel through one valley and the Ansar travelled through another valley, I would travel through the valley of the Ansar.' You know, Sa'd, that the Messenger of Allah ﷺ said while you were seated, 'Quraysh are the rulers in this business. Good people follow the good among them and the corrupt follow the corrupt among them.'" Sa'd said to him, "You have spoken the truth. We are the helpers and you are the rulers."

The Back-Breaking Disaster

Abu Bakr told Usama, "Carry out the command of the Messenger of Allah ﷺ." 'Umar demanded, "How can you send out this army when the Arabs are gathering against you?" Abu Bakr replied, "Even if the dogs were to play with the bangles of the women of Madina, I would still not bring back an army which the Messenger of Allah ﷺ had sent out."

In *al-Bidaya wa an-Nihaya*,[29] Ibn Kathir transmitted from Abu Bakr al-Bayhaqi the *hadith* of Muhammad ibn Yusuf al-Firyabi (al-Bukhari said that he was one of the best people of his time) from 'Ubbad ibn Kathir ar-Ramli, one of his shaykhs (Ibn al-Madini said that he was reliable and that there was no harm in him) from 'Abd ar-Rahman ibn Hurmuz al-A'raj (one of the *Tabi'un* who died in Alexandria) that Abu Hurayra said, "By Allah, there is no god but He! If Abu Bakr had not been appointed, Allah would no longer have been worshipped!" Then he repeated it two or three times. He was told, "Steady on, Abu Hurayra!" He said, "The Messenger of Allah ﷺ sent Usama ibn Zayd to Syria with seven hundred men. When he stopped at Dhu al-Khusub, the Messenger of Allah ﷺ died and the Arabs around Madina apostatised. The Companions of the Messenger of Allah ﷺ gathered around Abu Bakr and said, 'Abu Bakr, bring those men back. They have been sent to the Greeks when the Arabs around Madina have apostatised!' He said, 'By Allah, there is no god but He. Even if the dogs were to snap at the feet of the wives of the Messenger of Allah ﷺ, I would still not bring back an army which the Messenger of Allah ﷺ had sent out nor undo anything that the Messenger of Allah ﷺ had done.' So he sent out Usama and the army and they did not pass by a tribe who wanted to apostatise without them saying, 'If it had not been that those men had strength, they would never have sent out the like of these men. We will wait until after they have encountered the Greeks.' They encountered the Greeks and defeated and killed them and returned safe. So those tribes remained firm in Islam."

'Umar and others said to him, "If the Arabs refuse to pay you the *zakat*, then be patient with them." Abu Bakr said, "By Allah, if they deny me a single camel-halter which is due to the Messenger of Allah ﷺ, I will fight them for it. I will fight all those who make any distinction between *zakat* and the prayer!"

When Usama's army went on to eastern Jordan, the delegations of the tribes began to come to Madina. They confirmed the prayer but refused to pay *zakat*. Ibn Kathir said,[30] "Some of them used as a proof His words: '*Take* sadaqa *from their property by which to purify them and pray over them. Your prayer is a comfort for them.*'[31] They said, 'We only gave our *zakat* for his prayer which was a comfort for us.' The Companions spoke with Abu Bakr about leaving them alone in spite of the fact that they refused to pay *zakat* and to keep them unified until belief was firm in their hearts. Then after that, they would pay *zakat*. Abu Bakr refused to do this and rejected that course of action."

Most people – except Ibn Majah – related in their books from Abu Hurayra that 'Umar ibn al-Khattab told Abu Bakr, "How can you fight the people when the Messenger of Allah ﷺ said, 'I am commanded to fight people until they testify that there is no god but Allah and that Muhammad is the Messenger of Allah. When they say that, their blood and their property are protected from me except by a right.'?" Abu Bakr said, "By Allah, if they deny me a single camel-halter (or rein) which they used to give to the Messenger of Allah ﷺ, I will fight them for denying it." 'Umar said, "I saw that Allah had expanded Abu Bakr's breast to fight anyone who makes a distinction between the prayer and *zakat*. I recognised that it is the truth!" This *hadith* is in the *Musnad* of Ibn Hanbal[32] from the *hadith* of 'Ubayd ibn 'Abdullah ibn 'Utba from Abu Hurayra.

Al-Bidaya wa an-Nihaya[33] reports that al-Qasim ibn Muhammad ibn Abi Bakr as-Siddiq (and he is one of the seven *fuqaha'*) said, "The tribes of Asad, Ghatafan and Tayy' gathered with Tulayha al-Asadi and they sent a delegation to Madina and stayed with the notable people who put them up with the exception of al-'Abbas. They took them to Abu Bakr to ask him to allow them to do the prayer and not pay the *zakat*. Allah made Abu Bakr resolve on the truth and he said, "If they deny a single camel-strap to me, you must fight them."

He was asked, "With whom will you fight them?" He replied, "By myself until one side of my neck is parted from the other!"

The sides of the neck. There are two, one on each side. One of them is only separated from the other by death.

He appointed commanders over the armies and governors in the lands chosen for them with due consideration. That was one of the most correct and best things that he did for Islam.

The foremost of these leaders were Abu 'Ubayda 'Amir ibn 'Abdullah ibn al-Jarrah al-Fihri, 'Amr ibn al-'As as-Sahmi, Khalid ibn al-Walid al-Makhzumi, Khalid ibn Sa'id ibn al-'Asir al-Umawi, Yazid ibn Abi Sufyan, 'Ikrima ibn Abi Sufyan, 'Ikrima ibn Abi Jahl, al-Muhajir ibn Abi Umayya, the brother of Umm Salama, Shurahbil ibn Hasana, Mu'awiya ibn Abi Sufyan, Suhayl ibn 'Amr al-'Amiri, the *Khatib* of Quraysh, al-Qa'qa' ibn 'Amr at-Tamimi, 'Arfaja ibn Haritha al-Bariqi, al-'Ala' ibn al-Hadrami, the ally of the Banu Umayya, al-Muthanna ibn Haritha ash-Shaybani and Hudhayfa ibn Muhsin al-Ghatafani. Foremost among his governors were 'Attab ibn Usayd al-Umawi, 'Uthman ibn al-'As ath-Thaqafi, Ziyad ibn Labid al-Ansari, Abu Musa al-Ash'ari, Mu'adh ibn Jabal, Ya'la ibn Munabbih, Jarir ibn 'Abdullah al-Bajili, 'Iyad ibn Ghanim, al-Walid ibn 'Uqba ibn Abi Mu'ayt, 'Abdullah ibn Thawr of the Banu Ghawth and Suwayd ibn Muqarrin al-Muzani.

He told Fatima, 'Ali and al-'Abbas, "The Messenger of Allah ﷺ said, 'We do not leave legal inheritance. What we leave is *sadaqa*.'" The Companions remembered that."

The Book of the Virtues of the Companions in *Sahih Bukhari*[34] contains the *hadith* of az-Zuhri from 'Urwa ibn az-Zubayr from 'A'isha which states that Fatima sent to Abu Bakr to ask him for her inheritance from the Prophet ﷺ which was in Madina and Fadak and what remained of the fifth of Khaybar. Abu Bakr said, "The Messenger of Allah ﷺ said, 'We do not leave legal inheritance. What we leave is *sadaqa*.' Muhammad's family will have provision from this property (i.e. the property of Allah). They do not have more than that provision. By Allah, I will not change any of the *sadaqa* of the Prophet ﷺ which existed in the time of the Prophet ﷺ. I will act as the Messenger of Allah ﷺ acted." 'Ali said the *shahada* and then he said, "We recognise your virtue, Abu Bakr (and he then mentioned their relationship with the Messenger of Allah ﷺ and their right)." Abu Bakr said, "By the One in whose hand my life is, the family of the Messenger of Allah ﷺ are dearer to me than my own kin." There is more of this in the Book of Expeditions in the chapter on the raid on Khaybar in *Sahih Bukhari*.[35]

In the Book of Bequests from *Sahih Bukhari*[36] and the Book of the Division of the *Khums*[37] we find the *hadith* of Abu az-Zinad from al-A'raj from Abu Hurayra that the Messenger of Allah ﷺ said, "My heirs will not divide a single dinar between them. What I leave after ensuring the maintenance of my family and provision of my agent is *sadaqa*." In *Minhaj as-Sunna*, Ibn Taymiyya quoted the words of the Prophet ﷺ, "We do not leave legal inheritance. What we leave is *sadaqa*." It is related from him by Abu Bakr, 'Umar, 'Uthman, 'Ali, Talha, az-Zubayr, Sa'd, 'Abd ar-Rahman ibn 'Awf, al-'Abbas ibn 'Abd al-Muttalib, the wives of the Messenger of Allah ﷺ and Abu Hurayra. The *riwaya* from these people is firm in the *Sahih* collections and the *Musnads*.

He said before that:[38] "Allah protected the Prophets from bequeathing this world so that that would not be a cause of suspicion for anyone wanting to attack their prophethood by saying that they sought this world

The Back-Breaking Disaster

and bequeathed it to their heirs." The heirs of the Prophet ﷺ also included his wives. One of them was 'A'isha, Abu Bakr's daughter. She was denied her portion by this *hadith* of the Prophet ﷺ. If Abu Bakr had acted by his natural inclination, he would have wanted his daughter to inherit.

The Book of the Division of the *Khums* in *Sahih Bukhari*[39] contains the *hadith* of Ibn Shihab from 'Urwa ibn az-Zubayr in which 'A'isha stated that after the death of the Messenger of Allah ﷺ, Fatima, the daughter of the Messenger of Allah ﷺ, asked Abu Bakr as-Siddiq to allot to her her inheritance from what the Messenger of Allah ﷺ left from what Allah had given him as booty. Abu Bakr told her, "The Messenger of Allah ﷺ said, 'We do not leave legal inheritance. What we leave is *sadaqa.*'" Abu Bakr refused her request and said, "I will not abandon anything which the Messenger of Allah ﷺ did. I will also do it. I fear that if I were to leave anything he did, I would be misguided."

In the same chapter of *Sahih Bukhari*[40] we find the *hadith* of Imam Malik ibn Anas from Ibn Shihab from Malik ibn Aws ibn al-Hadthan an-Nasiri who said, "One day I was sitting with my family when the sun was high when a messenger from 'Umar ibn al-Khattab said, 'Respond to the Amir al-Mu'minin!' So I went. While I was sitting with him, the steward approached him and asked, 'Will you see 'Uthman, 'Abd ar-Rahman ibn 'Awf, az-Zubayr and Sa'd ibn Abi Waqqas who are all asking for permission to enter?' He said, 'Yes,' and gave permission. Then they came in and sat down. The steward approached him again after a short time and said, 'Will you see 'Ali and 'Abbas?' He said he would, giving them permission. They came in and gave the greeting and sat down. 'Abbas said, 'Amir al-Mu'minin! Decide between me and this one!' They were arguing about what booty Allah had given His Messenger ﷺ from the Banu an-Nadir. The group, 'Uthman and his companions, said, 'Amir al-Mu'minin! Decide between them and free them of each other!' 'Umar said, 'Gently! I ask you by Allah by whose permission the heaven and the earth are set up, do you know that the Messenger of Allah ﷺ said, "We do not leave legal inheritance. What we leave is *sadaqa*"?' The group replied, 'That is what he said.' He turned to 'Ali and 'Abbas and said, 'I ask you by Allah, do you know that the Messenger of Allah ﷺ said that?' They replied, 'That is what he said.' Then he mentioned that the Prophet ﷺ used to spend on his family for the year from their property. Then he made what remained the property of Allah. He asked them to testify to that and they testified. Then he said, 'Then Allah made His Prophet ﷺ die. Abu Bakr said, "I am the guardian of the Messenger of Allah ﷺ." He took it and acted as the Messenger of Allah ﷺ had acted. Allah knows that he was truthful in it, dutiful, right-guided, following the truth. Then Allah made Abu Bakr die. I am the guardian of the Messenger of Allah ﷺ. It is two years since I took on this command. I act in it according to what the Messenger of Allah ﷺ did and what Abu Bakr did. Allah knows that I am truthful concerning it, dutiful, right-guided, following the truth. Then you come to me and your words are the same and your business is the same. You come to me, 'Abbas, asking for your inheritance from your nephew. This one (meaning 'Ali) comes to me to ask for his wife's share from her father. I told you, "The Messenger of Allah ﷺ said, 'We do not leave legal inheritance. What we leave is *sadaqa*.'" Since it is clear to me that I have been given the leadership over you, I say, "If you wish, I will hand it over to you provided that you have the contract of Allah and His agreement that you will act in it according to how the Messenger of Allah ﷺ acted in it and how Abu Bakr acted in it and how I have acted in it since I was given it." If you say, "Give it to us on that condition," then I will give it to you. I ask you by Allah, have I given them this opportunity?' The group said, 'Yes.' Then he turned to 'Ali and al-'Abbas and said, 'I ask you by Allah, have I given you this opportunity?' They replied, 'Yes.' He said, 'Do you demand from me to carry out anything other than that? By Allah by whose permission the heaven and the earth are established, that is my only decision about it. If you are incapable of taking it on, then give it to me. I will spare you from it.'"[41]

Ibn Taymiyya said in *Minhaj as-Sunna*,[42] "Abu Bakr and 'Umar gave from the property of Allah many times over what the inheritance would have been to those who would have inherited it." He said, "He took a village from them which was not large. He did not take a city or a town from them." Then he said,[43] "'Ali was appointed after that and Fadak and other places were under his authority. He did not give any of the inheritance to Fatima's children nor to the children of al-'Abbas."

He said, "I heard the Messenger of Allah ﷺ say, 'A Prophet should only be buried in the place where he dies.'"

In the Book of Funerals in the *Muwatta'* of Malik,[44] it reports that Malik heard that the Messenger of Allah ﷺ died on a Monday and was buried on a Tuesday. People prayed over him one by one and none acted as Imam. Some people said that he should be buried near the minbar and some people said that he should be buried in al-Baqi'. Abu Bakr as-Siddiq came and said, "I heard the Messenger of Allah ﷺ say, 'A Prophet should only be buried in the place where he dies.'" Ibn 'Abd al-Barr said, "It is sound from different directions and the various *hadith*s which Malik gathered."

The Book of Funerals in the *Jami'* of at-Tirmidhi[45] contains the *hadith* of 'A'isha, "When the Messenger of Allah ﷺ died, they disagreed about his burial. Abu Bakr said, 'I heard something from the Messenger of Allah ﷺ which I have not forgotten. He said, "Allah only takes a Prophet in the place in which He wants him to be buried."'" They therefore buried him where his bed had been. In the Book of Funerals in the *Sunan* of Ibn Majah[46] it is reported that Ibn 'Abbas said, "The Muslims disagreed about where to bury him. Some said that he should be buried in his mosque. Others said that he should be buried with his Companions. Abu Bakr said, 'I heard the Messenger of Allah ﷺ say, "A Prophet should only be buried in the place where he dies."'" Ibn Ishaq related it in the *Sira* by Ibn Hisham[47] from the *hadith* of 'Ikrima from Ibn 'Abbas. Look at *al-Bidaya wa an-Nihaya* by Ibn Kathir.[48]

In all of these things, he was imperturbable, and demonstrated his knowledge and position in the *deen*.

Then he appointed 'Umar as his successor, and the *baraka* of Islam appeared. The true promise was fulfilled in the time of the two caliphs.

> What is being referred to is the promise of Allah in the *Surat an-Nur*,[49] "Allah has promised those of you who believe and do right actions that He will appoint them successors in the land as He made those before them successors, and will firmly establish for them their *deen* with which He is pleased and give them, in place of their fear, security. 'They worship Me, not associating anything with Me.' Any who disbelieve after that, such people are deviators."

Islamic society, under the direction of these two caliphs, was the most fortunate society history has known because people – from the rulers to the common people – preferred others to themselves in their dealings. An individual was content with what would fulfil his needs and would expend from himself as much as he could, striving to establish the truth in the earth and to make good between people universal. The good man among them would meet a man who had evil inclinations towards him and he would continue with him until he had numbed the elements of evil which beset him and had awakened in that man the elements of good which were concealed until he as well became one of the people of good. Among those claiming to be Muslim up until this very day are groups whose hearts are filled with malice, even towards Abu Bakr and 'Umar themselves, let alone those from whom Abu Bakr and 'Umar sought help among the people of excellence and doing good. Using false reports, they fabricated personalities for them other than their real personalities so that they are satisfied that the hatred they have for some people among them is actually deserved! This is why Islamic "history" is full of lies. There will be no new renaissance for the Muslims unless they recognise the reality of their predecessors and take them as models. They will not recognise the reality of their predecessors except by purifying Islamic history of what has become falsely attached to it.

Then 'Umar formed an electoral council. 'Abd ar-Rahman ibn 'Awf disqualified himself from being eligible so that he could be careful about who should be put forward.

In the Book of the Virtues of the Companions in *Sahih Bukhari*[50] we find the *hadith* of 'Amr ibn Maymun, one of the students of Mu'adh and Ibn Mas'ud and one of the shaykhs of ash-Sha'bi and Sa'id ibn Jubayr. This *hadith* contains an account of the murder of the Amir al-Mu'minin, 'Umar, and how 'Umar left the succession to the caliphate to the decision of a council of six men with whom the Messenger of Allah ﷺ was pleased when he died and how 'Abd ar-Rahman ibn 'Awf disqualified himself. Then he reached the point where he advanced 'Uthman. This *hadith* is the soundest and most excellent thing that is established on this subject. Then read what the *Shaykh al-Islam*, Ibn Taymiyya, wrote in the *Minhaj as-Sunna*[51] about the position of 'Umar when he made it a matter of consultation. In it is fine right guidance as to the agreement, love, and mutual help which existed between the Banu Hashim and the Banu Umayya in the days of the Prophet ﷺ, Abu Bakr and 'Umar. 'Uthman and 'Ali were closer to each other than the rest of the four were to the two of them. Ibn Taymiyya[52] quoted the words of Ahmad ibn Hanbal, "People did not agree on any allegiance as they agreed on the allegiance to 'Uthman." The Muslims appointed him after they had consulted one another for three days. They agreed and were in harmony and mutual love, all holding together to the rope of Allah. Allah informed them and made them victorious by the guidance and the *deen* of the truth with which He had sent His Prophet ﷺ and He gave them victory over the unbelievers. By means of them He conquered the lands of Syria and Iraq as well as some of Khorasan.

He preferred 'Uthman based on his opinion of him that he would not break a contract, violate an agreement, embark on anything disliked or oppose anything that was part of the *Sunna*.

> How can one not have a good opinion of 'Uthman when the Messenger of Allah ﷺ testified to the purity of his conduct and that he would have a good final seal? The Prophet ﷺ did not speak from caprice. *"It is only a revelation revealed."* Ibn Hajar said in 'Uthman's biography in the *Isaba*, "It has come by *mutawatir* transmission that the Messenger of Allah ﷺ gave 'Uthman the good news of the Garden and that he considered him one of the people of the Garden and testified that he would be a martyr." The *hadith* which are related by *mutawatir* transmission about that from the Messenger of Allah ﷺ are not in doubt. Anyone who inclines to something other than what they indicate is the one who is content to fling himself into the gates of Hell.
>
> At-Tirmidhi related by means of al-Harith ibn 'Abd ar-Rahman from Talha, one of the ten who were given the good news of the Garden, that the Messenger of Allah ﷺ said, "Every Prophet has a friend. My friend in the Garden will be 'Uthman." Ibn 'Abd al-Barr said in the biography of 'Uthman in the *Isti'ab*, "It is confirmed that the Prophet ﷺ said, 'I asked my Lord that none who became my in-law through marriage or to whom I became an in-law through marriage would enter the Fire (or 'go near it').'" Another testimony from the Messenger of Allah ﷺ about this excellent man is that he was one whose like Abu Bakr and 'Umar would hope for. Imam Muslim related in the Book of the Virtues of the Companions in the *Sahih*[53] from Nafi' that 'Abdullah ibn 'Umar ibn al-Khattab said, "In

the time of the Prophet ﷺ we did not think anyone equal to Abu Bakr, then 'Umar, then 'Uthman. After them we would bracket together the Companions of the Prophet ﷺ and not distinguish between them." Al-Muhallab ibn Abi Sufra was asked, "Why was 'Uthman called Dhu an-Nurayn?" He replied, "Because it is not known that anyone let down a curtain (to be alone) with two daughters of a Prophet but him." Khaythama narrated, in the Virtues of the Companions, from an-Nazzal ibn Sabra al-'Amiri (one of those who took from Abu Bakr, 'Uthman and 'Ali, and he was one of the shaykhs of ash-Sha'bi, ad-Dahhak), that he said, "We said to 'Ali, 'Tell us about 'Uthman.' He said, 'That is a man who is called Dhu an-Nurayn in the Highest Assembly.'"

Ibn Mas'ud said, when allegiance was paid to 'Uthman at the time when he became Caliph, "We have given allegiance to the best of us and we did not neglect anyone." 'Ali ibn Abi Talib described him after his term had passed and said, "'Uthman was the most given to maintaining ties of kinship among us and he was among those *'who believe, then are fearfully aware and do good. Allah loves those who do good'*[54]." Salim ibn 'Abdullah ibn 'Umar ibn al-Khattab related that his father said, "We censured 'Uthman for some things for which we would not have censured 'Umar." 'Abdullah ibn 'Umar was an eye-witness to the caliphate of 'Uthman from its beginning to its end. He was the strongest of people in clinging to the *Sunna* of Muhammad. In spite of that, he testified that everything for which 'Uthman was censured could have come from 'Umar, his father. If 'Umar had initiated them, no one would have blamed him for it. Mubarak ibn Fadala, the client of Zayd ibn al-Khattab said, "I heard 'Uthman saying, 'O people! Why do you take revenge on me? There has not been a day on which you have not divided up booty.'"

Al-Hasan al-Basri said, "I heard the herald of 'Uthman calling out, 'O people! Come in the morning for gifts!' They came and took them in full. 'O people! Come in the morning for your provision.' They came and took it in full until, by Allah, my ears heard, 'Come in the morning for your clothes,' and they took robes of honour. 'Come in the morning for your ghee and honey.'" Al-Hasan said, "Provision was abundant. There was much wealth. There was no believer on the earth who feared another believer, rather loving him, helping him, and being friendly to him." (That is related from him by Ibn 'Abd al-Barr).

Ibn Sirin, the colleague of al-Hasan al-Basri, was also a contemporary of 'Uthman. He said, "There was so much wealth in the time of 'Uthman that a slave-girl would be sold for her weight and a horse for 100,000 dinars and a palm-tree for 1000 dirhams." 'Abdullah ibn 'Umar ibn al-Khattab was asked about 'Ali and 'Uthman and he told the person who had asked him, "May Allah make you ugly! You ask about two men and both of them are better than you and you want me to denigrate one of them and elevate the other?"

The Prophet ﷺ said that 'Umar would be a martyr and that 'Uthman would be a martyr and that he would be given the Garden for the affliction which was going to befall him.

In the Virtues of the Companions from *Sahih Bukhari*[55] we find the *hadith* of Abu Musa al-Ash'ari who said, "The Prophet ﷺ entered a garden and commanded me to guard the garden door. A man came to ask permission to enter. The Messenger of Allah ﷺ said, 'Give him permission and give him the good news of the Garden.' It was Abu Bakr. Then another man came and asked for permission to enter. He said, 'Give him permission and give him the good news of the Garden.' It was 'Umar. Then another came and asked permission. The Prophet ﷺ was silent for a moment and then said, 'Give him permission and give him the good news of the Garden for an affliction which will strike him.' That was 'Uthman ibn 'Affan." (Look at *Sahih Bukhari*[56]).

A similar thing is in the Book of the Virtues of the Companions from

The Back-Breaking Disaster

Sahih Muslim[57] from the *hadith* of Abu Musa al-Ash'ari. Ibn Majah related[58] from Muhammad ibn Sirin, one of the Imams of the *Tabi'un*, from Ka'b ibn 'Ujra al-Balawi, the ally of the Ansar, one of those who were present at the *'umra* of Hudaybiya with the Messenger of Allah ﷺ in which the *ayat* of ransom was revealed (2:195). Ka'b ibn 'Ujra said, "The Messenger of Allah ﷺ mentioned sedition and said that it was near. A man with his head veiled passed by. The Messenger of Allah ﷺ said, 'On that day, this one will have guidance.' I got up and went to him and it was 'Uthman. Then I faced the Messenger of Allah ﷺ and said, 'This one?' He said, 'This one.'"

We find in the *Musnad* of Ahmad[59] from Abu Sahla, the client of 'Uthman (who is a reliable Tabi'i) that 'Uthman said on the 'day of the house' when he was surrounded, "The Messenger of Allah ﷺ took a pledge from me that I would be patient in it." The *hadith* is with at-Tirmidhi[60] by way of Waki'. He said, "The *hadith* is *hasan-sahih*." In Ibn Majah[61] there are two *hadith*. One of them is through Abu Sahla, the client of 'Uthman, the other is through 'A'isha. Al-Hakim presented them in the *Mustadrak* on the two *Sahih* volumes[62] from 'A'isha.

He and his wife Ruqayya, the daughter of the Messenger of Allah ﷺ, were the first emigrants after Ibrahim the Friend, by which he entered the category of "The first to..."

> As-Suyuti and other scholars before and after him wrote books in which they name the individuals who preceded others to particular praiseworthy actions and other things. They said, "'Uthman was the first to emigrate in the way of Allah in the first *hijra* to Abyssinia."

...which is a great knowledge that people have compiled.
Since his rule was sound, he was slain unjustly...

> Imam Ibn Hanbal related in his *Musnad*[63] from 'Abdullah ibn 'Umar ibn al-Khattab who said, "The Messenger of Allah ﷺ mentioned sedition. A

man passed by and the Prophet ﷺ said, 'This veiled man will be killed unjustly on that day.'" 'Abdullah ibn 'Umar said, "I looked and it was 'Uthman ibn 'Affan." Shaykh Ahmad Shakir said that at-Tirmidhi related the *hadith*[64] and his commentator quoted from Ibn Hajar that he said, "Its *isnad* is sound." Al-Hakim related the same in *al-Mustadrak*[65] from Murra ibn Ka'b and considered it sound according to the preconditions of the two shaykhs. Adh-Dhahabi agreed with him.

… **"*so that Allah might settle a matter whose result was preordained*".[66] He did not declare war…**

i.e. fighting the people of the *qibla*. As for his wars to elevate the word of Allah and spread the call of the truth, in this he was the most active of anyone known in Islamic history.

…nor put together an army…

to defend himself and to restrain those who acted unjustly against him.

…nor rise to civil war…

He was the strongest of Allah's creation in his dislike of it and striving to constrict its scope and sparing the blood of the Muslims, even if that would lead to himself being sacrificed for the sake of others.

…nor call others to homage…

People submitted to him without his looking for it. Ibn Taymiyya said in the *Minhaj as-Sunna*:[67] "The Companions agreed on 'Uthman because his appointment was the greatest in benefit and least in corruption compared with other rulers." Then he said, "There is no doubt that there were none better than the six with whom the Messenger of Allah ﷺ was pleased, i.e. those whom 'Umar had specified. If there was something to be disliked about each of them, others had more disliked things in them. This is why none better than him was appointed after 'Uthman nor any with better conduct than him."

...nor did anyone among his peers and equals fight or contend with him.

> The peers and equals of the Amir al-Mu'minin 'Uthman were his brothers whom 'Umar made part of the Council. As for those who obeyed 'Abdullah ibn Saba' and his followers when they plunged into the snares of sedition, the gap between them and the rank of the people of the Council is greater than that between the nadir and the apex, rather it is greater than that between good and evil. When they pandered to evil, they introduced it into the history of Islam by their stupidity and their shortsightedness. If its only result had been that because of what they did the outward movement of Islamic *jihad* stopped at its then borders for many years, that would have been enough of a wrong action and crime. Ibn Taymiyya stated in the *Minhaj as-Sunna*:[68] "None of the best Muslims were involved in the blood of 'Uthman. They did not kill him nor say that he should be killed. He was killed by a group of the rabble of the tribes and the people of sedition who corrupt the earth. 'Ali exclaimed, 'O Allah, curse the murderers of 'Uthman on land and sea, on the plains and the mountains!'"

He did not desire it for himself. There is no disagreement that no one should do it (i.e. murder) to someone other than 'Uthman, so how could it be done to 'Uthman?

The names of those who attacked him are known and we find that they were people of personal desires who used evil tricks to gain their designs.

> Those groups who shared in the crime against Islam on the 'Day of the House' fall into various degrees in their crime. Some were overcome by excess in the *deen*, so they thought that mistakes constituted terrible crimes and they in turn committed crimes in their objection. Some sided with the

Yemenis against the shaykhs of the Companions from Quraysh and they had no standing in Islam. They envied the people of Quraysh who had priority for the booty which they received according to the Shari'a as a reward for their *jihad* and their victories. They wanted to have the same without precedence in Islam or *jihad*. These included those who wanted blood money for the *hudud* of the Shari'a which had been carried out on some of their relatives. They harboured an old feud and rancour in their hearts because of it. They included the foolish people who the Saba'ites were able to gather because of their weak intellects and they then compelled them to sedition, corruption and false beliefs, and also those who were aggravated by the goodness of 'Uthman and his kindness towards them. Then they rejected the kindness of 'Uthman because they coveted leadership and advancement which they did not deserve, merely because they had grown up under his rule. They included those who had been punished by 'Uthman for things which they had done which were contrary to the proper behaviour of Islam and the punishment of the Shari'a made them angry at 'Uthman. If they had received a harsher punishment from 'Umar, they would have been content with it and submitted. They included those who were eager for leadership before they were ready for it because they were deceived by deceptive intelligence or eloquence and not nurtured by wisdom. They rebelled in order to make the business happen before its time.

In general, the mercy which formed the basis of 'Uthman's character and which filled his heart, made many envious of him. They wanted to make his mercy a mount for realising their passions. Perhaps if I have the time, I will devote myself to the study of those Kharijites who were against 'Uthman and organise the sound known facts which we still have about them so that it will be a lesson and instruction for all students of Islamic history.

They were warned about their conduct and rebuked.

The people of sound judgment, wisdom and good sense among

the notables of their cities and their scholars in Kufa, Basra and Fustat admonished them and forbade them what they were doing. Then Mu'awiya warned them and forbade them to behave as they were doing in some meetings which he had with them in Syria during their journey to 'Uthman as will come in the author's discussion of their attack on Madina with the pretext of performing the *hajj*. They turned their false *hajj* into an attack against the Caliph and ended by shedding his forbidden blood near the grave of the Prophet ﷺ.

They stayed with 'Abd ar-Rahman ibn Khalid ibn al-Walid...

> 'Abd ar-Rahman ibn Khalid ibn al-Walid was the agent of Mu'awiya in charge of Hums and that part of northern Syria around it up to the end of the island of Ibn 'Umar.

...and he threatened them until they repented.

> They pretended that they had repented but, *"But then when they go apart with their shaytans, they say, 'We are really with you...'"*[69]

Then he sent them to 'Uthman and they repented.

> 'Abd ar-Rahman ibn Khalid gave them a choice in going to 'Uthman. The greatest of them, al-Ashtar an-Nakha'i, went. That is a story which we will mention in its proper place in this book.

'Uthman gave them a choice and they chose to split up and go to different places, so he released them. When each had gone where he chose, then they organised the sedition and gathered their group together. They came to him all together.

> to 'Uthman.

He addressed them from the wall of his house, warning and reminding them and trying to make them beware of spilling his blood.

To make them beware of something is to restrain them and forbid them by proof and evidence.

Talha came out weeping and cautioning the people. 'Ali sent his sons.

So that they could guard the Amir al-Mu'minin, 'Uthman, and defend him with arms if he so wished.

They said to them, ...

i.e. the attackers said that they had spoken to 'Ali, Talha and az-Zubayr.

..."You sent to us saying, 'Come against those who have altered the *sunna* of Allah!'

The attackers claimed that they had received letters from 'Ali, Talha and az-Zubayr, calling them to rebel against 'Uthman under the pretext that he had altered the *sunna* of Allah. The fact that 'Ali, Talha and az-Zubayr denied that they had written any letters will come. It is clear that in fact both groups were truthful and that the Saba'ites who organised the sedition had forged the letters which the rebelling attackers mentioned.

"Now we have come, this one sits in his house (meaning 'Ali) and you come out...

addressed to Talha ibn 'Ubaydullah.

...with your eyes weeping. By Allah, we will not go until we have spilled his blood!"

This was immensely stressful and extremely distressing for the Companions. They lied to their faces and slandered them. If 'Uthman had so wished, he could have asked the Companions for help and they would have helped him immediately.

They approached him about that several times. Mu'awiya offered to

The Back-Breaking Disaster

move the seat of the caliphate to Syria or support him with the army from Syria which historically had only known advancement and victory.

People came alleging injustice and that they had been wronged...

> i.e. the rebels who put on the appearance of people who had been wronged. That is when people claim that there are matters which merit complaint. 'Uthman thought that he owed it to them to justify himself to them and to the people in general concerning the things they alleged, and to give his own view of the matters about which they claimed to have been wronged.

...and he admonished them, and they flared up. The Companions wanted to strike them with spears. 'Uthman directed that no one should fight on his account. He submitted and they left him to what he was content to do.

It is a weighty question in *fiqh*: whether a man may submit or is he obliged to defend himself? If he submits and forbids anyone to defend him by fighting, is it permitted for someone else to defend him and disregard his wishes? Scholars have different opinions regarding this matter.

'Uthman did not do anything objectionable either at the beginning of the affair nor at the end of it and the Companions are all agreed that he did nothing objectionable. Beware of paying any attention whatsoever to any false reports you may hear.

> The yardstick of reports regarding the history of any community is confidence in their sources and investigating their soundness by examining the character of the individuals to whom the account is ascribed. The reports of Islamic history are transmitted by eye-witnesses who mentioned them to those who came after them who related them to those after them. Biased people have crept into those transmitters, people who forged

reports, attributing them to the tongues of others, and circulated them in books, either to ingratiate themselves with some of the people of this world or out of partisanship for a particular position which they supposed to be part of the *deen*.

One of the virtues of Islamic history – following on from what the *hadith* scholars do – is that it singles out a group of scholars for the criticism of the *riwayas* and transmitters and distinguishes the truthful among them from the liars. This became a respected science which has its own rules and on which books have been written. Volumes filled with biographies have been written on the different transmitters, containing information about the degree of each transmitter in respect of truthfulness, firmness and trustworthiness in transmission.

One of them, for instance, might have a position based on a particular party or *madhhab* towards which he inclined. This will be mentioned in his biography so that anyone studying the reports of that man will be familiar with the areas of strength and weakness in his reports. Those who are too impetuous in writing about the history of Islam and compose books about it before they are fully ready – especially in respect of the criticism of the transmitters and the recognition of what scholars have verified about their integrity or lack of it – fall into an error which they would have been able to avoid if they had completed their studies in these areas.

Defamation

of 'Uthman

Following the transmission of the liars, many have maintained that 'Uthman committed some injustices and objectionable things while he was ruler. These include that:

1. He beat 'Ammar until his intestines split open.
2. He beat Ibn Mas'ud until his ribs were broken and denied him his stipend.
3. He introduced an innovation by collecting the Qur'an and compiling it and burning other copies of the Qur'an.
4. He set up the *hima* (sanctuary for animals).
5. He exiled Abu Dharr to ar-Rabadha.
6. He expelled Abu ad-Darda' from Syria.
7. He brought back al-Hakam after the Messenger of Allah ﷺ had exiled him.
8. He annulled the *sunna* of shortening the travel prayer.
9-12. He appointed Mu'awiya, 'Abdullah ibn 'Amir ibn Kurayz and Marwan. He appointed al-Walid ibn 'Uqba who was a deviant and not someone fit to rule.
13. He gave Marwan the *khums* (the fifth of the spoils due to the leader of the community) of North Africa.
14. 'Umar used to beat with a *durra* (stick) but 'Uthman beat with a staff.

> A *durra* is a small stick that the ruler carries for keeping people in check.

15. He went above the step of *minbar* used by the Messenger of Allah when Abu Bakr and 'Umar went below it.
16. He was not present at the Battle of Badr and was defeated on the Day of Uhud. He was not present at the Covenant of Ridwan (at Hudaybiya).
17. He did not execute 'Ubaydullah ibn 'Umar for killing al-Hurmuzan (who had given the knife to Abu Lu'lu'a and who incited him to murder 'Umar ibn al-Khattab).
18. He sent a letter with the slave in charge of his camels to Ibn Abi Sarh telling him to kill those mentioned in it.

DEFENCE

All of this is false both in *isnad* and in text. As for their words, "'Uthman committed injustices and objectionable things," that is false.

As you will see from the proofs which the author produces discrediting these allegations of theirs, one by one, until the last of them is reached.

1-2. As for his beating ['Ammar and Ibn Mas'ud] and denying him his stipend, that is a lie.

It has already been stated that when 'Uthman was given the oath of allegiance, 'Abdullah ibn Mas'ud said, "We have given allegiance to the best of us and we did not neglect anyone." Another version is, "We have appointed the highest of us and we did not neglect anyone." When 'Uthman was appointed, Ibn Mas'ud was the governor appointed by 'Umar over the people of Kufa and Sa'd ibn Abi Waqqas was in charge of the prayer and war affairs there. Sa'd and Ibn Mas'ud disagreed about a loan which Sa'd had asked him for – as will come later. Therefore 'Uthman dismissed Sa'd and kept Ibn Mas'ud on.

Up to this point, the relationship between Ibn Mas'ud and his Caliph was untroubled. When 'Uthman determined to make one copy of the

The Defamation of 'Uthman

Qur'an universal in the Muslim world, the Companions of the Messenger of Allah ﷺ agreed that it would be the complete copy, agreeing with the last form of presentation in which the Book of Allah was presented to His Messenger ﷺ before his death. Ibn Mas'ud wanted the writing of the *mushaf* to be entrusted to him. He also wanted his own copy of the Qur'an which he had written for himself in the past to remain in place. 'Uthman acted contrary to what Ibn Mas'ud wanted in both cases.

'Uthman chose Zayd ibn Thabit to write the unified *mushaf* that was because Abu Bakr and 'Umar had previously chosen him for this work during the khilafa of Abu Bakr. Indeed, Abu Bakr and 'Umar chose Zayd ibn Thabit in the beginning because he was the one who had memorised the final form in which the Book of Allah was presented to the Messenger ﷺ before his death. 'Uthman was correct in this. He knew, as all the Companions knew, the place of Ibn Mas'ud and his knowledge and he confirmed his belief. But 'Uthman was also right in purging all the other copies, including the copy of Ibn Mas'ud, because making the script of the *mushaf* the one with the most perfect form possible is by the consensus of the Companions the greatest of the things which 'Uthman did. Most of the Companions sided with 'Uthman in that against Ibn Mas'ud.[70]

In any case, 'Uthman did not beat Ibn Mas'ud and did not deny him his stipend. He continued to recognise his worth as Ibn Mas'ud continued to obey him as his leader to whom he had given allegiance and he believed that he was the best of the Muslims at the moment in which allegiance was offered.

That he beat 'Ammar in that way is also a lie. If his intestines had broken open, he would never have lived.

At-Tabari related[71] from Sa'id ibn al-Musayyab that there was a disagreement between 'Ammar and 'Abbas ibn 'Utba ibn Abi Lahab which moved 'Uthman to discipline them by beating them. I say that this is part of what someone in command does in cases like these and it happened both before and after 'Uthman. How frequently 'Umar did that to people like 'Ammar and to those who were better than 'Ammar by his right of rule over the Muslims.

When the Saba'ites organised the dissemination of rumours and began to send letters from every city to other cities with false reports, the Companions indicated to 'Uthman that he should send men in whom he had confidence to the cities so that they could return and tell him the true state of affairs. 'Uthman forgot what had taken place with 'Ammar and sent him to Egypt with his full confidence to investigate the state of affairs there. 'Ammar delayed for a time in Egypt, and the Saba'ites flocked to him to try to make him take their side. 'Uthman and his governor in Egypt took steps to remedy this and 'Ammar was brought back to Madina in full honour. 'Uthman censured him for what he had dared do.

According to what Ibn 'Asakir related in the *History of Damascus*,[72] he said to him, "Abu al-Yaqadhan! You slandered Ibn Abi Lahab when he slandered you and then you were angry with me because I took what was due from you and what was due from him. O Allah, I have dispensed justice between me and my community! O Allah, I draw near You by establishing Your *hudud* on everyone and I do not care! Leave me, 'Ammar!" He left. When 'Ammar met the common people, he defended himself and denied that he had done anything wrong. When he met someone he trusted, he admitted what he had done and showed regret. People censured him, parted from him and disliked him after that.

Ibn Taymiyya said in the *Minhaj as-Sunna*,[73] "'Uthman was better than all who spoke against him. He was better than Ibn Mas'ud, 'Ammar, Abu Dharr and others in many aspects as is confirmed by sound proofs. It is not more appropriate to regard the words of one who is surpassed as detracting from one who is better than doing the opposite. That is how what 'Ammar said against 'Uthman is transmitted as well as what al-Hasan said about 'Ammar. It is transmitted that 'Ammar said, "Uthman disbelieved along with other notorious unbelievers.' Al-Hasan ibn 'Ali objected to him saying that. It was the same with 'Ali who said to him, "Ammar, do you reject a Lord in whom 'Uthman believes?'"

Ibn Taymiyya said, "It is clear from this that a believing man who is a friend of Allah can believe another believing man who is a friend of Allah to be an unbeliever and that he can be mistaken in his opinion. That does not detract from the faith and *wilaya* of either of them. It confirmed in the *Sahih* that Usayd ibn Hudayr said to Sa'd ibn 'Ubada in the presence of the Prophet ﷺ, 'You are a hypocrite who argues for the hypocrites,' and that 'Umar ibn al-Khattab said of Hatib ibn Abi Balta'a, 'Messenger of Allah, let me cut off the head of this hypocrite!' The Prophet ﷺ said, 'He was at Badr. How do you know? Perhaps Allah has looked with compassion on the people of Badr and said, "Act as you like. I have forgiven you."' 'Umar was better than 'Ammar and 'Uthman was better than Hatib ibn Abi Balta'a by many degrees. 'Umar's proof in what he said to Hatib was more apparent than 'Ammar's proof. In spite of this, both of them are people of the Garden. How can 'Uthman and 'Ammar not be people of the Garden, even if one of them said what he said to the other? However, a group of scholars deny that 'Ammar said that anyway."

Ibn Taymiyya said, "In general, when it is said that 'Uthman beat Ibn Mas'ud or 'Ammar, this does not detract from any of them. We testify that these three men are in the Garden and that they are among the great fearful *awliya'* of Allah. A *wali* of Allah can do something which merits the punishment of the Shari'a, not to mention simple discipline. 'Umar ibn al-Khattab beat Ubayy ibn Ka'b with a stick when he saw people walking behind him. He said, 'This is abasement to the follower and a temptation for the followed.' If 'Uthman had disciplined them, either 'Uthman was correct in doing so by the fact that they deserved it and they repented of the thing for which they were punished and He expiated for them by the disciplining, by misfortunes, by their immense good actions or other things. If it is said that they were completely wronged, the statement about 'Uthman is like the statement about them and even more so. He was better than them and more entitled to forgiveness and mercy."

Scholars reject the allegations because of aspects of them that are based on falsehood.

> i.e. the claim of the liars, the enemies of the Companions of the Messenger of Allah ﷺ is that 'Uthman beat 'Ammar until his intestines split open and that he beat Ibn Mas'ud until his ribs were broken and denied him his proper stipend.

A truth cannot be based on something false. Do not spend time trying to keep up with the ignorant. That is something that has no end.

3. As for gathering the Qur'an, that would have been his greatest good work and greatest virtue, even if he had found it already completed. He made it known and brought people back to it and put an end to all dispute about it. The promise of Allah to preserve the Qur'an was carried out at his hand as we have made clear in our books on the Qur'an and elsewhere.[74]

All the Imams related[75] that Zayd ibn Thabit said, "Abu Bakr sent a message to me about the murderous fight against the people of Yamama...

> That was when the Banu Hanifa apostatised under Musaylima the Liar and at the instigation of the enemy of Allah, ar-Rajjal ibn 'Anfawa ibn Nahshal al-Hanafi. The generalship of the Muslims was in the hands of the 'Sword of Allah', Khalid ibn al-Walid. Zayd ibn al-Khattab, 'Umar's brother, was martyred in this bloody fight. The *huffaz* of the Qur'an among the Companions consulted among themselves and said, "O people of *Sura al-Baqara*, magic will be shown to be false today." The *Khatib* of the Ansar

and their banner-bearer, Thabit ibn Qays, shrouded himself and dug his feet into the ground up to the middle of his legs. He continued to fight remaining firm in his place with the banner until he was martyred. The Muhajirun said to Salim, the *mawla* of Abu Hudhayfa, "Do you fear we will advance before you?" He replied, "Then I would be an evil bearer of the Qur'an." He fought until he was martyred. Abu Hudhayfa said, "They have adorned the Qur'an by action." He continued to fight until he was struck down. One of those martyred on that day was Huzn ibn Abi Wahb al-Makhzumi, the grandfather of Sa'id ibn al-Musayyab.

The battle cry of the Companions on that day was, "Muhammad!" They were steadfast on that day with a fortitude which has never been matched, until the apostates sought refuge in the Garden of Death and Musaylima and his men sought shelter in it. Al-Bara' ibn Malik said, "O company of Muslims! Throw me into the garden and I will open its doors for you!" They carried him over the ditches and raised him with spears and threw him into the garden over its walls. He continued to fight the apostates by its door until he managed to open it and the Muslims entered and gained victory. Among those who plunged into the garden was Abu Dujana, one of the fighters of Badr. When he reached Musaylima, he got above him with his sword and killed him. Abu Dujana broke his foot in that battle and then obtained martyrdom. *Al-Bidaya wa an-Nihaya*[76] has the names of many of the martyrs of this terrible day in Islam. They included many who knew the Qur'an by heart.

...while 'Umar ibn al-Khattab was with him. Abu Bakr said, "Umar has come to us and said, "Fighting was intense in the Battle of Yamana and many of the reciters were killed. I fear that if many more reciters are killed in other places, then much of the Qur'an will be lost. I think that the Qur'an should be gathered together." Then I asked 'Umar how we could do something which the Messenger of Allah ﷺ did not do. 'Umar replied, "This is good, by Allah." He continued to argue with me until Allah opened my breast to it and I thought the same as 'Umar thought about it.'"

Zayd said that Abu Bakr went on, "You are a young man of intelligence and we do not suspect you. You used to write down the revelation of the Messenger of Allah ﷺ, so search out the Qur'an and gather it together." Zayd said, "By Allah, if they had asked me to move a mountain, that would not have been heavier on me than what they commanded me to do in assembling the Qur'an. I asked, 'How can you do something which the Messenger of Allah ﷺ did not do?' 'Umar said, 'By Allah, this is good.' He continued to argue with me until Allah expanded my breast in the same way that He had expanded the breast of Abu Bakr and 'Umar. I searched for the Qur'an in order to assemble it from palm branches, flat stones and the hearts of men...

> *'Usub*, the plural of *'asib*, are palm branches without leaves. They are the parts on which leaves do not grow. *Likhaf* (the plural of *lukhfa*) are thin white stones. They used to write on both of them when paper was scarce.

...until I found the end of the *Sura at-Tawba* with Khuzayma al-Ansari which no one else knew: '*A messenger from Allah has come from among you....*' to the end of the *sura*."

The pages remained with Abu Bakr until Allah caused him to die. Then they remained with 'Umar as long as he was alive. Then they were in the possession of Hafsa bint 'Umar until Hudhayfa ibn al-Yaman came to 'Uthman.

> His *hadith* regarding this is found in *Sahih Bukhari*[77] from Ibn Shihab az-Zuhri from Anas ibn Malik.

He had been on a raid with the people of Syria and taken part in the conquest of Armenia and Azerbaijan with the people of Iraq. Hudhayfa informed him about their differences regarding the recitation of the

Qur'an. Hudhayfa said to 'Uthman, "Amir al-Mu'minin, save this community before they disagree about the Book as the Jews and Christians disagree!" So 'Uthman sent a messenger to Hafsa saying, "Send us the pages of the Qur'an and we will make copies of it and then return them." Hafsa sent them to 'Uthman. He then commanded Zayd ibn Thabit, 'Abdullah ibn az-Zubayr, Sa'id ibn al-'As and 'Abd ar-Rahman ibn al-Harith ibn Hisham to make copies of the Qur'an.

> The two great men of Islam, Abu Bakr and 'Umar, were concerned with doing it. Their brother and in-law, Dhu an-Nurayn 'Uthman, completed it by gathering together the Qur'an and fixing it and making its text one. Thus they gave the greatest blessing to the Muslims. By it Allah fulfilled the promise He made when He said, *"We sent down the remembrance and We preserve it."*[78]

After these three shaykhs, the caliphate was given to the Amir al-Mu'minin, 'Ali, and he carried on their work and confirmed the *mushaf* of 'Uthman both in its text and recitation in all the cities he ruled. There is thus a consensus from the first Muslims that what Abu Bakr, 'Umar and 'Uthman established was their greatest good action.

One of the Shi'ite scholars relayed this consensus from the tongue of the Amir al-Mu'minin, 'Ali ibn Abi Talib. It has come in the book of the *History of the Qur'an* by Abu 'Abdullah az-Zanjani[79] that 'Ali ibn Musa, known as Ibn Tawus (589-664 AH), one of their scholars, transmitted in his book, *The Happiness of the Happy,* that ash-Shahrastani said in the preface of the *tafsir* from Suwayd ibn 'Alqama, "I heard 'Ali ibn Abi Talib, peace be upon him, say, 'O people! Allah! Allah! Beware of excess in the affair of 'Uthman and your statement regarding burning the copies of the Qur'an. By Allah, he only burned them with permission from the assembly of the Companions of the Messenger of Allah ﷺ. We agreed. He asked, "What do you say about this recitation about which people disagree? One man meets another man and says, 'My recitation is better than your recitation?'

This leads to disbelief." We said, "What is your opinion then?" He said, "I want the people to agree on one copy. If you disagree today, those after you will have a worse disagreement." We said, "What you think is good."'"

Something about which there is no doubt is that the aggressors themselves in the caliphate of 'Ali used to recite the *mushaf* of 'Uthman about which the Companions had agreed when 'Ali was among them. But some followers in succeeding generations have disgraced themselves by their idiocy and their rejection – like Shaytan at-Taq, Muhammad ibn Ja'far the Rafidite. According to what Imam Ibn Hazm related in the *Fasl*[80] from al-Jahiz, he said, "Abu Ishaq Ibrahim an-Nizam and Bishr ibn Khalid informed them that they said to Muhammad ibn Ja'far ar-Rafidi, known as Shaytan at-Taq, 'Woe to you! Are you not ashamed before Allah to say in your book on the Imamate that Allah did not say at all in the Qur'an, *"The second of the two when they were in the Cave when he said to his companion: Do not grieve. Allah is with us."*[81]. They said, 'By Allah, Shaytan at-Taq laughed a long time until it was as if we were the ones who had wronged him.'" This Shaytan at-Taq was one of the greatest of the propagandists regarding the two Imams, Zayd and his nephew, Ja'far as-Sadiq. He is the one who originated the lie that the Imamate is covenanted to certain individuals. No one had ever said that before this Shaytan at-Taq. Imam Zayd objected to his saying that in Ja'far's assembly.

The Rafidites attempted to alter the Qur'an when 'Ali clearly stated that the Companions agreed to what 'Uthman had undertaken. Abundant material has gone to the Christian missionaries who have cited it as evidence. Ibn Hazm said to them in the *Fasl*,[82] "The Rafidites were not Muslims. They are a group who followed the course of the Jews and the Christians in lying and rejection." I say that the last of them who disgraced himself by this business and disgraced the Shi'a by it was Husayn ibn Muhammad Taqi an-Nuri at-Tabarasi in his book about an assembly ascribed to the Amir al-Mu'minin, 'Ali, which was published in an-Najaf in

1292 and published in Iran in 1298. I have a copy of it. Part of the nature of factionalism, partisanship and bias is that it destroys both the intellects of people who ascribe to it and their character. It also strips them of their modesty and their *deen*.

'Uthman said to the group of the three Qurayshis, "When you and Zayd ibn Thabit disagree about some part of the Qur'an, write it down in the dialect of Quraysh. It was revealed in their tongue." So they did that.

When they had copied the pages out and made copies of the Qur'an, 'Uthman returned the pages to Hafsa and sent one of their copies to each province and commanded that every page and copy of any other Qur'an should be burned.

Ibn Shihab said,[83] "Kharija ibn Zayd informed me that he heard Zayd ibn Thabit say, 'One *ayat* of 'the Parties' (*Ahzab*) was missing, when we copied out the *mushaf*, which I heard the Messenger of Allah ﷺ recite. We looked for it and found it with Khuzayma al-Ansari: *'Among the believers are men who have been true to the contract they made with Allah.*[84] We inserted it in its *sura* in the copy of the Qur'an.'"

As for what is related that he burned them or ripped them (with *ha'* or *kha'*), both are possible since there would have been corruption in letting them remain, or something which was not part of the Qur'an was in them or something abrogated from it, or it was not in the proper order. All the Companions submitted to that, although it is related that Ibn Mas'ud spoke in Kufa and said, "Allah says, *'Whoever defrauds will bring what he has defrauded (ghalla) on the Day of Rising.'*[85] I am going to lock up (*ghaall*) my copy of the Qur'an. Whoever of you is able to lock his copy of the Qur'an away should do it." Ibn Mas'ud wanted his copy of the Qur'an to be taken and what he knew about it to be reliably established. When that was not done with his, he said what he said. Therefore 'Uthman forced him to remove his copy of the Qur'an and he erased its marks, so that a recitation would never reliably be ascribed to him. Allah helped 'Uthman and the truth by removing it from the earth (i.e. Ibn Mas'ud's version).

> 'Abdullah ibn Mas'ud was one of the great scholars of the Companions and one of those who were the most excellent in the recitation of the Book of Allah. The Messenger of Allah ﷺ once praised the good recitation of Ibn Mas'ud of the Qur'an. Abu Bakr and 'Umar raced to convey the good news of this prophetic praise.[86] Ibn Mas'ud used to write down what was revealed in the Qur'an in his copy whenever the revelation of *ayats* of it reached him. He differs in the order of some of these *ayats* from the 'Uthmani copies which were based on the last presentation to the Messenger of Allah ﷺ according to the *ijtihad* of the Companions who were entrusted with gathering it. It is possible that in his copy, Ibn Mas'ud missed out some of the *ayats* from the other reciters of the Qur'an which Zayd ibn Thabit and his colleagues had searched out. Furthermore, Ibn Mas'ud was dominated by the dialect of his people, Hudhayl. The Prophet ﷺ allowed people like Ibn Mas'ud to recite in their own dialects, but it was not for Ibn Mas'ud to compel the community in his time and times after him to use his particular dialect. Part of the blessing was to unify the community in the recitation of the Book of their Lord in the Mudari dialect which the Messenger of Allah ﷺ spoke.

4. As for the *hima* (a place of pasture and water forbidden to the public), it already existed.

> When a nobleman in the time of the *Jahiliyya* settled on a piece of land, he had a dog bark and then made the area as far as the dog's bark extended exclusively for his horses, camels and beasts, and no one else shared in it. When Islam came, the Prophet ﷺ forbade that. He set the *hima* aside for the camels of the *zakat* that were earmarked for *jihad* and general use. The Prophet ﷺ said, "There is no *hima* except for that of

Allah and His Messenger." Al-Bukhari related it in his *Sahih*.[87] Ahmad ibn Hanbal related it in his *Musnad*[88] from the *hadith* of as-Sa'b ibn Jaththama. The Messenger of Allah ﷺ made a *hima* at a place called an-Naqi'. This refers to Naqi' al-Khadmat, as is found in the *Musnad* of Ibn Hanbal[89] from the *hadith* of Abu 'Abd ar-Rahman ibn 'Umar al-'Umari from Nafi' from Ibn 'Umar that the Prophet ﷺ made an-Naqi' a *hima* for horses. Hammad ibn Khalid, the transmitter of this *hadith* from 'Abdullah ibn 'Umar al-'Umari, said, "O 'Abd ar-Rahman, his horses?" He replied, "The horses of the Muslims (i.e. those kept for *jihad* or owned by the Treasury)." This an-Naqi' is about twenty parasangs from Madina. Its area was one mile by eight as is recorded in the *Muwatta'* of Malik in the *riwaya* of Ibn Wahb.

It is known that this continued during the caliphate of Abu Bakr the same as in the time of the Prophet ﷺ because Abu Bakr did not abandon anything which had existed in the time of the Prophet ﷺ, especially as there was more need of horses and camels for *jihad* than before. In 'Umar's time, the *hima* was widened and it included Sarf and ar-Rabadha. 'Umar put an agent in charge of the *hima* who was a client of his called Hani'. In The Book of *Jihad* in *Sahih Bukhari*[90] from the *hadith* of Zayd ibn Aslam from his father is the text of the instruction of 'Umar to his agent who was in charge of the *hima* to bar the animals of the wealthy people like 'Abd ar-Rahman ibn 'Awf and 'Uthman ibn 'Affan, but to be indulgent with the one with sheep and the one whose land had been reaped so that their animals would not die.

As 'Umar extended the *hima* to more than what it had been in the time of the Prophet ﷺ and Abu Bakr due to the increase of the animals of the Treasury in his time, so 'Uthman expanded it because of the expansion of the state and the increase in conquests. That which the Prophet ﷺ permitted for the animals of the Treasury and which Abu Bakr and 'Umar continued was permitted for the Treasury in the time of 'Uthman. Any objection to it is an objection to a matter which is included in the Islamic

Shari'a. When 'Uthman replied to the question about the *hima* when he defended himself before the assembly of the Companions, he announced that those who were in charge of the *hima* limited it to the *zakat* animals of the Muslims in order to protect them so that there would not be any conflict with other animals next to it. They did not deny or push anyone away from it. He mentioned about himself before he was appointed caliph that he had the greatest number of camels and sheep among the Arabs. Then that time passed and he did not have more than two camels for his *hajj*. He asked those of the Companions who knew that, "Is that not the case?" They answered, "O Allah, yes!"

It is said that 'Uthman added to it due to the increase in herds. If the origin of its permission was that need, then it is permitted to increase its size when the need has increased.

5. As for his exiling Abu Dharr to ar-Rabadha, he did not do it.

Abu Dharr chose to retire to ar-Rabadha and 'Uthman agreed with him about it as will be seen. He honoured him and gave him provisions which would give him ease.

Abu Dharr was an ascetic. He used to scold the governors of 'Uthman and recited to them: *"Those who treasure up gold and silver and do not spend it in the way of Allah, given them the good news of a painful punishment."*[91] He saw them increasing in the quantity of their mounts and clothes and he objected to them doing that and wanted them to distribute everything in their possession that was not necessary. 'Umar and the other Companions said, "That on which *zakat* has been paid is not treasure."

Look at the clarification of *fiqh* and the details of the Shari'a on this question in the *Minhaj as-Sunna* by Ibn Taymiyya.[92]

In Syria, there were some words between Abu Dharr and Mu'awiya.

At-Tabari (5:66)[93] and most Islamic sources reported that when Ibn as-Sawda' ('Abdullah ibn Saba') came to Syria, he met Abu Dharr. He said, "Abu Dharr, aren't you amazed at Mu'awiya saying, 'The property is the property of Allah. Doesn't everything belong to Allah?' as if he means to cut it off from the Muslims and erase the name of the Muslims?" Abu Dharr therefore went to him and said, "What leads you to call the property of the Muslims the 'property of Allah'?" Mu'awiya said, "May Allah have mercy on you, Abu Dharr! Are we not the slaves of Allah and all property is His property and all creation is His creation and all the affair is His affair." Abu Dharr said, "Do not say that." Mu'awiya said, "I do not say that it does not belong to Allah, but I will say, 'The property of the Muslims.'" Ibn as-Sawda' ('Abdullah ibn Saba') came to Abu ad-Darda' who said to him, "Who are you? By Allah, I think that you are a Jew." Ibn Saba' came to 'Abdullah ibn as-Samit who took hold of him. 'Abdullah brought him to Mu'awiya and said, "By Allah, this is the one who sent Abu Dharr to you!"

Abu Dharr went to Madina and people gathered around him. He began to act in that way. 'Uthman told him, "If you were to retire..." meaning that you have a position which is not conducive to keeping the company of people. Keeping company with people has preconditions and retirement has preconditions as well. Whoever follows the path of Abu Dharr has a state which demands that he should be on his own or that he should mix with people, allowing everyone their state, provided that it is not unlawful in the Shari'a.

Therefore Abu Dharr went out to ar-Rabadha as an excellent man of asceticism and left excellent men behind him. All of them had good, blessing and excellence. The state of Abu Dharr was better, but it was not possible for everyone. If they had based themselves on it, they would have been destroyed.

What I think after studying the texts of the Shari'a about property and seeing how the texts were applied during the lifetime of the early Community and how they acted, is that the Muslim can own property for himself and his kin which will be sufficient for him and them according to what is customary for people like him and them among the people of integrity, contentment and *deen*. For anything beyond that, he must pay the *zakat* on it demanded by the *Shari'a*, directly according to his own *ijtihad* if he does not pay it to the Islamic government acting by the rules of the Shari'a. After paying *zakat* on it, the owner of the property remains in a state of trial from Allah to see if he will deal with it in a manner which is pleasing to Allah and which will increase the Muslims in strength, happiness and might. If he is a merchant, it is by the path of trade, or if he is a farmer, it is by the ways of agriculture. If he is someone with a craft, it is by way of his craft. In the areas where Islam was established, it benefited from the wealth of the wealthy Companions in help, aid, and strength. When the commerce of the Muslim merchant enables the Muslims to dispense with the commerce of their enemies, it is considered to be a strength for them according to the extent that the one who has it spends it with this intention. It is the same with the craft of the Muslim craftsman and the agriculture of the Muslim farmer. The intention in these matters is a big thing. Its measure is according to action where there is need for it. In general, Muslims can be rich without limit provided that it is part of what they can properly dispose of and that they take enough from it according to what is commonly considered to be adequate, and always try to free themselves from servitude and yielding to luxuries, let alone the trivia and nonsense of civilisation. After they have paid the *zakat* on what they own, what is more than their needs is like the trust of Allah in their possessions. They do with it what will increase the Muslims in wealth, strength, ease, might and happiness. As for the path of Abu Dharr that the Muslim does not spend the night with any money in his possession, that is not now in the best interests of the Muslims. The path of the wealthy Muslims now – when they provide for themselves and their pleasure without any concern for the power of Islam and the strength of its domain and the needs of its people – is not part of Islam. Islam does not recognise those who do not recognise it.

Glory be to the One who ordered the ranks!

It is strange that he should be criticised for something which 'Umar did. It is related that 'Umar ibn al-Khattab confined Ibn Mas'ud and some of the Companions for a year in Madina before he was martyred. Then 'Uthman released them. He had imprisoned them because people were narrating a lot of *hadith*s from the Prophet ﷺ.

> In the Book of the Judgments in the *Principles of the Judgments* by Ibn Hazm[94] is the *mursal* report which Ibn Shu'ba related from Sa'd ibn Ibrahim ibn 'Abd ar-Rahman ibn 'Awf from his father, Ibrahim ibn 'Abd ar-Rahman ibn 'Awf, who said, "'Umar said to Ibn Mas'ud, Abu ad-Darda' and Abu Dharr, 'This *hadith* is not from the Messenger of Allah ﷺ.' I believe that he did not let them leave Madina until he died." Ibn Hazm noted that this report is *mursal* and to use it as proof is not allowed. Shaykh Ahmad Shakir added to it that al-Bayhaqi agreed with Ibn Hazm that Ibrahim ibn 'Abd ar-Rahman ibn 'Awf (d. 65 or 66 when he was 75 years old) did not take directly from 'Umar. I do not know whether in this passage Ibn al-'Arabi relied on this *mursal* report or on another report which we have not read.

Some words passed between Abu Dharr and Mu'awiya. Abu Dharr used words which were not said in the time of 'Umar. Mu'awiya relayed that to 'Uthman. He feared that sedition would arise among the common people. Abu Dharr used to encourage them to take on asceticism and other things which not everyone can bear. They are only for a few. 'Uthman wrote to him, as we have already said, to come to Madina.

When he came, people gathered to him. He said to 'Uthman, "I want to go to ar-Rabadha." 'Uthman told him, "Do so," so he retired. That alone was appropriate for him due to the path he had taken.

> Ibn Khaldun mentioned in the *'Ibar*[95] that Abu Dharr asked 'Uthman for permission to leave Madina. He said, "The Messenger of Allah ﷺ commanded me to leave it when the buildings reached Sal'." 'Uthman allotted him a herd of camels and gave him two slaves and provided him with some provision. He used to visit Madina. There were three miles between Madina and ar-Rabadha. Yaqut said, "It was one of the best houses on the road to Makka."

6. Some words passed between Abu ad-Darda' and Mu'awiya. Abu ad-Darda' was an excellent man of asceticism, one of the qadis.

> i.e. in Damascus.

When he was harsh in the truth and made the path of 'Umar public with the people, they could not bear it and they dismissed him...

> Mu'awiya himself tried to act in the path of 'Umar as Ibn Kathir transmitted in *Al-Bidaya wa an-Nihaya*[96] from Muhammad ibn Sa'd. He said, "'Arim related to us from Hammad ibn Yazid from Ma'mar from az-Zuhri that Mu'awiya acted for two years as 'Umar acted and did not leave any of it. He was far from that." Someone who has not looked into the lives of people and their politics supposes that the ruler does whatever he likes wherever he is. This is an error. The environment has an effect on the ruler and the organisation of the ruler more than the effect that the ruler and the organisation of the ruler have on the environment. This is one of the meanings of the words of Allah, *"Allah never changes a people's state until they change what is in themselves."*[97]

...so he went to Madina."

All of these are benefits which do not diminish the *deen*. They do

The Defamation of 'Uthman

not affect the position of any of the Muslims at all. Abu ad-Darda' and Abu Dharr were free from fault. 'Uthman was completely and utterly innocent and had more integrity. If someone else relates that he exiled someone and told of a cause for it, that is entirely false.

7. As for his bringing back al-Hakam, it is not true.

> i.e. the claim of 'Uthman's attackers was not true when they said that 'Uthman opposed what the Shari'a demanded in that respect.

Our scholars said in answer to it, "When the Messenger of Allah ﷺ gave him permission for it, 'Uthman spoke to Abu Bakr and 'Umar and they said, 'If there is a witness with you, we will return him.' When he was appointed, he made the judgment according to his knowledge to bring him back. 'Uthman would not bring back anyone sent away by the Messenger of Allah ﷺ, even if it had been his own father, nor would he have overturned his judgment."

> Ibn Taymiyya said in the *Minhaj as-Sunna*,[98] "Many of the people of knowledge attacked the story of his exile (i.e. al-Hakam's exile by the Prophet ﷺ) and said that he went by his own choice. The story of al-Hakam's exile is not found in the *Sahih* volumes, nor does it have any *isnad* by which the affair is known." Then he said, "The Makkans who did not become Muslim until the conquest of Makka did not live in Madina. His banishment was that he had him banished from Makka, not from Madina. If he had exiled him from Madina, he would have sent him to Makka. Many of the people of knowledge attacked the story of his exile as has already been stated and then said that he went by his own choice. When the Prophet ﷺ disciplined a man by exile, he did not demand that he remain in exile forever. This is not known for any wrong action. The Shari'a does not mention any wrong action which leaves the one who does it in exile forever. 'Uthman interceded for 'Abdullah ibn Sa'd ibn Abi Sarh and the Prophet ﷺ accepted his intercession for him and took his homage.

How could he not then accept his intercession for al-Hakam? They related that 'Uthman asked him to return him and he gave him permission to do that. We know that his wrong action was less than the wrong action of 'Abdullah ibn Sa'd ibn Abi Sarh. The story of 'Abdullah is confirmed and known by *isnad*s. Al-Hakam's story is mentioned by *mursal*. The historians who fabricated many lies mentioned it in what they related. There is no firm transmission here demanding one to detract [even] from someone inferior to 'Uthman."

"The virtues of 'Uthman are known as well as the love of the Prophet ﷺ for him, his praise of him, his singling him out for his two daughters and his testifying that he would have the Garden. He sent him to Makka and took the pledge on his behalf. The Companions advanced him for the caliphate. 'Umar and others testified that the Messenger of Allah ﷺ died while he was pleased with him. Things like this prove definitely that he was one of the great *awliya'* of Allah, the godfearing with whom Allah is pleased and who are pleased with Him. This is not rejected because of a transmission whose *isnad* is not firm and the manner of whose occurrence is not known, and by saying that 'Uthman did something wrong in a matter whose reality is not known."[99]

Imam Abu Muhammad ibn Hazm transmitted it in the book, *Al-Imama wa al-mufadala*, included in part 4 of his book, *al-Fasl*,[100] the words of the one who gives 'Uthman a proof against the one who objected to him doing that: "The exile imposed by the Prophet ﷺ did not have a necessary limit, nor is there anything in the Shari'a to make it last forever. The punishment is for a wrong action which is deserved but the door to repentance is open. If the perpetrator repents, that punishment falls from him. There is no disagreement about them among the people of Islam. The whole earth becomes permitted." The *mujtahid* of the Zaydis, Sayyid Muhammad ibn Ibrahim al-Wazir al-Yamani (d. 840 AH) quoted in his book, *The Smiling Meadows in the Defence of the Sunna of Abu al-Qasim*[101] the words of al-

Hakam al-Muhsin ibn Kirama al-Mu'tazili al-Mutashayyi' from his book, *The Free Springs,* that the Messenger of Allah ﷺ gave 'Uthman permission for that. Ibn al-Wazir said, "The Mu'tazilites and the Shi'a from the Zaydis must accept this *hadith* and not object to 'Uthman doing that because the opinion of the transmitter of the *hadith* was famous for reliability, knowledge and sound belief." Then Ibn al-Wazir spoke extensively on this subject with proofs and evidence filling three pages in defence of the Amir al-Mu'minin 'Uthman in his recalling al-Hakam. These proofs are from one of the Imams of the Zaydis and their *mujtahids* after he had transmitted that *hadith* from the Mu'tazilite Imam. It had its particular proofs which I heard after that from two of the Imams of the people of the *Sunna,* the Shaykh al-Islam Ibn Taymiyya and Qadi Ibn al-'Arabi and from the Imam of the people of the Dhahir, Abu Muhammad ibn Hazm.

8. As for abandoning the shortening of the prayer, that is *ijtihad* because he heard that some people were tempted by the shortening and did that in their own homes. He thought that the *sunna* might lead to omitting the obligatory. Therefore he left it fearing that it would be the cause of that happening.

> That was in Mina in the *hajj 'Id* in 29 AH. 'Abd ar-Rahman ibn 'Awf censured 'Uthman for performing the full prayer while they were in Mina. ('Uthman made an excuse that some of those who were among the *hajjis* included people from the Yemen and coarse people who had said the previous year, "The prayer for the one at home is two *rak'ats*. This is your Imam, 'Uthman, and he prays two *rak'ats*." Then 'Uthman told 'Abd ar-Rahman ibn 'Awf, "I have taken family in Makka (i.e. that he had entered under the judgment of the resident, not the traveller). I think that I should pray four *rak'ats* out of the fear that I have for the people." Then 'Abd ar-Rahman ibn 'Awf left 'Uthman and met 'Abdullah ibn Mas'ud and spoke to him about that, Ibn Mas'ud said, "Dispute is evil. I have heard that he

prayed four, so I pray four with my companions." 'Abd ar-Rahman ibn 'Awf said, "It reached me that he had prayed four but I prayed two *rak'ats* with my party, but now, it will be as you say." He meant that today "we pray four with him".[102]

However, a group of scholars said, "The traveller can choose between shortening the prayer and performing it in full."

How excellent is what Qadi Abu Bakr said about 'Uthman leaving off shortening the prayer in the journey and making *ijtihad*. In the *hadith* it says, "When the judge strives and is right, he has two rewards. If he errs, he has one reward." 'Uthman erred in this instance. The transmissions about that are clear. It is better to follow the truth. In spite of that, he is rewarded for his *ijtihad*.

The proof of his error lies in the words of Ibn 'Umar, "I kept the company of the Prophet ﷺ and he did not add more than two *rak'ats* to the travel prayer." Abu Bakr, 'Uthman and 'Umar were like that. Al-Bukhari and Muslim related that.

Imam ash-Shawkani said, "His words, 'He did not add more than two *rak'ats* to the travel prayer' contains the fact that the Prophet ﷺ kept to the shortened prayer and did not pray it in full."

The *hadith* of 'A'isha is agreed upon, "The prayer when it was first made obligatory was two *rak'ats* then the travel prayer was confirmed [as two] and the prayer at home was completed [as four]."

There is a strong proof in these two *hadith* that it is obligatory to shorten it and not recommended as some have claimed.

'Ali, 'Umar and most of the scholars of the Salaf and the *fuqaha'* of the community and 'Umar ibn 'Abd al-'Aziz, Qatada, al-Hasan and the Hanafis believe that it is obligatory to shorten the prayer. Hammad ibn Sulayman said, "The one who prays four *rak'ats* in the journey must repeat it." Malik said, "He repeats it as long as it is still in its time."

Those who said that shortening was recommended and not obligatory, have no definite proof and the *hadith* which they use as evidence are not sound. The one who wants to verify that should refer to the book, *Obtaining the Desires* by ash-Shawkani.[103]

A group of the Companions objected to 'Uthman when he did the full prayer at Mina. They gave it various interpretations. Ibn al-Qayyim said, "The best [interpretation] was that it was because he had family at Mina. When the traveller stays in a place and marries in it or has a wife, then he performs a full prayer." Ahmad ibn Hanbal related that 'Uthman said, "O people! When I came, I had family here. I heard the Messenger of Allah ﷺ say, 'When a man marries in a land, he should pray the prayer of the one who resides in it.'" Al-Bayhaqi faults this *hadith* since it is cut off and 'Ikrima ibn Ibrahim is in the *isnad*. He is weak as al-Bayhaqi said. He said in the *Fath*, "This *hadith* is not sound because it is cut off and one of its transmitters is someone who is not used as a proof." Similarly, what is ascribed to 'Uthman is not sound when it is said that he left off shortening fearing that some of the bedouins would think that the prayer was two *rak'ats* for the one at home.

Then if it is sound that 'A'isha interpreted it the same way as 'Uthman interpreted it and he used to pray four *rak'ats* on a journey, the preceding is true of her as we said about 'Uthman, that she made *ijtihad* and erred just as the Rightly-guided Caliph erred. Complete protection from erring is only possessed by the Prophets.

"The Companions disagreed about that."

Muhammad ibn Yahya al-Ash'ari al-Maliki, known as Ibn Bakr (674-741 AH), quoted in his book, *The Preface and the Clarification of the Murder of the Martyr 'Uthman*,[104] that he related from a group of the Companions that the prayer was done in full on a journey. They included 'A'isha, Salman and fourteen Companions. In the chapters of shortening from

Sahih Bukhari[105] is the *hadith* of az-Zuhri from 'Urwa ibn az-Zubayr that 'A'isha said, "The first obligatory prayer was two *rak'ats*, so that the travel prayer is confirmed and the prayer of the one in residence is done in full." Az-Zuhri said, "I asked 'Urwa, 'Why did 'A'isha do it in full then?' He said, 'She interpreted the same as 'Uthman interpreted.'" In the *Musnad* of Ibn Hanbal[106] we find that 'Abbad ibn 'Abdullah ibn az-Zubayr said, "When Mu'awiya came to us on the *hajj*, we went with him to Makka. He prayed *Dhuhr* with two *rak'ats* with us. Then he went to Dar an-Nadwa. On the other hand, 'Uthman would do the full prayer when he came to Makka and prayed *Dhuhr*, *'Asr* and *'Isha'* there with four *rak'ats* each. When he went to Mina and 'Arafat, he shortened the prayer. When he finished the *hajj* and stayed at Mina, he did the full prayer until he left Makka. When Mu'awiya prayed *Dhuhr* with us with two *rak'ats*, Marwan and 'Umar ibn 'Uthman went to him and said, 'No one ever disgraced the son of your uncle in a worse way than you disgraced him.' He asked them, 'How is that?' They told him, 'Don't you know that he did the full prayer in Makka?' He mentioned to them that he had prayed them with the Prophet ﷺ, Abu Bakr and 'Umar. They said, 'Your cousin did it in full.'" It is clear that Mu'awiya thought that shortening the prayer was allowed and that the traveller could choose. He prayed *'Asr* with four *rak'ats*.

9. As for Mu'awiya, 'Umar appointed him. He put him in charge of all of Syria and 'Uthman confirmed him. Indeed, Abu Bakr as-Siddiq appointed him because he had appointed his brother Yazid. Yazid delegated him, so 'Umar confirmed him since he was connected to the government of Abu Bakr because the ruler had appointed him. 'Uthman followed 'Umar and confirmed him. Look at this chain and how reliable it is.[107] No one will ever bring the like of it after it.

The state of Islam in the caliphate of Abu Bakr and 'Umar reached its pinnacle in might. Examples were made of the human success and happiness of that society because by the light of Allah, Abu Bakr and 'Umar uncovered the depths of character in its people and the elements of manliness in the men. The people appointed them to lead them and provided them with the keys of mastery and entrusted them with the community of Muhammad ﷺ. These men knew that they were answerable for that before Allah, the Mighty. You saw in the footnotes that Yazid ibn Abi Sufyan and his brother Mu'awiya were among the men of the state of Abu Bakr whom he selected to bear the burdens of the community in their wars and peace. They did it very well indeed. When Yazid was appointed to lead one of the armies. Abu Bakr went out walking with him to see him off.[108]

Mu'awiya was mentioned in history after his brother Yazid because he was younger than him, not because he was inferior to him in the perfection of the qualities of leadership and mastery. It is accepted that Mu'awiya was one of the men of the government of Abu Bakr and 'Umar. He was one of those whom the Messenger of Allah employed and from whom he sought help. He called him to him once while Mu'awiya was eating and he was insistent in calling him and sent to him time after time to make him hurry to come to him. The Prophet ﷺ appointed Mu'awiya to serve him before Abu Bakr and 'Umar had appointed him. He also appointed Yazid ibn Abi Sufyan, as recorded in the *Futuh al-buldan* by al-Baladhuri.[109]

Those who are filled with hate and rancour for the Companions of the Messenger of Allah ﷺ, especially the Banu Umayya among them, cannot fail to acknowledge the fact that the Prophet ﷺ appointed Mu'awiya to be his scribe. They said that he used to write for him, but that he did not write down the revelation. They say this by a revelation which has been revealed to them from Shaytan. They have no historical text in their possession of proof of the Shari'a to which they refer. They make a distinction between matters for which they have no proof to make that distinction. If the Prophet ﷺ had made a distinction between his scribes in a certain matter rather than other matters, that would have been found in multiple transmissions from him and the transmitters would have transmitted it as has occurred with things less important than this. One of the young Muslims of whom I have a good opinion once asked me, "What do you say about Mu'awiya?" I said to him, "Who am I that I should be asked about one of the great ones of this community and a Companion who was one of the best Companions of Muhammad ﷺ? He was one of the lamps of Islam. But this lamp shone at the side of four suns that filled the world with their lights. Their lights overcame his light."

Ibn Kathir said in *al-Bidaya wa an-Nihaya*[110] from al-Layth ibn Sa'd (and he was the Imam, scholar and leader of Egypt, d. in 175 AH) from Bukayr (who was Ibn 'Abdullah al-Ashajj al-Madini al-Misri, d. 127 AH, and an-Nasa'i said that he is reliable) from Busr ibn Sa'id al-Madini (d. 100 AH and Ibn Ma'in said that he is reliable and al-Layth ibn Sa'd said that he was one of the devoted people of worship and one of the people of scrupulousness and asceticism in this world) that Sa'd ibn Abi Waqqas (one of the ten promised the Garden) said, "I did not see anyone who fulfilled a right after 'Uthman more than the owner of this door," i.e. Mu'awiya. Ibn Kathir also related[111] from 'Abd ar-Razzaq ibn Humam as-San'ani, one of the notable Imams and *huffadh*[112] (he was ascribed to the Shi'a) from Ma'mar ibn Rashid, Abu 'Urwa al-Basri, then al-Yamani, who was one of the notables, from Humam ibn Munabbih as-San'ani (who was reliable). He said, "I heard Ibn 'Abbas say, 'I have not seen a man more suited to rule than Mu'awiya.'" Is there a man who is the most suited of people other than the one who is just, wise, and forbearing and strong in defence of his kingdom and one who seeks help from Allah to spread the call of Allah in other domains and to undertake the trust in the community over which Allah has entrusted him? Should 'Uthman be censured for appointing the most suitable of people to rule? What an extraordinary wonder! How can 'Uthman be censured for appointing him when 'Umar appointed him

The Defamation of 'Uthman

before him and he was appointed by Abu Bakr before 'Umar? He was also appointed to an office by the Messenger of Allah ﷺ before the caliphate went to Abu Bakr, 'Umar and 'Uthman.

There is no doubt that a mind which Shaytan plays with and seduces by whisperings like this is an unsound mind. It perverts people's intellects and their logic before it perverts their *deen* and history for them. It is obligatory for those who love the truth and good to avoid all who carry a brain like this in their heads as they would avoid a leper. At-Tirmidhi related from Abu Idris al-Khawlani, one of the great scholars of the Tabi'un and the most knowledgeable of the people of Syria after Abu ad-Darda', that when 'Umar ibn al-Khattab dismissed 'Umayr ibn Sa'd al-Ansari al-Awsi from Hums and appointed Mu'awiya, people said, "He has dismissed 'Umayr and appointed Mu'awiya." (Al-Baghawi said in the *Collection of the Companions*, "'Umayr used to be called the 'unique'"). Ibn Sirin said that 'Umar used to call him that due to his administration for him. 'Umayr was one of the people of asceticism. 'Umayr said, "Do not mention Mu'awiya with anything but good. I heard the Messenger of Allah ﷺ say, 'O Allah, guide by means of him!'" It is related that the person who gave this testimony for Mu'awiya was the Amir al-Mu'minin 'Umar. He was the one who testified to it for him and he related the supplication of the Messenger of Allah ﷺ for Mu'awiya that Allah should guide by means of him. That is a very big thing because of the greatness of 'Umar's position. If the one who testified to that was 'Umayr ibn Sa'd al-Ansari and he was dismissed in favour of Mu'awiya from his appointment over Hums, that still does not detract from its greatness if it had been 'Umar himself who gave that testimony for Mu'awiya.

You know that 'Umayr was one of the Companions of the Messenger of Allah ﷺ and that he was among the ascetics of the Ansar. Ibn Taymiyya said in the *Minhaj as-Sunna*:[113] "The conduct of Mu'awiya with his people was one of the best ever seen in rulers. His people loved him. It is confirmed in the *Sahih* volumes that the Prophet ﷺ said, 'The best of your Imams are those you love and who love you. You pray for them and they pray for you. The worst of your Imams are those whom you hate and who hate you. You curse them and they curse you.'" There is no room here for more than this. We will elaborate the real form of Mu'awiya when his caliphate is mentioned so that you will know to what extent we have been deceived by the lies of the enemies of the first generations of Islam. This is a portion from a sound *hadith* as you will see later.

10. As for 'Abdullah ibn 'Amir ibn Kurayz, he appointed him, as he said, because he was noble in both his maternal and paternal aunts.

> He was from 'Abd Shams by parentage, Hashimi by relationship through his maternal aunt. His father's mother was Arwa ibn Kurayz. Her mother was al-Bayda' by 'Abd al-Muttalib ibn Hashim, the paternal aunt of the Prophet ﷺ. When he was born, he was brought to the Prophet ﷺ who said to Banu 'Abd Shams, "This one is more like us than you." Then he spat in his mouth and he swallowed it. The Prophet ﷺ said, "I hope that he will be a water-giver." He did not cultivate any land without water appearing in it. He grew up generous, noble, brave, blessed in nature with many virtues. He conquered all of Khorasan, the ends of Persia, Sijistan and Kerman until he reached the districts of Ghazna. He put an end to Yazdegerd ibn Shariyar, the last of the Persian kings. The Iranians believe that the dynasty of their kings started with their Adam whom they called Jiumart. The kingdom of his sons continued in a straight line until the last of them died by the force of Islam in the caliphate of the Amir al-Mu'minin, 'Uthman, by the *jihad* of this man who was Abd Shams by parentage, Hashimi by his maternal aunt, 'Abdullah ibn 'Amir ibn Kurayz. It is a fire in the hearts of the people of the Magian sect against Islam and against 'Uthman and Ibn Kurayz. They had rancour towards them and fought with them up until the present day with the weapons of lies, hate and intrigue.

The Defamation of 'Uthman

That will continue until the Day of Rising. Were not those who confirmed Islam among those to whom Iran gave birth in the days when it was Shafi'i in *madhhab,* when scholars of the Muhammadan *Sunna* emerged from it. They included great Imams, *hadith* scholars and *fuqaha'*. They stripped their hearts of any rancour they had towards those who believed and struggled with their property and themselves until Allah opened the lands at their hands. He guided the community because of them. The Muslims love and respect them for their merits. We do not claim partisanship for anyone after the Messenger of Allah ﷺ and we remove error from every Companion or Tabi'i or those who followed them by thinking the best of them.

As for those who filled this world with mountains of good deeds, some are blind to them and stick their noses in the garbage in order to extract from it something which they can use to cast blame. If they do not find it, they will invent and lie. Part of the nobility of the Muslim towards himself is that he lifts himself above listening to the likes of those men and is not deceived by them. You have enough in the victory of 'Abdullah ibn 'Amir ibn Kurayz which reached the furthest east and his demolition of the Magian empire. There is also documentation of the large quantity of good deeds he performed. Ibn Kathir said in *al-Bidaya wa an-Nihaya*,[114] "He was the first to make cisterns at 'Arafat for the *hajjis* to the House of Allah and to make spring water flow to them." Ibn Taymiyya said about him in the *Minhaj as-Sunna*,[115] "He is known for good deeds and the love people had for him in their hearts and that cannot be ignored." If men like them had been among the ancients of the English and French, their greatness would still be found in the books of history, culture and education. Our sciences have been decimated and we tend to transmit that in our scholarly books so that our generation believes in the greatness of the forebears of the colonialists. As for the greatness of our forebears, Shaytan has overpowered it by means of false hearts which overflow with evil. Many of us confirm the lies and we proceed like a community without glory, asleep to the inheritance of a glory whose like humanity has never known.

11. As for his appointment of al-Walid ibn 'Uqba, people, according to their false intentions, hastened to do evil things before good things. The liars mentioned that he appointed him for the reason that was already stated. 'Uthman said, "I did not appoint al-Walid because he is my brother.

> He was his brother by his mother, Arwa bint Kurayz. Her mother was al-Bayda' bint 'Abd al-Muttalib ibn Hashim.

"I appointed him because he is the son of Umm Hakim al-Bayda', the aunt of the Messenger of Allah ﷺ and the twin of his father." This will be made clear, Allah willing.

> Anyone who has no recognition of the beginning of this community would suppose that the Amir al-Mu'minin 'Uthman brought al-Walid ibn 'Uqba from the gutter and appointed him over Kufa. As for those whom Allah has blessed with the blessing of intimate knowledge of the circumstances of that time and its people, they know that the first Islamic state from the time of the caliphate of Abu Bakr seized on this energetic, resolute youth of pleasing character and truthful belief. His gifts were employed in the way of Allah until Abu Bakr died. The first office that he held in the caliphate of Abu Bakr was that he was entrusted with the secret messages of war which passed between the Caliph and his general, Khalid ibn al-Walid, in the Battle of al-Madhar against the Persians in 12 AH.[116] Then he sent him to help his general, 'Iyad ibn Ghanm al-Fihri.[117] In 13 AH, al-Walid was put in charge of the *zakat* for the tribe of Quda'a for Abu Bakr.
>
> Then when Abu Bakr decided to conquer Syria, al-Walid was with him in the place of 'Amr ibn al-'As in respect, trust and honour. He wrote to 'Amr ibn al-'As and to al-Walid ibn 'Uqba to call them to lead the *jihad*. Ibn al-'As bore the banner of Islam towards Palestine and al-Walid ibn

'Uqba went as a general east of the Jordan (at-Tabari 4:29-30). Then we see al-Walid in 13 AH as governor of the lands of the Banu Taghlib and the Arabs of the peninsula.[118] He protected the fighters in the north of Syria so that no one could come at them from the rear. The tribes of Rabi'a and Tanukh, both the Muslims and the unbelievers among them, were under his leadership. Al-Walid ibn 'Uqba made full use of the opportunity of his appointment and his generalship over this area which was still full of Christians from the Arab tribes, because in addition to his military *jihad* and administrative office, he also called the people to Allah, using all of the means of wisdom and good warning to encourage the Christians of Iyad and Taghlib to become Muslim like the rest of the Arabs. Iyad fled from him to al-Andul which was still under Byzantine rule. Al-Walid persuaded his caliph, 'Umar, to write a letter threatening the Byzantine Emperor so he would return them to the borders of the Islamic state. Taghlib tried to revolt against al-Walid when he spread the Islamic call among their young people and children. He became very angry with the anger that the people of Mudar had, which was supported by Muslim belief. He uttered his famous words about them:

When I wrapped my head with a turban,
   Taghlib, the daughter of Wa'il, lured you from me.

These words reached 'Umar and he was afraid that his general would fall upon the young Christian men of Taghlib, so he took the reins from his hand at the moment when they were fighting with the Muslims. Therefore he restrained the hand of al-Walid from them and moved him from their area. Al-Walid came into the caliphate of 'Uthman with this excellent past record. 'Uthman appointed him over Kufa. He was one of its best governors as far as justice, compassion and charity are concerned. While he was in charge of Kufa, his armies went to the east in conquest and victory as we will mention later.

Appointment is by *ijtihad*...

At the end of this book, the author has a section in which he indicates the meaning and realities which someone in command should take into consideration in his *ijtihad* when appointing or dismissing governors. That has great *fiqh* and wondrous knowledges which the Imams and scholars clarified in the details that they wrote about leadership and the politics of the state. This is found in their books about the bases of the *deen*. The tyrant, the forger al-Hasan ibn al-Mutahhar al-Hulli, claimed in his book, *The Path of Generosity*, that 'Uthman appointed someone who was not suited to govern the affairs of the Muslims. Ibn Taymiyya answered him in *Minhaj as-Sunna*[119] that 'Ali appointed Ziyad ibn Abi Sufyan and he appointed al-Ashtar an-Nakha'i and he appointed Muhammad ibn Abi Bakr and others like them. The intelligent man knows beyond doubt that Mu'awiya ibn Abi Sufyan was better than all of these. He said, "It is a wonder that the Shi'a object to 'Uthman appointing his relatives from his father's side and his mother's side. He appointed 'Abdullah ibn 'Abbas over Yemen. He appointed Qutham ibn al-'Abbas over Makka and Ta'if. As for Madina, it is said that he appointed Sahl ibn Hanif over it, and it is said that he appointed Thumana ibn al-'Abbas. He appointed 'Abdullah ibn 'Abbas over Basra. He appointed his foster son, Muhammad ibn Abi Bakr over Egypt. He had raised him in his own house since he had married his mother after Abu Bakr had died when Muhammad was still a child. The Imamiyya claim that 'Ali specified his sons for the caliphate, or his son and then his son and then his son and so on. It is known that the appointment of relatives was disliked. Then appointing a relative to the greatest caliphate would be worse than appointing someone to be governor.

When the speaker says that 'Ali had a proof for what he did, we say to him, "The proof of 'Uthman for what he did is greater still." When he claims divine protection from wrong action and things like that for 'Ali to stifle the tongues of the attackers, *ijtihad* is claimed for 'Uthman which also stifles the tongues of the attackers and which is more easily understood and conveyed. Then he says, "The Banu Umayya were employed by the Messenger of Allah ﷺ while he was alive. After him, they were employed in the government by Abu Bakr and 'Umar. It is not known that any of the tribes of Quraysh provided more governors for the Messenger of Allah ﷺ than the Banu 'Abd Shams because they were numerous and they had nobility and leadership." In the beginning of Islam, the Prophet ﷺ appointed 'Attab ibn Usayd ibn Abi al-'As over the best place on earth, Makka. He appointed Abu Sufyan ibn Harb ibn Umayya over Najran. He appointed Sa'id ibn al-'Asi over the *zakat* of the Banu Madhhij and over Sana' and the Yemen until the Messenger of Allah ﷺ died. He appointed 'Uthman ibn Sa'id al-'As over Tayma', Khaybar and Qura 'Urayna. He appointed Aban ibn Sa'id ibn al-'As over some of the captives and then he appointed him over Bahrayn. He continued in charge of it after al-'Ala' ibn al-Hadrami (the ally of the Banu Umayya) until the Prophet ﷺ died.

'Uthman said, "I only appoint from among those the Prophet ﷺ appointed and those like them and from their tribe." It the same with Abu Bakr and 'Umar after him. The evidence for the permission to appoint men from the Banu Umayya is a confirmed text from the Prophet ﷺ. This is clear to every man of intellect, setting apart the claim that the caliphate is by stipulation for one particular individual from the Banu Hashim because, according to the consensus of the people of knowledge by transmission, this is a lie. That is confirmed by the agreement of the people of the science of transmission.[120] Anyone who considers the life of the governors of 'Uthman and their *jihad* and their virtues will see that they are at the highest pinnacle of the men of government. He will feel no hesitation in confirming that they were among the architects of the strong basis of the administrative and military glory of Islam in the reward of the successful results of conquest and in spreading the call of Islam in what history recognises to be one of the most extraordinary miracles ever witnessed.

... and 'Umar had dismissed Sa'd ibn Abi Waqqas and advanced someone whose rank was less than his.

> That was in 21 AH. Those who were appointed after Sa'd were 'Abdullah ibn 'Abdullah ibn 'Uthman (and in his time the Battle of Nihawand took place), then Ziyad ibn Hanzala (and he asked to be retired and was dismissed) and after them 'Ammar ibn Yasir was appointed.[121]

12. As for their statement about Marwan and al-Walid, it is an attack on them, and their judgment that they were deviant (*fasiq*) is in fact a deviation on their part.

Marwan was a just man, one of the great ones of the community in the opinion of the Companions, the Tabi'un and the *fuqaha'* of the Muslims. As for the Companions, Sahl ibn Sa'd as-Sa'idi related from him.

> His *riwaya* from him is in *Sahih Bukhari* and elsewhere.

As for the Tabi'un, they are the same age as him, although he surpassed them by having "Companionship" according to one of two statements.

> In the forefront of those who related from him among the great Tabi'un was Zayn al-'Abidin 'Ali ibn al-Husayn as-Sibt. Ibn Taymiyya in *Minhaj as-Sunna*[122] and Ibn Hajar in *al-Isaba* quoted that. You will see its details in the *Greater Tabaqat of the Shafi'is* by as-Subki in the biography of the linguist, Abu Mansur Muhammad ibn Ahmad ibn al-Azhar, the author of *Tadhhib al-Lugha* (282-370 AH). Among those whom Ibn Hajar quoted in the *riwaya* from Marwan were: Sa'id ibn al-Musayyab, the chief of the scholars of the Tabi'un, his brothers from among the seven *fuqaha'*, Abu Bakr ibn 'Abd ar-Rahman ibn al-Harith ibn Hisham al-Makhzumi, 'Ubaydullah ibn 'Abdullah, 'Utba ibn Mas'ud, 'Urwa ibn az-Zubayr and others like them, such as 'Arak ibn Malik al-Ghifari al-Madini, the *faqih* of the people of

Dahlak (who used to fast constantly) and 'Abdullah ibn Shaddad ibn al-Had, one of those who transmitted from 'Umar, 'Ali and Mu'adh. The *riwaya* of 'Urwa ibn az-Zubayr from Marwan is in the *Musnad* of Imam Ahmad ibn Hanbal.[123] The *riwaya* of 'Arak from Marwan is transmitted by the Imam of the people of Egypt, al-Layth ibn Sa'd from Yazid ibn Hudayba in the *Musnad* of Ibn Hanbal.[124] The *riwaya* of 'Abdullah ibn Shaddad ibn al-Had from Marwan is in the *Musnad* of Ibn Hanbal.[125]

Anyone who considers the *hadith* which are related from Marwan will find that those who relate it are reliable Imams whose *riwaya* has a chain from him over a period of two generations or more. All of them hold higher ranks in Islam than those who cooled the rancour in their hearts by attacking Marwan and those better than Marwan. Among the transmitters of Marwan's *hadiths* was 'Abd ar-Rahman, the Imam of the people of Yemen, even though he has some Shi'ite tendencies. In the *Musnad* of Ibn Hanbal[126] is the *hadith* of 'Abd ar-Rahman ibn al-Harith ibn Hisham that he was the messenger of Marwan to the Umm al-Mu'minin Umm Salama to verify some of the judgments of the Shari'a. In the *Musnad* of Ibn Hanbal[127] is a sample that shows the great concern Marwan had for the *Sunna* of the Messenger of Allah ﷺ, as far as he was capable of bringing it out from the Imams and leaders of the Muslims.

As for the *fuqaha'* of the cities, all of them esteemed him, had respect for his caliphate, accepted his *fatwa* and followed his *riwaya*. As for the fools among the historians and men of letters, they speak according to their merits.

As for al-Walid, one of the commentators related that Allah called him *fasiq* (deviant) when He says: *"When a deviant brings you news, then make it clear, lest you afflict a people by ignorance."* (49:6) According to them, that *ayat* was revealed about him. The Prophet ﷺ sent him to the Banu al-Mustaliq, and he reported that they had apostatised. For this reason, the Messenger of Allah ﷺ sent Khalid ibn al-Walid to them and he ascertained what had happened and the invalidity of his words became clear. There is some disagreement about this. Some say that it was revealed about this incident.

I was astounded at how this *ayat* could have come down about al-Walid ibn 'Uqba and Allah calling him a deviant and yet after that the two Caliphs of the Messenger of Allah, Abu Bakr and 'Umar, would still give him the position which history has written that he had. We quoted examples of it in the margin earlier when we presented what passed in the ten odd years before 'Uthman appointed him over Kufa. This contradiction between the trust that Abu Bakr and 'Umar had for al-Walid ibn 'Uqba and how one should deal with him if Allah had called him a deviant, moved me to doubt that this *ayat* was sent down about him, not because it is unlikely that al-Walid did something by which he could be considered deviant, but because it is unlikely that the one described by *fisq* in the Clear Qur'an would be the confidant of two men of the friends of Allah who were such that we do not know of anyone closer to Allah than them after His Messenger.

Then after I was assailed by this doubt, I looked again at the reports that have come about the reason for the revelation of this *ayat*: *"When a deviant brings you news."* When I applied myself to studying it, I found that it stopped with Mujahid, or Qatada, or Ibn Abi Layla or Yazid ibn Ruman. None of them mentioned the names of the narrators of these reports in the period of a hundred years or more which passed between their time and the time when this event took place. Those hundred years are full of narrators from different sources. Those who have a tendency to injure the reputation of people like al-Walid and those of greater rank than al-Walid have filled this world with suspicious reports that have no scholarly worth. The transmitters of those reports regarding the reason for the revelation of the *ayat* are still unknown among scholars who consider people to be just witnesses or not (*ta'dil*) after the men to whom these reports reached. The scholars who consider people to be just witnesses or otherwise do not know anything about them, not even their names. It is not permitted in the Shari'a and history to judge that these sourceless, broken reports are sound.

There are two direct reports. One of them is from Umm Salama. Musa ibn 'Ubayda claimed that he heard it from Thabit, the client of Umm Salama. An-Nasa'i, Ibn al-Madini, Ibn 'Adi and a group considered Musa ibn 'Ubayda to be weak. This Thabit who is claimed to be the client of Umm Salama is not mentioned in any of the books of knowledge. He is not mentioned in the *Tadhhib at-Tadhhib* nor in the *Taqrib at-Tadhhib* nor in the summary of the *Tadhhib al-Kamal*. I did not find him nor do I have any suspicions about the *Balance of Justice* and the *Tongue of the Balance*. I went to the collection of the *hadith*s of Umm Salama in the *Musnad* of Ibn Hanbal and I read them one by one, but I did not find this report among them. I did not find any report from Umm Salama in which the name of a client of hers called Thabit was mentioned. In addition to all this, Umm Salama did not say in the report, if it is indeed sound – and there is no way to verify that it came from her – that the *ayat* was revealed about al-Walid. She said (i.e. it is ascribed to her), "The Messenger of Allah ﷺ sent a man for the *zakat* of the Banu al-Mustaliq."

The second report is related by at-Tabari from Ibn Sa'd from his father from his uncle from his father from his father from Ibn 'Abbas. At-Tabari did not meet Ibn Sa'd and did not take from him because when Ibn Sa'd died in Baghdad in 230, at-Tabari was a child of six years and at that time had not left his home, Amal, in Tabaristan for Baghdad or anywhere else. If Ibn Sa'd himself was one of the people of integrity in the *deen* and majesty in knowledge, scholars who judge integrity or its opposite do not know the names of most of people in this chain before him, let alone anything about their circumstances. All of these reports from first to last cannot censure an industrious man who was trusted by Abu Bakr and 'Umar. He carried out services for Islam for which the greatest reward is expected, Allah willing.

I add to all that has preceded the fact that at the time when this event occurred with the Banu al-Mustaliq about which the *ayat* was revealed, al-Walid was still young, as will come in the following passage.

It is said that it is about 'Ali and al-Walid in another story. It is said that on the day of the Conquest of Makka, al-Walid went ahead in a group of youths to the Messenger of Allah. He said, "There was *khaluq* (coloured perfume) on my head, so the Messenger of Allah ﷺ refused to pat it." When someone is that young, one sends someone else to verify what he says.

> This *hadith* about the age of al-Walid ibn 'Uqba on the Day of the Conquest of Makka is related by Ibn Hanbal in his *Musnad*[128] from a shaykh of his, Fiyad ibn Muhammad ar-Raqqi, from Ja'far ibn Barqan ar-Raqqi from Thabit ibn al-Hajjaj al-Kilabi ar-Raqqi from 'Abdullah al-Hamdani (and he is 'Abdullah ibn Malik ibn al-Harith) from al-Walid ibn 'Uqba. It is apparent that al-Walid ibn 'Uqba related this *hadith* when he withdrew from people in the last two years of his life, choosing to remain in a village he owned in the Raqqa area. The *riwaya* of the report has a chain in the transmitters of Raqqa, and Imam Ibn Hanbal took it from a shaykh he knew among them. 'Abdullah al-Hamdani is reliable, but his name is confused in other *riwayats* than these with another Hamdani whose *kunya* is Abu Musa and whose name is Malik ibn al-Harith (i.e. according to the name of the father of 'Abdullah al-Hamdani). He is unknown to the people who judge integrity or lack of it. As for 'Abdullah al-Hamdani who is in the *riwaya* of Ibn Hanbal, he is known and trusted. Qadi Abu Bakr ibn al-'Arabi relied on this *riwaya* and others like it in his judgment regarding the age of al-Walid ibn 'Uqba, saying that he was a child when Makka was conquered and that the one about

The Defamation of 'Uthman

whom the *ayat*, "If a deviator brings you a report..."¹²⁹ (see below) was sent down is someone else. It is extraordinary that those who tend to slander the reputation of this young Companion, who was a man of *jihad*, cheerfulness and good conduct among people, have tried to refute the proof of his youthfulness in that time by another report about him coming to Madina with his brother, 'Umara, in the seventh year of the *Hijra* to ask the Prophet ﷺ to return their sister, Umm Kulthum, to Makka. The fact of this report, even if it is sound, is that in it the name 'Umara is put ahead of al-Walid. From this it is gathered that 'Umara was the mainstay of this journey and that al-Walid came along to accompany him. What would prevent al-Walid from coming as a child with his older brother? Indeed, that is a common occurrence everywhere. Al-Walid's statement that he was a child in the year of the conquest is not contradicted by the report about him coming to Madina with his older brother in the seventh year of the *Hijra*. So it should be clear to you that none of the reports which have come about al-Walid ibn 'Uqba being the reason for the revelation of the *ayat*, " If a deviator brings you a report ..." allow a learned person to base a judgment in the Shari'a or historical judgment on them. When you add to that the *hadith* of the *Musnad* of Ibn Hanbal about the age of al-Walid in the year of the Conquest of Makka, then the wisdom of Abu Bakr and 'Umar appointing al-Walid and their trust in him and their reliance on him although he was still a youth will be clear to you.

Through this disagreement, scholars will drop strong *hadith*s. How could a man be considered *fasiq* because of words like these? How could that be the case with a man from among the Companions of Muhammad ﷺ?

As for the *hadd* carried out on him for drinking wine, 'Umar carried out the *hadd* punishment for wine on Qudama ibn Maz'un while he was governor and dismissed him. It is said that he later made up with him.

Qudama ibn Maz'un al-Jumahi was one of the first of the forerunners. He went on *hijra* twice and he was at Badr. He was the in-law of the Umm al-Mu'minin Hafsa bint 'Umar and her brother, 'Ubaydullah. While Qudama was in charge of Bahrayn during the caliphate of 'Umar, al-Jarud, the master of the Banu 'Abd al-Qays, came to 'Umar from Bahrayn and claimed that Qudama drank and became drunk. 'Umar said to him, "Who will testify with you?" He said, "Abu Hurayra." He asked Abu Hurayra to testify. He said, "I did not see him drink, but I did see him vomiting." 'Umar told him, "You have been excessive in the testimony." He sent for Qudama from Bahrayn and al-Jarud said to 'Umar, "Carry out the Book of Allah on this one." 'Umar said to him, "Are you an opponent or a witness? He replied, "A witness." 'Umar said, "You have given your testimony." Al-Jarud was silent. Then he came in the morning to 'Umar and said, "Carry out the *hadd* of Allah on this one." 'Umar said, "You hold your tongue or I will deal severely with you!" He said, "'Umar, this is not proper! Your nephew drinks wine and then you treat me severely!" He brought one of Qudama's wives and she gave testimony against her husband. 'Umar wanted to carry out the *hadd* on him. The Companions said to him, "We do not think that you should carry out the *hadd* on him while he is ill." Then he came again and they said what they had said to him before. 'Umar said, "I prefer that he meet Allah under the whip than I meet Him while he is on my neck." He had him flogged. Qudama was cross with him. When they returned from *hajj*, he was brought to 'Umar. 'Umar spoke to him and sought forgiveness for him. Part of the good fortune of Qudama ibn Maz'un was that he was a Qurayshi from the Banu Jumah. If he had been a Qurayshi from the Banu 'Abd Shams, evil tongues would have uttered their contempt for him and fabricated lies about him for as long as there is a lie in this world.

Wrong actions do not remove integrity when there is repentance.

The Defamation of 'Uthman

This is true, but it is like what happened to Qudama ibn Maz'un and like what is well known with the people about Abu Mihjan ath-Thaqafi, the poet-horseman who had a glorious day in the Battle of Qadisiyya. As for al-Walid ibn 'Uqba the *mujahid*, the just but wronged conqueror who made every effort to do all the good that he was able to do for his community, he saw with his own eyes how the liars attacked the righteous and how their falsehood was perpetrated against them. He withdrew from people after the murder of 'Uthman to an estate he owned, cut off from the clamour of society. It was about fifteen miles from the city of Raqqa in the land of Jazira where he had fought and where he had called its Christians to Islam during 'Umar's caliphate. Now the intrigues of the liars about him unveil their faults. It does not harm a man if the truth about him is uncovered some thirteen centuries later. The truth is old but evidence is not affected by age.

When al-Walid ibn 'Uqba was governor of Kufa for 'Uthman, he wanted to be a model ruler in justice, nobility and good conduct with the people as he was a model warrior in his *jihad* and establishing for Islam what was fitting in those who defended its call, those who bore its banner and spread its message. He governed Kufa for five years and up until the day in which he left Kufa his house did not have a door between him and the people, whether he knew them or not. Whoever wanted to could visit him whenever they liked, night or day. Al-Walid did not have any need to be veiled from the people.

The veil covers foul actions.
No veil except the good is thrown over you.

All people ought to have loved their good ruler because he set up houses of hospitality for strangers and brought good to people. He began to distribute property to male and female slaves and gave each slave extra money every month through which they could find ease without making their masters pay for their provisions. In fact, the majority of the people had no choice but to love this model ruler for the length of the period of his rule – except for a party of the evil ones, the people of corruption whose tribe received the whip of the Shari'a for punishment at the hands of al-Walid. They devoted their lives to lying in ambush to harm him. These men include one who is called Abu Zaynab ibn 'Awf al-Azdi and another called Abu Mawra'. The third was called Jundub ibn Abi Zuhayr. The authorities had seized their sons because of the night in which they took revenge on Ibn al-Haysaman and murdered him. One of the Companions of the Messenger of Allah ﷺ had settled in his neighbourhood. He had been in charge of the army of Khuza'a on the day of the conquest of Makka. He and his son had come from Madina to Kufa to travel with one of the armies of al-Walid ibn 'Uqba which was going towards it in the direction of the east for conquest and to spread the call of Islam. This Companion and his son testified that on that night those evil men had attacked the house of Ibn al-Haysaman. He and his son gave testimony against those murderers. Al-Walid therefore carried out the judgment of the Shari'a on them at the door of the castle in the courtyard. Their fathers made a contract against themselves with Shaytan that they would work devices against this good and merciful ruler. They sent observers and spies to watch his movements, although his house was constantly open. One day he had some of the poets of the north come as his guests. There was a Christian among his uncles from Taghlib in the land of Jazira and he had become Muslim through al-Walid. The spies of those who sought revenge thought that this poet who had been a Christian must be one of those who drink wine and perhaps al-Walid honoured him because of that. They called Abu Zaynab, Abu al-Mawra' and their companions and broke into al-Walid's house from the mosque-side, even though the house did not have a door. When they burst in, he pushed something under the bed. One of them reached under with his hand and brought it out without the permission of the owner of the house. When he got it out from under the bed, it was a plate on which there were some separated grapes. Al-Walid had put it away out of modesty lest the plate be seen with only separated grapes on it. They began to blame each other out of shame. People heard the story and began to curse and abuse them, but al-Walid covered up for them, kept it from 'Uthman and was silent and patient about it.

Then the machinations of Jundub, Abu Zaynab and Abu al-Mawra' were repeated. They seized on every event and gave it a bad interpretation and forged lies. Some of those had been§ officials in the government whom al-Walid had removed from their offices due to their bad behaviour. They went to Madina and began to complain about al-Walid to 'Uthman and to seek his dismissal from Kufa. While these men were in Madina, Abu Zaynab and Abu al-Mawra' entered the governor's house in Kufa with some other gullible people. They remained in it until al-Walid came back to rest. The rest of the people left and Abu Zaynab and Abu al-Mawra' remained until they were able to steal al-Walid's ring from his house and then they left. When al-Walid woke up, he could not find his ring. He asked his two wives about it. They were in a bedroom looking at the visitors of al-Walid from behind a curtain. They said that the last who remained in the house were two men and they described their appearance and clothes to al-Walid. He recognised that they were Abu Zaynab and Abu al-Mawra' and realised that they had only stolen the ring for some trick they were contriving. He sent someone to look for them, but they were not to be found in Kufa. They had set out immediately to Madina as witnesses against al-Walid, stating that he drank wine (and I think that they took their false testimony from the details of the event which had already happened to Qudama ibn Maz'un during the caliphate of 'Umar). 'Uthman said to them, "How did you see him?" They said, "We were in his retinue and came in and he was vomiting wine." 'Uthman said, "Only the one who drinks wine vomits it." Al-Walid was brought from Kufa and he swore to 'Uthman and told him about that. 'Uthman said, "We carry out the *hudud* and the false witness invites himself to the Fire."

This story about al-Walid being suspected of drinking wine, as in the events of 30 AH in the *History* of at-Tabari, had nothing in it except for this according to various old sources. The elements of the report according to at-Tabari are that the witnesses against al-Walid were two of the men who sought revenge and there are many witnesses to their rancour against him.

No mention of the prayer has come in the testimony at all, let alone whether it was two or four *rak'ats*. The addition of the mention of the prayer is something else extraordinary. Its report is transmitted from al-Hudayn ibn al-Mundhir (one of the followers of 'Ali). He was with 'Ali and 'Uthman when the *hadd* punishment was carried out on al-Walid. This report is transmitted from him. Muslim wrote it in his *Sahih*[130] with the words, "I saw 'Uthman ibn 'Affan when al-Walid was brought to him. He had prayed *Subh* with two *rak'ats*. Then he said, 'Shall I make it more?' One of them testified that he drank wine and the other testified that he vomited. As for the prayer of *Subh* with two *rak'ats* and then him saying, 'Shall I make it more?' that is something which Hudayn said. Hudayn was not one of the witnesses and he was not in Kufa at the time of the alleged event. This particular cause of suspicion does not have any *isnad* to anyone who is known. It is a wonder that the same report that is in *Sahih Muslim* comes in three places in the *Musnad* of Ibn Hanbal, related from Hudayn. What he heard from Hudayn in *Sahih Muslim* is what was heard from him in the *Musnad* of Ibn Hanbal in three places. The first and second places[131] contain no mention of the prayer on the tongue of Hudayn, let alone from anyone else. Perhaps one of the transmitters after him knew the discussion about the prayer was not the words of the two witnesses and was content to mention the *hadd* punishment.

As for the third place from the *Musnad* of Ibn Hanbal,[132] it comes on the tongue of Hudayn that "al-Walid prayed *Subh* with four *rak'ats* with

The Defamation of 'Uthman

the people." It contradicts what comes on the tongue of Hudayn himself in *Sahih Muslim*. There is a change in one of the two *riwayats* and Allah knows best the reason for it. In both cases, the mention of the prayer is only according to the words of Hudayn, and Hudayn was not a witness and he did not relate from a witness, so this part of what he said is not considered.

After informing you about the affair of those who sought revenge from what at-Tabari transmitted from the shaykhs, I will add for you the knowledge of the affair of Humran. He was one of the slaves of 'Uthman who rebelled against Allah before he testified against al-Walid. In the city of the Messenger ﷺ, he married a divorced woman and went to her while she was still in *'idda* from her first husband. 'Uthman got angry at him for this and for other matters before it and he drove him out of his courtyard and expelled him from Madina. He went to Kufa to spread corruption there. He visited the right-acting slave, 'Amir ibn 'Abd al-Qays and forged lies against him with the men of the government and he was the reason that he travelled to Syria.

I will leave the business of this witness and the other two witnesses before him to the conscience of the reader who can best judge what he thinks of them. By my *ijtihad*, I think that witnesses like these do not cause the *hadd* of Allah to be carried out on anyone who is under suspicion, even among the ordinary people, so how could it be with a strong striving Companion in whose hands the caliph had placed the trust of an area and the leadership of armies? Part of the opinion regarding him is good conduct with the people and sincere preservation of the trusts of Allah. He was trusted by three of the most perfect caliphs of Islam: Abu Bakr, 'Umar and 'Uthman. The kinship of al-Walid to 'Uthman that the liars claim was the reason for his partiality was the proof according to them that 'Uthman showed preference to his relatives. We think that those who delight in people's honour will be amused by the six verses ascribed to a vile madman which come on page 85 of his *diwan*. Natural critical faculty does not make them aware that these verses contain inconsistency and contradiction. Where is the praise in it for al-Walid when he says:

> When they saw the qualities of the one who is glorious,
>   and gives in hardship and ease,
> I removed a lie against you and you did not
>   frequent penury or poverty,

Part of the rest of its verses is:

> He called out when their prayer was completed,
>   "I will increase you", in intoxication when he was not
>   in command of his senses.

It is not logical to put the last verse with the first two verses, so he praises and blames in the same section which is not more than six verses long. I wrote a long treatise on *Mixture in Poetry* in which I cited examples of the inclusion of foreign verses with the same meter and rhyme in *qasida*s by someone other than their author. In any case, the witnesses who testified before 'Uthman did not allege the story of the prayer, even though they were not people who feared Allah and the Last Day. Now I will tell it for the face of Allah clearly and without any mistakes. If al-Walid had been one of the men of European history like St. Louis IX whom we captured in the house of Ibn Luqman in Mansura, he would have been a saint to his enemy because Louis IX was not as good to France as al-Walid was to his community. He did not conquer for the Christians as al-Walid conquered for Islam. How strange is a community that deals badly with its heroes and spoils the splendour of their history and destroys its glorious ones as the evil ones among us do. Then the subterfuges of these evil men spread until even the good ones supposed that it was the truth.

It was said to 'Uthman, "You appointed al-Walid because he is your brother by your mother, Arwa bint Khurayz ibn Rabi'a ibn Habib ibn 'Abd Shams." He said, "Rather it was because he is the nephew of the Messenger of Allah ﷺ by the Prophet's aunt, Umm Hakim al-Bayda'," who was the grandmother of 'Uthman and the grandmother of al-Walid by their mother Arwa. Umm Hakim was the twin of 'Abdullah, the father of the Messenger of Allah. How can a man be forbidden to appoint the brother of his kin?

It preceded in the margin, p. 70, that in his caliphate the Amir al-Mu'minin, 'Ali ibn Abi Talib, appointed governors in many cities under his rule from people who were his kin, and that the Messenger of Allah ﷺ appointed men of the Banu Umayya and their youths. That is how Abu Bakr and 'Umar acted. 'Uthman only acted according to what the Prophet ﷺ and his two Companions had done before him. When 'Uthman carried out the *hadd* on his brother for the sake of his community, he did something we do not think anyone else would have done on the testimony of biased witnesses who did not desire Allah by their testimony. The witnesses against al-Walid were of this biased type. One of the greatest *qadis* of Islam in knowledge, excellence and justice, Imam 'Amir ibn Sharahil ash-Sha'bi heard in the *Awa'il* about the bravery of Maslama ibn 'Abd al-Malik, the grandson of al-Walid ibn 'Uqba in his *jihad*. Ash-Sha'bi said, "How would it be if you were to meet al-Walid when he commanded a raid? He used to reach such-and-such and such-and-such which is not insignificant. No one said anything against him until he was dismissed from his office when he was at the Door (i.e. at ad-Daraband which is beyond the Caspian Sea in Russia and is one of the greatest fortresses in the world) by means of 'Abd ar-Rahman al-Bahili who is the greatest of the generals of al-Walid. Some of what 'Uthman gave to people at the hand of al-Walid was that he returned to every slave in Kufa some of the extra money in the treasury three times every month which they could enjoy without any cost to their masters."

This is a testimony from ash-Sha'bi for al-Walid about his victorious *jihad* and his kindness to his people. The false ones are dealt a heavy blow and the righteous are delighted. The Amir al-Mu'minin 'Uthman confirmed the state of his wronged brother's heart when he said, "We carry out the *hudud,* and the false witness brings upon himself the Fire. *'Our Lord, forgive us and our brothers who preceded us in faith and do not put any rancour in our hearts towards those who believe. Our Lord, You are forgiving, merciful.'"

13. As for his giving the *khums* (fifth) of North Africa to one person, that is not true...

> The truth is that he gave a fifth of the *khums* to 'Abdullah ibn Abi Sarh as a reward for his *jihad*. Then he retracted it and asked for him to return it. It comes in the events of 27 AH of the *History* of at-Tabari[133] that when 'Uthman commanded 'Abdullah ibn Sa'd ibn Abi Sarh to advance from Egypt to Tunis to conquer it, he said to him, "Allah will open North Africa to you tomorrow and you shall have a fifth of the fifth (*khums*) of the booty which Allah gives to the Muslims." He went out with the army until he passed through Egypt and pressed into the land of North Africa and conquered it, both the flatland and the mountains. 'Abdullah shared with his army what Allah had given him as booty, taking a fifth of the fifth and sent the four-fifths [of the fifth] to 'Uthman with Wuthayma an-Nasri. A delegation of those who came with him complained to 'Uthman about what 'Abdullah ibn Sa'd had taken. 'Uthman said to them, "I commanded him to do that. If you resent it, it will be returned." They said, "We resent it." So 'Uthman commanded 'Abdullah ibn Sa'd to return it and he did so. 'Abdullah ibn Sa'd returned to Egypt having conquered North Africa.

...even though Malik and a group believe that the Imam can have his own opinion regarding the *khums* and use it however his own *ijtihad*

The Defamation of 'Uthman

leads him to. If he gives it to someone, that is permitted. We have made this clear in its proper place.

i.e. in his other books when he goes into details about this question regarding the rules of Islamic *fiqh*. Imam 'Amir ibn Sharahil ash-Sha'bi said, "Land grants take the form of booty making up a fifth of what Allah gives as booty." He said, "'Umar gave Talha, Jarir ibn 'Abdullah and ar-Rabbil ibn 'Amir land grants. 'Umar gave Abu Mufazzar a grant of Dar al-Fil." Among those to whom 'Umar ibn al-Khattab gave a land grant was Nafi', the brother of Ziyad and Abu Bakra by their mother. He gave them a grant of some land in Basra whose area was ten *jurba*s for pasturing his horses and camels. (Look at the biography of Nafi' in the *Isaba*).

Qadi Abu Yusuf said in the *Book of Kharaj*,[134] "The Messenger of Allah ﷺ gave land grants and brought people close to Islam. The caliphs after him gave fiefs to those they thought it was correct to give grants." Abu Yusuf gives examples of this. Look at the Book of Land Grants, of the *Book of Kharaj* by Yahya ibn Adam al-Qurashi.[135] Imam ash-Sha'bi mentioned some of those to whom 'Uthman gave grants. He said, "Grants were given to az-Zubayr, Khabbab, 'Abdullah ibn Mas'ud, 'Ammar ibn Yasir and Ibn Habbar in the time of 'Uthman. If 'Uthman was mistaken, those before him erred as well, and they were those from whom we take our *deen*[136]. 'Ali ibn Abi Talib gave a land grant to Kardaws ibn Hani' al-Kardawsiyya and he gave a grant of land to Suwayd ibn Ghafala and his relatives. How can they object to 'Uthman and then be silent about 'Umar and 'Ali? Qadi Abu Yusuf has some apt discussion on this subject in the *Book of Kharaj*.[137]

As for what people claim about 'Uthman loving his relatives and giving things to them, his love for his kin was one of his virtues. 'Ali praised 'Uthman for being one who was closer to his family than the other Companions. 'Uthman explained this position of his when he said, "They say that I love the people of my house and give to them, but it has not led to injustice. I give them what they are due. As for my giving to them what

I give to them, it is from my own property. I do not make the property of the Muslims lawful for myself or anyone else. I gave the great desired gift, the bulk of my own property during the time of the Messenger of Allah ﷺ, Abu Bakr and 'Umar. Should I be avaricious and stingy today? Is it a time that when the nobles from the people of my house come to me and when my life has passed, that I should omit that which I owe my family simply because the deniers say what they say?"[138]

'Uthman divided up his property and his land among the Banu Umayya and he gave his son the same as he gave the others. He began with the Banu Abu al-'Asi, the Banu al-'Is and the Banu Harb. Ibn Taymiyya took the broadest view and he said in the *Minhaj as-Sunna*[139] that some of the *fuqaha'* believed that the portion of the relatives is by virtue of their kinship to the Imam, as al-Hasan and Abu Thawr said. The Prophet ﷺ used to give to his relatives by the principle of guardianship. It was said that that was the privilege of those appointed to rule after him. He said, "In general, most of those who undertook to rule after 'Umar singled out some of their relatives, either for appointment or money."

Then he said, "What 'Uthman did regarding the property has three sources. One of them is that he was the agent for it and the agent has a due even when he is wealthy. The second is that those of kinship are those with kinship to the Imam. The third is that they (i.e. the relatives of 'Uthman) were a numerous tribe unlike the tribe of Abu Bakr and 'Umar. He needed to give to them and appoint them more than Abu Bakr and 'Umar needed to appoint their relatives and give to them. This is part of what is transmitted from 'Uthman in evidence for him."[140]

14. As for their statement that he beat people with a staff, I have not heard that from anyone – neither rebel nor obedient. It is a falsehood that is related and a lie that is divulged. By Allah, it is prohibited.

> The report and *hadith* are *natha*: made public and evident. *Natha* is like praise, but it is for both good and evil. Praise is only for good.

15. As for his going above the step of the Messenger of Allah ﷺ, I did not hear it from any of those who have *taqwa*. It is an objectionable rumour that is related and mentioned. The heart of the one who changes is changed. Scholars said, "If it is sound, this does not contain anything that makes his blood allowable." It is not impossible that that is true, but if that is the case, then the Companions did not object to his doing it, so they must have thought that it was permissible in the beginning or there must have been a reason that called for that. If that was not the case, then there is no discussion.

> The mosque of the Prophet ﷺ had a narrow courtyard in the time of the Prophet ﷺ and the caliphate of Abu Bakr. One of the virtues of 'Uthman in the time of the Prophet ﷺ was that when the number of Companions increased, he purchased some land for a courtyard with his own money by which the mosque of the Prophet ﷺ was enlarged. Then the Amir al-Mu'minin 'Umar widened it and included the house of al-'Abbas ibn 'Abd al-Muttalib in it. Then the number of those who prayed increased with the number of the inhabitants of Madina and those who came to visit. The Amir al-Mu'minin 'Uthman widened it again and made its length 160 cubits and its width 150 cubits and renewed its foundations. The capacity of the mosque and the increase in the number of those who attended it and the distance of some of them from the minbar in the *khutba* could be one reason making it necessary to raise the speaker so that he could see them and they could see him and listen to him.

16. As for his being routed in the Battle of Hunayn, his flight on the day of Uhud, his absence from Badr and the Homage of Ridwan, 'Abdullah ibn 'Umar clarified the principle of the judgment about the Homage, Badr and Uhud. In the Battle of Hunayn there were only a handful who stayed with the Messenger of Allah ﷺ. There is no explanation in the *Sahih* volumes of the matter regarding those who

stayed. There are various statements. One of them is that the only ones who remained with him were al-'Abbas and his sons, 'Abdullah and Quthum. This disagreement is all you need know. The Companions shared in this event and Allah and His Messenger ﷺ forgave it. It is not lawful to mention what Allah and His Messenger and the believers have dropped. Al-Bukhari related, "A man came to Ibn 'Umar and asked him about 'Uthman. He mentioned the good things that he had done. He said, 'Perhaps that vexes you?' He said, 'Yes.' He said, 'May Allah spite you.' Then he asked him about 'Ali and he mentioned the good things which he had done. He said, 'He is that in his house, the best of the houses of the Prophet ﷺ.' He said, 'Perhaps that vexes you?' He said, 'Certainly.' He said, 'May Allah spite you. So go away and strive with all your might and main against me'".[141] Some extra material on 'Ali and 'Uthman has already been shown in the *hadith*, "Islam is built on five", by al-Bukhari.[142]

Al-Bukhari also related[143] that 'Uthman ibn 'Abdullah ibn Mawhab said, "A man came from the people of Egypt, intending to go on *hajj* to the House. He saw some people sitting and said, 'Who are these people?' They said, 'Those are Quraysh.' He asked, 'Who is the old man in their midst?' They said, 'Abdullah ibn 'Umar.' He said, 'Ibn 'Umar, I will ask you something. Relate it to me! Do you know that 'Uthman fled on the day of Uhud?' He replied, 'Yes.' He said, ' You know that he was absent from Badr?' He said, 'Yes.' He said, 'Do you know that he was absent from the Pledge of Hudaybiya and did not attend it?' He said, 'Yes.' He said, 'Allah is greater.' Ibn 'Umar said, 'Come and I will make it clear to you. As for his flight on the day of Uhud, I testify that Allah has forgiven him and pardoned him. As for his absence from Badr, the daughter of the Messenger of Allah ﷺ was his wife and she was ill. The Messenger of Allah ﷺ told him, "You will have the reward and share of a man of those who are present at Badr."

The Defamation of 'Uthman

The Prophet ﷺ sent the good news of the victory at Badr with Zayd ibn Haritha to 'Uthman in Madina. Usama ibn Zayd said (in what at-Tabari[144] related), "The news came to us while we were levelling the earth over Ruqayya, the daughter of the Messenger of Allah ﷺ who was married to 'Uthman ibn 'Affan. The Messenger of Allah ﷺ left me in charge of her along with 'Uthman ibn 'Affan. Then in Rabi' al-Awwal, the year following the Battle of Badr, 'Uthman married Umm Kulthum, the daughter of the Messenger of Allah. She went to live with him in Jumada al-Akhira.

As for his absence from the Homage of Ridwan, if anyone had been more respected in Makka than 'Uthman, he would have sent him in his place. The Messenger of Allah ﷺ sent 'Uthman...

Before he sent 'Uthman, the Prophet ﷺ had wanted to send 'Umar ibn al-Khattab to Makka to convey what he brought to the nobles of Quraysh. 'Umar said, "Messenger of Allah, I fear for myself with Quraysh. None of the Banu 'Adi ibn Ka'b are in Makka to protect me. But I will show you a man who is more esteemed than me there: 'Uthman ibn 'Affan." The Messenger of Allah ﷺ summoned him and sent him to Abu Sufyan and the nobles of Quraysh. On the day when the Islamic states write the history of the embassies in Islam, the name of 'Uthman will be the first of the ambassadors of Islam.

...and the Homage of Ridwan took place after 'Uthman had gone to Makka.

Because when 'Uthman conveyed his message in that journey, he was detained for some days and did not return to the Messenger of Allah ﷺ at the time he was meant to return. The Prophet ﷺ heard his ambassador had been killed. Therefore the Prophet ﷺ summoned the Companions to the Homage of Ridwan to help 'Uthman. He had the intention to go with his Companions to Makka and deal with the idol-worshippers because of the news of 'Uthman's murder. The Homage of Ridwan was one of the marks of honour awarded to 'Uthman. What honour could be greater? The forces of Islam gathered under the leadership of the greatest Messenger to take revenge for this man who was beloved to the Muslims and who had the high position with the first and the last. When the Prophet ﷺ later learned that 'Uthman was alive at the moment in which the Companions had gathered to take the Pledge, he proceeded to complete the pledge according to his *Sunna*. When he began a business, he completed it, even if the reason for it had gone. Then 'Uthman had a doubled honour since the hand of the Messenger of Allah ﷺ represented his hand in the contract of the pledge for him. So the Homage of Ridwan was to help 'Uthman and all of the Companions took a contract with their own hands except for 'Uthman. The noblest hand in existence took his place and gave his pledge for him. If 'Uthman had no other honour in his life except this, it would have been enough.

The Messenger of Allah ﷺ held out his right hand, saying, "This is the hand of 'Uthman." He struck one of his hands on his other hand and said, "This is for 'Uthman.'" Then Ibn 'Umar said to him, 'Take this with you now.'"

If the Amir al-Mu'minin 'Uthman had been one of the apostles of the Messiah, and had received the like of this honour from 'Isa ibn Maryam which Allah bestowed on him from the Prophet of Mercy, Muhammad ﷺ, the Christians would have worshipped him because of it. It is extraordinary to find a community where ignorant men, in his own time, censure 'Uthman for being absent from the Homage of Ridwan when they include men who felt very sure of his own courage when advancing to shed the blood of this merciful caliph for various reasons of which this was one. Then a man, who came to worship Allah by performing the obligations of the *hajj*, had this sort of ignorance which he openly stated to a group of the Companions of Quraysh whose leader was 'Abdullah ibn 'Umar. Then there still was a need for examination to clarify the truth in the time of Qadi Abu Bakr Ibn al-'Arabi. People like us in this time are aware that 'Uthman still is in a position in relation to part of his community which demands justice and he still needs to be defended from bad words. We are truly a poor community. That which leaves us in our current state among the nations and the state in which we will continue to sink is *"Allah does not change a people until they change what is in themselves."*¹⁴⁵

17. As for his preventing 'Ubaydullah ibn 'Umar ibn al-Khattab being killed for al-Hurmuzan, that is false.

By the testimony of his son al-Qamadhban, at-Tabari related¹⁴⁶ from Sayf ibn 'Umar with his *isnad* to Abu Mansur. He said, "I heard al-Qamadhban relate about the killing of his father: 'When 'Uthman was appointed, he summoned me and gave me power over him (i.e. 'Ubaydullah ibn 'Umar ibn al-Khattab). Then he said, "My son, this is the one who killed your father. You are more entitled to him than me, so go and kill him." I took him out and everyone in the land went with me. They were begging for him. I said to them, "Can I kill him?" They replied, "Yes," and they abused 'Ubaydullah. I said, "Do you have any right to prevent it?" They said, "No," and they abused him. So I left him for the sake of Allah and for them and they carried me away. By Allah, I only reached the house on the heads and shoulders of men.'" These are the words of the son of of al-Hurmuzan. Every just person believes (and perhaps the son of al-Hurmuzan also believed) that the blood of the *Amir al-Mu'minin* 'Umar was the responsibility of al-Hurmuzan and that Abu Lu'lu'a was only an implement in the hand of this Persian politician. The station of 'Uthman and his brothers, the Companions of the Messenger of Allah ﷺ, in this event has no like in the history of human justice.

If he did not do it, there were many Companions and this business also occurred at the beginning (of his caliphate).

'Uthman acted in this matter after he had consulted the Companions about it. At-Tabari said,[147] "'Uthman sat at the side of the mosque and called 'Ubaydullah while he was sitting in the house of Sa'd ibn Abi Waqqas. He is the one who took the sword from his hand. 'Uthman said to a group of the Muhajirun and the Ansar, 'Tell me what I must do in this matter which splits Islam.' 'Ali said, 'I think that you should kill him.' One of the Muhajirun said, "Umar was killed yesterday and then his son is to be killed today!' 'Amr ibn al-'As said, 'Amir al-Mu'minin, Allah would forgive you if this had happened while you have power over the Muslims. However, this took place before you had power.' 'Uthman said, 'I am their guardian. I make it a blood-wit and I will pay it with my own money.'"

It was said, "Al-Hurmuzan strove to provoke the murder of 'Umar. He carried the dagger and it showed under his garment."

In the *History* of at-Tabari,[148] there is the *hadith* of Sa'id ibn al-Musayyab. He related that 'Abd ar-Rahman ibn Abi Bakr as-Siddiq said on the morning when 'Umar was attacked, "Yesterday evening, I passed by Abu Lu'lu'a, and Jufayna (who was a Christian from the people of Hira and a tutor to Sa'd ibn Abi Waqqas) and al-Hurmuzan were with him. They were speaking secretly. When I approached them, they jumped up and they dropped a dagger. It had two heads and the handle was in the middle. Look and see what dagger he was killed with." A man from the Banu Tamim went out to investigate. The Tamimi came back to them. He had pursued Abu Lu'lu'a when he left 'Umar and caught him. He brought the dagger which 'Abd ar-Rahman ibn Abi Bakr had described. 'Ubaydullah ibn 'Umar heard that. He held back until 'Umar died. Then he girded on his sword and went to al-Hurmuzan and killed him.

The Defamation of 'Uthman

'Ubaydullah killed him when 'Uthman had become the ruler. Perhaps 'Uthman did not think that 'Ubaydullah deserved punishment since the state of al-Hurmuzan and what he did was proven.

Similarly, the sage of the community, 'Abdullah ibn 'Abbas, held the opinion that it was permitted to kill the unbelieving Persians who were in Madina without exception. Ibn Taymiyya said in the *Minhaj as-Sunna*,[149] "'Abdullah ibn 'Abbas spoke when 'Umar was attacked and 'Umar said to him, 'You and your father used to want many infidels to come to Madina.' Ibn 'Abbas said, 'If you had wished, we would have killed them.' 'Umar said, 'You lied. Now you speak out with your tongue when they have reached your *qibla*?'"

Ibn Taymiyya said, "Ibn 'Abbas had more *fiqh* and more *deen* than 'Ubaydullah ibn 'Umar and was much more excellent, and he asked 'Umar for a general permission to kill the infidel Persians who were in Madina when they were suspected of corruption. He believed that this sort of thing was permitted. If al-Hurmuzan was one of those individuals who had assisted in 'Umar's murder, he was definitely one of those who corrupt the land and wage war. Therefore he should have been killed on that account. If he had found that the slain man was someone whose blood was protected, then it would have been forbidden to kill him. However, the killer thought and believed that it was lawful to kill him by his clear suspicion. That suspicion which he had averts (punishment) from the killer (i.e. 'Ubaydullah ibn 'Umar)." I said: 'Uthman believed this when he spared him the blood-wit and paid it from his own property.* If something like the murder of the Amir al-Mu'minin 'Umar ibn al-Khattab had occurred in any other land, no matter what the level of its peak in civilisation, they would not have done what the Companions did in their forbearance which went to the very limit, even to the extent of killing the son of the Amir al-Mu'minin who had been murdered by treachery, depravity and blameworthy attack.

* When 'Ubaydullah ibn 'Umar killed al-Hurmuzan, he also killed the daughter of Abu Lu'lu'a. He also killed Jufayna an-Nasrani because he was also suspected of that. 'Uthman's enemies say that he did not take any retaliation from 'Ubaydullah for that. The answer is that the daughter of Abu Lu'lu'a was a Magian and Jufayna was a Christian. The Prophet ﷺ, as has reported al-Bukhari, said, "A Muslim is not killed for an unbeliever." 'Uthman paid their blood-wit when he paid the blood-wit of al-Hurmuzan after al-Hurmuzan's son had forgiven 'Ubaydullah as we saw elsewhere.

If no one undertook to demand it, how could it be sound to look into an unproven business when all these possibilities exist?

18. As for their statement that a letter was found with the rider or with his slave (and no one at all says that it was his slave)...

They said that he was the slave in charge of the *zakat*, i.e. he was one of the herdsmen of the *zakat* camels. The camels of the *zakat* numbered many thousands and they had hundreds of herdsmen. If it is said that he was one of the herdsmen of the *zakat* camels, even their leaders did not know their names because of their great number, let alone the Amir al-Mu'minin, his great agents and helpers. Assuming that he actually was one of the herdsmen of the *zakat* camels, it could be very easy for those rebels to hire him for their purposes. It is proven that al-Ashtar and Hukaym ibn Jabala remained behind in Madina when the rebels left after they were content with the answers and proofs of 'Uthman. While al-Ashtar and Hukaym ibn Jabala remained, the plot involving the letter and its carrier was implemented as a means for renewing the sedition and bringing back the rebels. None except al-Ashtar and his companions would profit by renewing the sedition. How many tricks they used which were more tortuous than simply hiring a herdsman who tended the *zakat* camels!

They have mentioned that Muhammad ibn Abi Hudhayfa, the fosterling of 'Uthman al-Abiq who was out of favour, was at that very moment in

The Defamation of 'Uthman

Egypt provoking people against the Amir al-Mu'minin and forging false letters ascribed to the wives of the Prophet. He took camels and emaciated them and put men outside the houses in Fustat with their faces towards the sun so that they would look like travellers. Then he commanded them to go out to the Hijazi road in Egypt to tell people that they were coming. When they met them, they said that they were bringing letters from the wives of Prophet ﷺ complaining about the rule of 'Uthman. These letters were read out in the mosque of 'Amr in Fustat to the assembly of people even though they were forged and false. Those who carried them had been in Egypt the entire time and they had not gone to the Hijaz at all.[150] Forging letters in the tragedy of the attack on the Amir al-Mu'minin 'Uthman was one of the weapons that the attackers used on every side. We have had an example of that. Some of it will come later.

...addressed to 'Abdullah ibn Sa'd ibn Abi Sarh telling him to kill its bearers.

> How can he have written to 'Abdullah ibn Sa'd ibn Abi Sarh when he had given 'Abdullah permission to come to Madina and knew that he had left Egypt[151] and he knew that the one with power in Fustat was Muhammad ibn Abi Hudhayfa, the head of the rebels and their chief in this region? The transmitters of the reports are also confused about the contents of the forged letter when they try to specify its contents. That will be discussed later.

'Uthman said to them, "Bring two witnesses to that. If not, I swear that I never wrote it nor did I command that."

> Ibn Taymiyya said in the *Minhaj as-Sunna*,[152] "Everyone who knows anything about what 'Uthman was like knows that he was not the type of person who would command the death of Muhammad ibn Abi Bakr or men like him. It is unknown of him to have killed anyone like this. These

men strove to kill him (i.e. to kill the Amir al-Mu'minin 'Uthman) and Muhammad attacked him with them. He did not command that they be killed in order to protect himself, so why would he instigate the execution of someone whose blood was protected?"

It might have been written in 'Uthman's language, done in his handwriting and sealed with his seal.

Something similar happened in the time of 'Umar, as al-Baladhuri related in the *Futuh al-Buldan*[153] and Ibn Hajar in the *Isaba*.[154]

They said, "Then surrender Marwan to us." He replied, "I will not do it." If he had surrendered him, he would have been unjust.

Ibn Taymiyya said in the *Minhaj as-Sunna*,[155] "If 'Uthman had commanded that Muhammad ibn Abi Bakr be killed, he deserved to be obeyed more than those who sought to kill Marwan, because 'Uthman was an Imam of guidance and a rightly-guided Caliph who must put people in order and kill those whose evil can only be averted by execution. As for those who sought to kill Marwan, they were Kharijites who were corrupting the earth. They did not have the right to kill anyone nor to carry out any *hadd* punishment. Marwan was not nearer to sedition and evil than Muhammad ibn Abi Bakr. Ibn Abi Bakr was not more famous in knowledge and the *deen* than Marwan was. The people of the *Sahih* volumes related a number of *hadith* from Marwan. He spoke with the people of *fatwas*. They disagree about whether he was a Companion. Muhammad ibn Abi Bakr did not have this position with the people. Furthermore, Marwan was one of the associates of Ibn az-Zubayr, etc."

They must seek their right against Marwan and others from him [i.e. from the caliph]. It is confirmed that the caliph executes and takes [what is due to people]. He empowers the person who takes his due. In addition to his precedence, excellence and position, nothing was proven

The Defamation of 'Uthman

against him to necessitate that he be dismissed, let alone killed.

The most exemplary part of what is related in his story is that because of the previous decision, certain people conspired against him with rancour they were determined on, those who had sought posts of command and did not get them and who harboured a great envy whose sickness is apparent, moved to that by lack of the *deen*, lack of certainty, and preference for this world over the Next World.

> The Amir al-Mu'minin 'Ali ibn Abi Talib described it in a similar way in the speech which he addressed to the new men in his army in Kufa when the Companion and warrior of *jihad*, al-Qa'qa' ibn 'Amr at-Tamimi, was seeking to finish the task which 'A'isha, Talha and az-Zubayr had sought to complete. At-Tabari related[156] that 'Ali mentioned Allah's blessing to the community through agreement on the Caliph after the Messenger of Allah ﷺ and the next after and the next after him. He said in the presence of those who had murdered 'Uthman, "Then this event took place. Those who desired this world brought it on the community. They envied the excellence Allah had given him and wanted to reverse things." Then he mentioned that he would travel the next day to Basra to meet with ['A'isha] the Umm al-Mu'minin and his brothers, Talha and az-Zubayr. He said, "None should travel tomorrow who abetted matters against 'Uthman, may Allah be pleased with him, in any of the people's business. Let the fools protect themselves from me."

When you look at this, you will clearly see the baseness of their hearts and the falseness of their business.

> We already summarised the qualities of those who attacked 'Uthman. The first to uncover their secret and look at their faces with the light of Allah and think ill of them was the man of Islam, the inspired one (*muhaddath*), Amir al-Mu'minin 'Umar ibn al-Khattab. He possessed perspicacity that did not err. At-Tabari related[157] that when 'Umar reviewed

the armies for *jihad* in 14 AH, the tribes of the Yemeni inhabitants passed before him with Kinda. They were led by Husayn ibn Numayr as-Sakuni and Mu'awiya ibn Hudayj, one of the Companions who conquered Egypt and later was one of its governors. 'Umar was before them. There were some young men among them with dark lank hair. He turned away from them and then he turned away again and turned away a third time until he was asked, "What is wrong between you and those men?" He said, "I am doubtful about them. No people from the Arabs have passed by me whom I disliked more than them." They included Safwan ibn Haran and Khalid ibn Miljam. Both of them were among those who attacked 'Uthman.

Al-Ghafiqi al-Misri was in charge of the people.

He is al-Ghafiqi ibn Harb al-'Ukki, one of the sons of the nobles of the Yemeni tribes who stayed in Egypt after it was conquered. When Ibn Saba' displayed his partisanship for 'Ali and did not find a breeding-ground for his occupation in the Hijaz, nor in Syria, he contented himself with some helpers in Basra and Kufa. He chose to reside in Fustat. This al-Ghafiqi was one of his recruiters. They won him over by means of his desire for leadership and rank. Muhammad ibn Abi Hudhayfa ibn 'Utba al-Umawi was the fosterling of 'Uthman al-Abiq. He was his right hand in carrying out the plans of the Saba'ites in Egypt, and al-Ghafiqi in taking the lead and being to the front. In Shawwal, 35 AH, they made their preparations to advance from Egypt to Madina with four groups whose men numbered about six hundred altogether. There was a leader in charge of every group. Their general leader was this al-Ghafiqi. They pretended that they were intending to go on *hajj*. In Madina, their agitators developed until the business got out of control and they prevented 'Uthman leading the people in prayer in the Prophet's Mosque. Al-Ghafiqi was the one who led the people in prayer.[158] When Shaytan induced them to undertake the greatest crime, al-Ghafiqi was one of those who dared to do it and struck 'Uthman with a sword he had and struck the Qur'an with his foot and turned it around.[159] After 'Uthman's murder, Madina remained for five days with al-Ghafiqi ibn Harb as its governor.[160]

Kinana ibn Bishr at-Tujibi...

This was also one of the recruiters of Ibn Saba' in Egypt. When 'Uthman sent 'Ammar to Egypt to investigate the rumours and to ascertain the true situation, the Saba'ites won him over. Kinana ibn Bishr was one of them.[161] When the mobs from the tribes gathered to attack Madina under the pretext of the *hajj* in Shawwal 35 AH, they split up into four groups in Egypt. Each group had a leader. Kinana ibn Bishr was the leader of one of these groups.[162] Then he was in the front of those who attacked the house of 'Uthman, holding a torch soaked in naphtha in his hand. He entered from the house of 'Amr ibn Hazm and the torches were carried in after him.[163] Kinana at-Tujibi reached 'Uthman and stabbed him with a broad arrowhead and blood splashed on the *ayat*, *"Allah will be enough for you against them."*[164][165] Kinana cut the hand of Na'ila, 'Uthman's wife and he leaned with his sword on 'Uthman's breast and killed him.[166] Muhammad ibn 'Umar al-Waqidi said that 'Abd ar-Rahman ibn Abi az-Zinad al-Madini related to him that 'Abd ar-Rahman ibn al-Harith ibn Hisham al-Makhzumi al-Madini (d. 43 AH) said, "The one who killed the Amir al-Mu'minin 'Uthman was Kinana ibn Bishr ibn 'Attab at-Tujibi."[167] Al-Walid ibn 'Uqba ibn Abi Mu'ayt says on it:

> Isn't the best of creation after the three, the one who
> was murdered by the Tujibi from Egypt?

Kinana's end was that he was slain in the war which broke out in Egypt in 38 AH between Muhammad ibn Abi Bakr as-Siddiq, the representative of 'Ali and 'Amr ibn al-'As and men from the army of Mu'awiya ibn Hudayj as-Sakuni.[168]

...Sudan ibn Humran,...

He was as-Sakuni, from one of the tribes of Murad of Yemen who stayed in Egypt. It was already stated that in 14 AH he was one of those who came during 'Umar's caliphate to do *jihad* with the armies of the Yemen under the leadership of Husayn ibn Numayr and Mu'awiya ibn Hudayj. When the Amir al-Mu'minin reviewed them, his glance fell on Sudan ibn Humran and his colleague, Khalid ibn Miljan. He felt that there would be calamity from them and so he disliked them. When the Amir al-Mu'minin 'Uthman sent 'Ammar to Egypt to investigate the source of the false rumours and ascertain the real situation for him, the Saba'ites embraced 'Ammar. Sudan ibn Humran was one of them.[169] When the Saba'ites moved the volunteers in the sedition from the Yemeni mobs in Egypt, in Shawwal 35 AH, towards Madina and they divided them into four groups, Sudan was the leader of one of these groups.[170] When those rebels reached Madina and Muhammad ibn Maslama went out to them to stress the right of 'Uthman and pointed out that they were bound by the homage which they had given to him, he saw that they followed four men. This man was one of them.[171] In the *History* of at-Tabari,[172] he describes how Sudan and some others scaled the wall from the house of 'Amr ibn Hazm to reach 'Uthman's house. Then there are some of the details of what Sudan did when they committed this terrible crime.[173] When they finished murdering the Amir al-Mu'minin, Sudan left the house shouting, "We have killed 'Uthman ibn 'Affan!"[174]

...'Abdullah ibn Budayl ibn Warqa' al-Khuza'i,...

His father was an aged man among those who became Muslim at the conquest of Makka. 'Abdullah ibn Budayl will be mentioned in the terrible sedition against 'Uthman. At-Tabari[175] mentioned that al-Mughira ibn al-Akhnas ibn Shariq ath-Thaqafi, the ally of the Banu Zuhra, went out with 'Abdullah ibn az-Zubayr, Marwan and others to defend the Amir al-Mu'minin at the door of his house. 'Abdullah ibn Budayl attacked al-Akhnas ibn Shariq and killed him.

Ibn Hajar transmitted in his biography in the *Isaba*[176] from al-Kalbi that 'Abdullah ibn Budayl and his brother, 'Abd ar-Rahman, were present at Siffin with 'Ali and killed there. It is clear that his brother was killed before him. Ibn Hajar transmitted in the *Isaba*[177] from Ibn Ishaq in the *Kitab al-Firdaws* that when 'Ubaydullah ibn 'Umar ibn al-Khattab came to Kufa (i.e. with the army of the people of Syria), he met 'Abdullah ibn Budayl. Ibn Budayl advised him not to shed his blood in this sedition. 'Ubaydullah used the excuse that he was seeking to avenge the blood of the Amir al-Mu'minin and that 'Uthman had been wrongly murdered. Ibn Budayl offered the excuse that he was seeking revenge for the blood of the brother who had been wrongly killed. How could his brother have been wrongly killed when he was killed in a sedition in which he had voluntarily participated of his own free will while 'Uthman, who was the Amir al-Mu'minin and ruled them by right of rule, was attacked by Ibn Budayl and men like him and men who were less important than him? In spite of that, 'Uthman did not fight anyone and he did not defend himself. He forbade people to defend him against the mob who had come to the city of the Messenger of Allah from different lands to perpetrate evil. Where is 'Abd ar-Rahman ibn Budayl who is practically unknown in history in relation to 'Uthman, whose good deeds filled the heavens and the earth?

...Hukaym ibn Jabala from the people of Basra,...

Hukaym ibn Jabala al-'Abdi was from the tribes of the 'Abd al-Qays. Their root was in Oman and the coasts of the Persian Gulf. He lived in Basra after it was settled. This Hukaym was a brave young man. The Islamic armies that set out towards the west to spread the call and conquest came from Basra and Kufa. Hukaym ibn Jabala accompanied these armies and risked himself in one of the dangerous attacks just as commandos do now.

The armies of the Amir al-Mu'minin 'Uthman used him in one of these operations in its attempt to conquer India as I mentioned in my treatise, *The Precursors of Islam in India*. The shaykhs of Sayf ibn 'Umar at-Tamimi (who is the most famous of the historians of the history of Iraq) confirmed what he quoted from at-Tabari[178] i.e. that when the armies returned, Hukaym ibn Jabala hid from them. He went into Persia and changed the people of the *Dhimma* for the worse and alienated them. He corrupted them in the land, took what he wanted and then came back. The people of the *Dhimma* and the people of the *qibla* both complained to 'Uthman. 'Uthman wrote to 'Abdullah ibn 'Amir that he should jail him and those like him. They were not to be allowed to leave Basra until right guidance could be seen in them. They jailed him (i.e. kept him from leaving Basra). When 'Abdullah ibn Saba' came to Basra, he stayed with Hukaym ibn Jabala and some individuals gathered to him and he spat his poison into them. From there, Ibn Saba' travelled to Fustat and remained there. He began to correspond with them and some of them disagreed.

At-Tabari[179] mentioned that when the Saba'ites decided to advance from the cities against the city of the Messenger of Allah, the number of those who came from Basra was the same as the number that came from Egypt. They were also divided into four groups. The Amir of one of these groups was Hukaym ibn Jabala. They stopped at place called Dhu Khusub. Then they threw pebbles at the Amir al-Mu'minin while he was speaking on the minbar of the Prophet ﷺ. Hukaym ibn Jabala was one of them.[180] When the rebels travelled from Madina the first time after their debate with 'Uthman and listening to his defence and being content with it, they left al-Ashtar and Hukaym ibn Jabala behind in Madina.[181] This indicates a strong suspicion that they could have been involved in the business of fabricating the letter ascribed to the Amir al-Mu'minin.

When 'A'isha, Talha and az-Zubayr came to Basra and were about to reach an agreement with the Amir al-Mu'minin 'Ali to put things in order, Hukaym ibn Jabala was the one who started the fighting so that the understanding and agreement would not be completed.[182] He vilely murdered a woman from his own people. She had heard him reviling the Umm al-Mu'minin, 'A'isha, and she said to him, "Son of a wicked woman, you are more suited to that!" So he attacked and killed her.[183] Then his people withdrew from helping him except for some fools among them. He continued to fight until his foot was cut off. Then he was killed and all those who were in the battle from those who had attacked 'Uthman were killed. The herald of az-Zubayr and Talha called out in Basra, "Whoever has anyone in your tribes who are among those who attacked Madina should bring them to us." They were brought as dogs are brought and then killed. The only one among them who was missed out was Harqus ibn Zuhayr as-Sa'di, one of the Banu Tamim.[184] 'Amr ibn Hafs related from one of his shaykhs, "A man from al-Haddad struck the neck of Hukaym ibn Jabala. This man was called Dukhaym. Hukaym's head hung down by the skin and his face turned around to the back of his neck.[185]

…and Malik ibn al-Harith al-Ashtar…

From an-Nakha'. That is a Yemeni tribe from the tribes of Madhhij. He was a brave hero, one of the heroes of the Arabs. His first military battle was at Yarmuk. He lost one of his eyes there. Then he wanted to unsheathe his sword against his brother Muslims in the sedition. If he had not been one of those who conspired against the Amir al-Mu'minin 'Uthman and if Allah had written that his military battles were for the spread of Islam and to widen the conquest, he would have another position in history. That which moved him to his course was his excess in the *deen*, and his love of leadership and rank. I do not know how they were both combined in him. Al-Ashtar was one of those who took Kufa as their place of residence. When al-Walid ibn 'Uqba was governor of Kufa, al-Ashtar felt himself worthy of leadership and government. He slipped in with those who blamed the state and its men, from the highest caliph in Madina down to his governor over Kufa, al-Walid ibn 'Uqba. When Abu Zaynab and Abu Mawra' stole al-Walid's ring from his house and took it to Madina and they testified that al-Walid had drunk wine as was already stated, al-Ashtar and others rushed to Madina to enlarge the area of sedition. When 'Uthman dismissed al-Walid for Sa'id ibn al-'As, al-Ashtar returned with Sa'id to Kufa.[186] 'Uthman had established a system for the transfer of lands. Whoever had some land from the booty in a place which was far from him could change it for land closer to him with the consent of the two people who made the transfer. By this means, Talha ibn 'Ubaydullah renounced his shares in Khaybar and used them to purchase some of the booty of the people of Madina in Iraq. That land was called an-Nashastaj.[187]

While Sa'id ibn al-'As was in the governor's house in Kufa with some people, a man praised Talha ibn 'Ubaydullah for his generosity. Sa'id ibn al-'As said, "If I had the like of the land of an-Nashastaj, I would let you live a life of plenty for Allah."'Abd ar-Rahman ibn Khumays al-Asadi said to him, "I wish that you had al-Miltat." Al-Miltat was some land on the side of the Euphrates that had belonged to the family of Khosrau. Al-Ashtar and his companions became angry. They said to the Asadi, "You wish that he had some of our good land!" His father said, "He wants the double of it for you." Al-Ashtar and his companions attacked the Asadi and his father and beat them in the assembly of the governor until they fainted. The Banu Asad heard about that and came and surrounded the castle to defend their men. Sa'id ibn al-'As stopped this feudal flare-up and turned the Banu Asad away from al-Ashtar and his group. The nobles of Kufa and their men of right action wrote to 'Uthman to ask him to expel these troublemakers from their land. He sent them to Mu'awiya in Syria.[188] Then Mu'awiya expelled them and they came to the peninsula of Ibn 'Umar. They were in the castles of 'Abd ar-Rahman ibn Khalid ibn al-Walid until they showed regret. Then al-Ashtar went to Madina to tell 'Uthman of their repentance.

The Defamation of 'Uthman

'Uthman was satisfied with him and allowed him to go wherever he liked. He chose to return to his colleagues who were with 'Abd ar-Rahman ibn Khalid ibn al-Walid in the peninsula.[189] While he was telling 'Uthman that he and his colleagues repented in 34 AH, the Saba'ites in Egypt were corresponding with their agents in Kufa and Basra. They told them to rebel against their governors and to make ready for a certain day. Only the group situated in Kufa did that. Yazid ibn Qays al-Arhabi stirred them up.[190]

When al-Ashtar came from Madina to his brothers with 'Abd ar-Rahman ibn Khalid ibn al-Walid, he found that they had received a letter from Yazid ibn Qays al-Arhabi. It said, "Come as soon as you put down this letter." They felt uneasy about this summons and preferred to remain where they were. Al-Ashtar opposed them and returned as a rebel after his repentance. He joined the rebels of Kufa who had alighted at al-Jar'a, a place overlooking Qadisiyya. There they met Sa'd ibn al-'As, the governor of Kufa, when he was returning from Madina and turned him back. Al-Ashtar met a client of Sa'd ibn al-'As and struck him down. It reached 'Uthman that they wanted to dismiss Sa'd for Abu Musa al-Ash'ari and he gave them what they asked for.[191] When the date in 34 AH proved unsuccessful and the sedition was confined to what took place in al-Jar'a, the Saba'ites prepared for the following year (35). They arranged things so that they went to Madina with the *hajjis* as if they were going on *hajj*. Al-Ashtar was one of the leaders who left Kufa. He was in charge of one of their four groups.[192] After they reached Madina, the Amir al-Mu'minin 'Uthman debated with them and made his proof clear to them in all that they thought. Most of them were satisfied with that and forced the leaders of the sedition to be content with 'Uthman's answers. They travelled from Madina again, except for al-Ashtar and Hukaym ibn Jabala. They remained in Madina and did not travel with them.[193]

When the Egyptians reached a place called al-Buwayb, a rider stopped them playing the part of the bearer of the alleged letter. The story about that will come later. At-Tabari[194] mentioned that al-Ashtar was involved in the Saba'ite plot which they had hatched before 'Ali travelled from Kufa to Basra trying to reach an understanding with Talha, az-Zubayr and 'A'isha. The Saba'ites had plotted to start the war between the two parties before peace could be made between them. In the Battle of the Camel, 'Abdullah ibn az-Zubayr and al-Ashtar fought and exchanged blows. 'Abdullah ibn az-Zubayr uttered his famous words, "Kill me and Malik!" Al-Ashtar got away from him. At-Tabari related[195] from ash-Sha'bi that people did not know al-Ashtar by the name of Malik. If Ibn az-Zubayr had said, "Kill me and al-Ashtar," and al-Ashtar had had a million men, none of them would have been saved. He continued to reel back before Ibn az-Zubayr until he managed to slip away. At-Tabari[196] related that when 'Ali finished the oath of allegiance after the Battle of the Camel and appointed 'Abdullah ibn 'Abbas over Basra, al-Ashtar heard about that appointment. He became angry and said, "For what did we kill the old man then? Yemen is for 'Ubaydullah, the Hijaz is for Quthum, Basra is for 'Abdullah and Kufa is for 'Ali!" Then he called his mount and rode back. 'Ali heard about that and he called out, "Departure!" Then he rushed to travel and caught up to him. He did not tell him what he had heard about him. He said, "What is this journey? You have gone ahead of us?" He feared that if he left and went out, evil would befall the people. Then al-Ashtar participated in the war of Siffin and 'Ali appointed him over Egypt after Qays ibn Sa'd ibn 'Ubada left it. When he reached Suez, he had a drink of honey and died. It is said that the honey was poisoned. That was in 38 AH.

...were in the group of their leaders, as well as others.

They stirred up the sedition, so 'Uthman expelled them by his *ijtihad*. They were in a group who were sent to Mu'awiya.

They stirred up the sedition on the day when they beat up 'Abd ar-Rahman ibn Khunays al-Asadi and his father while they were in the house of the Amir in Kufa. The nobles and men of right action of Kufa wrote to

The Defamation of 'Uthman

'Uthman asking him to expel them to another land and he sent them to Mu'awiya in Syria. Those who were sent to Mu'awiya were: al-Ashtar an-Nakha'i, Ibn al-Kiwa' al-Yashkari, Sa'sa'a ibn Sawhan al-'Abdi, his brother Zayd, Kumayl ibn Ziyad an-Nakha'i, Jundub ibn Zuhayr al-Ghamidi, Jundub ibn Ka'b al-Azdi, Thabit ibn Qays ibn Munaqqa', 'Urwa ibn al-Ja'd al-Bariqi and 'Amr ibn al-Humq al-Khuza'i.

He reminded them by Allah and by *taqwa* against perverting the situation and breaking up the community…

> The text of what Mu'awiya said is found in at-Tabari,[197] "You are people from the Arabs. You have importance (lit. teeth) and a say. You have obtained nobility by Islam. You have conquered the nations and you have won their positions and their inheritance. I have heard that you resent Quraysh. If it had not been for Quraysh, you would have been considered abased as you were before. They are your Imams up until today and your shelter, so do not destroy your shelter. Your Imams are patient with you in your injustice and put up with trouble from you. By Allah, you will cease or Allah will try you with one who will be hard on you. Then you will not be praised for patience. Then you will share with them in what you brought upon the populace while you were alive and after your death."

…until Zayd ibn Suhan said to him (according to what is related)…

> The speaker was actually his brother, Sa'sa'a.

…"How much you go on at us about authority and Quraysh! The Arabs were eating from the hilts of their swords while Quraysh were only merchants!"

> He also said to Mu'awiya, "As for what you mentioned of the shelter, when the shelter is pierced, then come to us," i.e. when we kill our governors, then we will be the rulers." If any rebel had uttered these

words while he was in the power of his ruler since the time governments appeared until the Last Day, he would not have experienced the judiciousness and patience that Sa'sa'a experienced from Mu'awiya.

Mu'awiya said to him, "You have no mother! I remind you by Islam and yet you mention the *Jahiliyya* to me! May Allah make ugly those who come frequently to the Amir al-Mu'minin on your behalf! You are not among those who are helped or harmed. Leave me!"

The answer Mu'awiya gave to the words of Sa'sa'a in the description of Quraysh and their position is very long and excellent. At-Tabari quoted it.[198]

Ibn al-Kiwa' informed him about the people of sedition...

The speaker might say, "Don't the events which occurred in the tragedy of the martyrdom of the caliph 'Uthman indicate his negligence since he did not know what was happening in the secret conspiracy of the plotters?"

In reality, in spite of his occupation with the vast conquests that were completed in his time, this caliph was not unaware of the plots that were hatched against him in order to directly harm Islam. As far as the events are concerned, he was free of any suspicion of weakness repeated by his opponents.

The historian Muhammad 'Izza Daruza said, "Ibn Sawda (i.e. 'Abdullah ibn Saba') and his groups worked to spread the agitation against 'Uthman and his governors until they enlarged their base as has come in the transmission of at-Tabari. They wrote secret letters and sent them to the people in the cities. The people of Madina heard about that and they went to 'Uthman to ask him whether he heard what they had heard from the cities. He said, "By Allah, only peace has come to me, so tell me what it is." Then he told them, "You are my partners and the witnesses of the believers. Give me advice." They indicated that he should send certain individuals who were trustworthy to the cities to tell the people

The Defamation of 'Uthman

that neither his notable men nor the common people objected to anything that 'Uthman had done. The governors were just to the people.[199]

Then he wrote a general letter to the people of the cities in which he mentioned what he had heard about the rumours and attacks on the governors. He said, "The Amir al-Mu'minin is appointed to undertake to command the correct and forbid the objectionable. He appoints his governors to do that. He is prepared to listen to every complaint about himself and about his governors and to give justice to the one with the complaint and give everyone with a due his due." He summoned anyone with a complaint to come to him in the Festival. At-Tabari[200] was quoted to say that in the *History of the Arab Race*.[201] Then he summoned the governors of the cities and asked them for news about the affair. He said, "I fear that it will be proven against you." They assured him that they were following the path of truth and correct behaviour, and that what he had heard was nothing but intrigue and whisperings spread by stealth. One of them proposed that the propaganda agents be punished and executed. 'Uthman commanded his governors to be prudent, compassionate and indulgent as long as that did not entail the loss of the rights of the community. One of the governors was Mu'awiya ibn Abi Sufyan.[202]

The historians mentioned that 'Uthman gathered some of his elite and consulted them about the business of the people. He listened to them and then said to them, "I have heard all that you have pointed out to me. Every business has a door. This business which is feared for the community is still hidden and its closed door can be opened. We will hold it back by leniency and by being obliging except where the *hudud* of Allah are concerned. Then if the door opens, no one will have any proof against me. Allah knows that I have treated the people well. If the millstone of sedition turns around, then 'Uthman will have bliss if he dies without having been the one to move it. Calm people and give them their rights. When the rights of Allah are damaged, then do not be lax!"[203]

One of the clearest proofs of the strength of 'Uthman and his self-composure was his position with the rebels and people of the sedition when they were intense in their attack on him. They attacked him in his house to kill him while the great valiant Companions and their sons wanted to defend him as we stated elsewhere. He ordered everyone who thought that 'Uthman was owed obedience to restrain their hands and throw away their weapons." This was due to his solicitude for the blood of the Muslims, even if that involved offering his life to death and murder.

Would that I knew what personal courage and what patience people could seek beyond this? If courage is self-control in calamities without any apprehension, steadfastness in adversities without anxiety, patience in events without complacency, and firmness in great misfortunes without being shaken, the sources could not omit someone like 'Uthman in his courage, self-composure, the strength of his certainty and his firmness in his opinion. No one in a situation similar to that in which 'Uthman found himself would endure the like of what 'Uthman endured, not even part of it. No one could endure affliction and trial as 'Uthman endured it. How could someone endure something which would lead to them being murdered with full knowledge and insight? If he had been fearful and had wanted to do anything other than endure with both certainty and contentment, he had means by which he could have escaped and lived in comfort. However, 'Uthman was neither weak nor abject, as is claimed by those who are incapable and negligent. He was strong in faith, great in certainty, high-minded, with great courage, noble in patience and piercing in insight. He ransomed the community and established its greatest support of order in social formation.[204]

...in every land and their conspiracies.

Ibn al-Kiwa' said, in what Ibn 'Asakir quoted in his biography in the *History of Damascus*[205] and Abu Ja'far at-Tabari quoted in his *History*[206]

The Defamation of 'Uthman

in describing the people of misdeeds: "The people of misdeeds in Madina were the most eager for evil in the community and the most incapable of them. The people of misdeeds in Kufa were the ones who most frequently dwell on minor wrong actions although they commit the greatest wrong actions. The people of misdeeds from the people of Basra rejected everyone and went out in separate groups. As for the people of misdeeds from the people of Egypt, they were the people with the fullest portion of evil and the quickest to repent. As for the people of misdeeds from the people of Syria, they were the people who were the quickest to obey their guide and rebel against the one who would misguide them.

He wrote to 'Uthman to inform him about that. He sent some of their individuals to them. Mu'awiya expelled them...

> He wrote about them to 'Uthman, "Some people have come to me who have neither intellect nor *deen*. Islam is burdensome to them and justice vexes them. They do not aim for Allah in anything nor do they speak by any proof. They are busy with sedition and taking the property of the people of the *dhimma*. Allah is the One who will test and try them. Then He will be the One to disgrace them and humiliate them. They are those who injure people. Restrain Sa'id and those with him among them. They do not have the most strife or repugnant behaviour."[207]

...and then they went to 'Abd ar-Rahman ibn Khalid ibn al-Walid...

> He was appointed over Homs for Mu'awiya and the area of Jazira, Harran and ar-Raqqa.

...who imprisoned them and rebuked them. He told them, "Remember what you said to Mu'awiya!"

> That was after he said to them, "Tools of Shaytan! You have no welcome!

Shaytan has returned in sorrow and yet you are still active! May Allah disappoint 'Abd ar-Rahman if he does not discipline you until he makes you feel regret! O company of a people whom I do not know to be Arab or non-Arab, you will not say to me what I heard you said to Mu'awiya! I am the son of Khalid ibn al-Walid. I am the son of the one who was tested by the teeth. I am the son of the one who knocked out the *Ridda*. By Allah, Sa'sa'a, son of abasement, if I were to hear that any of those with me had broken your nose and then given something to you, I would have made you fly down an abyss!"[208]

He held them and kept them abased until they repented after a year had passed.

> Whenever he rode, he made them walk. When he passed by Sa'sa'a, he said, "Son of a mean woman, don't you know that the one who is not put right by good is put right by bad? Why don't you tell me what I heard that you said to Sa'id and Mu'awiya?" They said, "We repent to Allah! Release us, may Allah release you!"[209]

He wrote about them to 'Uthman and 'Uthman told him to send them to him. When they stood in front of him, they re-iterated their repentance and they took an oath that they were telling the truth and said that they were innocent of what they were accused of.

> The one who went to the Amir al-Mu'minin 'Uthman in Madina was al-Ashtar an-Nakha'i alone. He is the one who represented the sons of Suhan, Ibn al-Kiwa' and others in re-stating their earlier repentance to 'Abd ar-Rahman ibn Khalid ibn al-Walid. However, the sedition was not confined to these men. It originated with Ibn Saba' who chose to reside in Fustat. It had a branch in Basra. Al-Ashtar and his brothers left some men in Kufa. While al-Ashtar was in Madina, re-stating his repentance and the repentance of his brothers, the agents of Ibn Saba' were writing

to Basra and Kufa to set the time to attack their governors. When al-Ashtar returned to his brothers who were with 'Abd ar-Rahman ibn Khalid ibn al-Walid, they had received a letter from their brothers in Kufa calling them to participate in the plot. Only al-Ashtar, who had not yet even forgotten his repentance, was happy about that summons to sedition and evil. He sped to Kufa and joined the sedition which history calls "The Day of al-Jar'a." That was in 34 AH.

He let them choose where they wanted to go. Each of them chose a city – Kufa, Basra, or Egypt. He sent them out. Wherever they went, they rebelled and agitated until other groups joined them.

When the Saba'ites were unsuccessful in their attack on their governors in 34 AH in the sedition of the Day of Jar'a, they plotted another sedition with a wider scope. They set it for the following year (35) when the *hajjis* were preparing to go from Egypt, Basra and Kufa to Madina and Makka. The *hajjis* went on *hajj* to obey Allah, but the protagonists of the sedition went to proclaim a rebellion against Allah. They had organised themselves into twelve groups: four from Egypt, four from Basra and four from Kufa. There were about 150 people in each group, i.e. about 600 men from every city.

Those who went to 'Uthman...

i.e. to the Amir al-Mu'minin 'Uthman in the city of the Messenger.

...were 'Abd ar-Rahman ibn 'Udays al-Balawi in charge of the people of Egypt, ...

The warrior poet. He stayed with the conquering army in Egypt. It is not known that he was distinguished by anything after his participation in this sedition, even though he claimed he was one of those who took the Pledge of the Tree. I do not think that he was one of the leaders who organised the sedition. However, their organizers took advantage of his desire for leadership. They made use of his age and rank among the warriors of the Arab tribes of Egypt. They appointed him to lead one of the four groups that left Egypt for Madina. (The leaders of the other three groups were: Kinana ibn Bishr at-Tujibi, Sudan ibn Humran as-Sakuni and Qutayra as-Sakuni. Their general-in-chief was al-Ghafiqi ibn Harb al-'Ukki.) During the siege, 'Abd ar-Rahman ibn 'Udays was very cruel to the Amir al-Mu'minin 'Uthman and the people of his house. He ended by being killed at Hebron, close to Hums. A bedouin met him. When he admitted that he was one of 'Uthman's murderers, the bedouin leapt up and killed him.[210] Whoever said that Ibn 'Udays was related to Tujib made a mistake. He was a Balawi from Quda'a. As for Tujib bint Thawban al-Madhhijiyya, only the sons of her sons are ascribed to her and 'Adi, the sons of Ashras ibn Shubayb ibn as-Sukun from Kinda. Where is Kinda in relationship to Quda'a?

...Hukaym ibn Jabalah in charge of the people Basra,...

The information was already given earlier. He was the Amir of one of the four groups from Basra (the three others were Dhurayh ibn 'Abbad al-'Abdi, Bishr ibn Shurayh "al-Hatm" and Ibn al-Mahrash al-Hanafi. Their commander was Harqus ibn Zuhayr as-Sa'di.

...and al-Ashtar Malik ibn al-Harith an-Nakha'i in charge of the people of Kufa.

He was already mentioned earlier. He was the leader of one of the four groups of Kufa. The three others were Zayd ibn Suhan al-'Abdi, Ziyad ibn an-Nadr al-Harithi and 'Abdullah ibn al-Asamm. Their commander was 'Amr ibn al-Asamm.

They came to Madina at the beginning of Dhu al-Qa'da 35 AH.

They alighted three stages outside of Madina. Then the rebels of Basra advanced and camped at Dhu Khushub. The rebels of Kufa camped at al-A'was. Most of them camped at Dhu al-Marwa.

'Uthman received them. They said, "Call for a copy of the Qur'an." He called for it. They said, "Open to the ninth,"...

> It is like that in the Algerian edition.[211] Perhaps he erred and the correct version is the "seventh" as in the *History* of at-Tabari.[212] It is said that that was the position of *Sura Yunus* in the Qur'an of Ibn Mas'ud according to the *Fihrist* of Ibn an-Nadim.[213]

...meaning the *Sura Yunus*. They said, "Read." He read until he reached the words, *"Has Allah given permission, or do you forge lies against Allah?"* They told him, "Stop." They said to him, "Do you think that Allah has given you permission for the *hima* which you have made or have you forged lies against Allah?" He said, "Finish the *ayat*. It was revealed about such-and-such. 'Umar made the *hima* and when there were more camels, he enlarged the *hima*."

> The discussion on the *hima* has already been given.

They began to interrogate him in that way, but he defeated them. Finally he said to them, "What do you want?"

They made an agreement with him and wrote down five or six stipulations in it:

> They made five or six stipulations with the following meanings.

...that the exile be returned, that the ruler give to the one who was deprived, that the booty be given in full, that he be just in the division and that he appoint those who had trustworthiness and strength. They wrote all of that in a document. He enjoined them not to break from the Community nor leave the Community. Then they went back content.

Those who came from the cities against the city of the Messenger ﷺ consisted of two groups: deceitful leaders and their deluded followers. They were many. Biased propaganda had spread among them until they truly believed that there were exiles who had been wronged, deprived individuals who had been stripped of their rights, etc. You have already seen the testimony of the two most truthful witnesses in Iraq at that time: al-Hasan al-Basri and his brother, Ibn Sirin. They testified to the abundance of gifts, provisions and various blessings in 'Uthman's time when people were summoned to accept them. He did not refuse anyone. You already saw the testimony of Imam ash-Sha'bi regarding general provision and bounty, even for slaves. When the rebels heard 'Uthman's answers and recognised the truth, they were satisfied and retreated. They went home by different routes since their cities lay in opposite directions. The Egyptians headed for the northwest so as to travel along the coast of the Red Sea to Suez and Egypt. The Iraqis, both the Basrans and Kufans, headed northeast in order to go by the Najd highlands to Basra and Kufa in Iraq.

It was said that he sent 'Ali to them and they agreed on the above-mentioned five stipulations and went back well content. While they were on their way, …

> i.e. while the Iraqis from Basra and Kufa were on their way to the northeast and the Egyptians were on their way to the northwest, and while there were many stages between the two groups because they had already been travelling for sometime and very far from each other.

…a rider stopped before them…

> i.e. the Egyptians alone.

…and he went back and forth between them several times.

The Defamation of 'Uthman

He only stopped them so that they would look at him. He deliberately made them suspicious of him. This is what those who had employed this man wanted. He was meant to play this role. The organisers of this plot wanted to rekindle the sedition after Allah had quelled it and relieved the Muslims of their evil. It would not be reasonable to assume that this drama could originate with 'Uthman, Marwan, or any man connected to them because they would not profit by rekindling the sedition after Allah had averted it. Those who stood to benefit by that were the first propagandists who wanted to provoke this strife. They included al-Ashtar and Hukaym ibn Jabala who did not travel with their people. They had remained behind in Madina.[214] The only reason for them to remain in Madina would be to conspire with these measures. It was their sole desire.

They said, "What is wrong with you?" He said, "I am the messenger of the Amir al-Mu'minin to his governor in Egypt."

They clearly stated that it was 'Abdullah ibn Sa'd ibn Abi Sarh.[215] It is not reasonable to suppose that 'Uthman or Marwan would have written to 'Abdullah because he had already left Egypt after the rebels and had left for Madina. He had written to 'Uthman to ask for his permission to come.[216] He had actually left Egypt for al-'Arish, Palestine, and Ayla ('Aqaba), and Muhammad ibn Abi Hudhayfa had taken over in Egypt. He was an enemy to Allah and His Messenger. He came out against the Caliph of the Muslims. How could 'Uthman or Marwan have written to 'Abdullah ibn Sa'd when they had already received his letter in which he asked for permission to come to Madina?

Therefore they examined the letter. They found a letter addressed to the governor of Egypt which was ascribed to 'Uthman and bore his seal. It ordered him to crucify them and cut off their hands and feet.

The reports which have come on it state that the rider was 'Uthman's slave and that the camel was one of the *zakat* camels and that 'Uthman admitted that, are all *mursal* reports whose speaker is unknown or else they are lies spread by those whose truthfulness and trustworthiness are doubted. The *riwayats* are confused regarding the contents of the letter. One of the *riwayats* has, "When 'Abd ar-Rahman ibn 'Udays comes to you, flog him a hundred times, shave his head and beard, and imprison him for a long time until my command comes to you. Do the same to 'Amr ibn al-Humq, Sudan ibn Humran and 'Urwa ibn an-Nabba' al-Laythi." One version has, "When Muhammad ibn Abi Bakr as-Siddiq and so-and-so and so-and-so come to you, kill them and consider their document invalid. Remain in your post until my opinion reaches you." A third version says that the contents of the letter commanded his governor to kill them, cut off their hands and crucify these rebels. This disagreement about the contents of the same letter increases its doubtfulness.

They advanced on Madina.

The most extraordinary thing is that the caravans of the rebels which were far from each other in the east and the west returned together to Madina at the same time, i.e. the caravan of the Iraqis which had been many stages away from the caravan of the Egyptians, learned of this staged transmission at the very same moment in which the drama was being played out in al-Buwayb. They returned to Madina at the very moment that the Egyptians returned. They reached Madina together as if it was arranged. This means that those who hired the rider to play the role of the bearer of the letter for the caravan of the Egyptians, also hired another rider to leave Madina with him to go to the caravans of the Iraqis to inform them that the Egyptians had discovered a letter which 'Uthman had sent to 'Abdullah ibn Sa'd in Egypt, ordering him to kill Muhammad ibn Abi Bakr. At-Tabari said,[217] "'Ali said to them, 'How did you learn, people of Kufa and people of Basra, what the people of Egypt had found out when you had already travelled several stages? Now you come back to us? By Allah, this is something which was fabricated in Madina!" 'Ali indicated that al-Ashtar and Hukaym had remained in Madina and they were responsible for this drama. The Iraqi rebels said, "Take it however you like. We do not need this man. Let him leave us alone." They admitted that the letter was forged and that their first and last desire was to depose the Amir al-Mu'minin 'Uthman and to shed his blood, although Allah had protected it by the Shari'a of His Messenger ﷺ.

They went to 'Ali and said to him, "Do you not see that the enemy of Allah has written such-and-such about us? Allah has made his blood lawful." Then they said, "Join us." He said, "By Allah, I will not join you!" They asked, "Then why did you write to us?" He said, "By Allah, I did not write to you." They looked at each other.

All the *riwayats*[218] agree about this conversation between 'Ali and the rebels. It is a definite strong text showing that the hand which forged the letter against 'Uthman and informed the Iraqis about that and asked them to return to Madina was the same hand which forged the letter ascribed to 'Ali and sent it to the Iraqi rebels, asking them to return. We already said that the rebels were in two groups: deceiving and deceived. Those who were deluded looked at each other when 'Ali swore that he had not written to them. They wondered how it could be that 'Ali had not written to them when they had received it. Who had written the letter ascribed to him if he had not written it? You will learn that Masruq ibn al-Ajda' al-Hamdani (who was one of the notable Imams of guidance) censured the Umm al-Mu'minin 'A'isha for writing to people to command them to come out against 'Uthman. She swore to him by Allah in whom the believers believe and whom the rejecters reject that she had not written anything to them. Sulayman ibn Mahran al-A'mash, one of the great Imams, said, "They thought that it was written by her and ascribed to her."

O Muslims of this age and every age! The criminal hands who forged the false letters ascribed to 'A'isha or 'Ali, Talha and az-Zubayr are the same hands which organised all of this iniquity. They are the ones who cooked up the sedition from beginning to end. They are the ones who forged the so-called letter ascribed to the Amir al-Mu'minin 'Uthman, addressed to his governor in Egypt at the moment when he knew that he did not have a governor in Egypt. They forged the letter that was ascribed to 'Uthman with the same pen they used to forge the other letter ascribed to 'Ali. All of that was done in order to make the rebels return to Madina after they had been content with the soundness of the position of their Caliph and satisfied that what had been spread about him was all lies and they were assured that he acted in every matter according to what he thought to be true and good. The son-in-law of the Messenger of Allah ﷺ, who gave him the good news of martyrdom and the Garden, was not the only one harmed by this foul Saba'ite conspiracy. Islam itself was injured by that. The pure clean history which generations of Islam learned was distorted and twisted. Those generations have among them those injured by that foul Jew and those who surrendered to him in their passions and appetites.

Then 'Ali left Madina.

They went to 'Uthman and said to him, "You wrote such-and-such about us." He told them to bring two of the Muslims as witnesses or he would take an oath as we already mentioned. They did not accept this.

> Because they did not come to accept the truth or refer to the Shari'a. They came either to depose him or to shed his blood.

They broke their covenant and laid siege to him.

> That which was already stated is that they had bound themselves not to leave that community or part from the community.

The Defamation of 'Uthman

It is related that al-Ashtar was brought to 'Uthman. Al-Ashtar said to him, "People want you either to abdicate or to offer yourself for retaliation. If not, they will kill you." He said, "As for my abdicating, I will not leave the community of Muhammad while they are against each other. As for retaliation, my two Companions (Abu Bakr and 'Umar) before me did not offer themselves for retaliation. My body will not bear that."

This report is in the *History* of at-Tabari,[219] in *al-Bidaya wa an-Nihaya*[220] and in the *Ansab al-Ashraf* by al-Baladhuri.[221]

It is related that a man said to him, "I have vowed to take your blood." He said, "Take my shirt." He made a slit in it with his sword and his blood flowed through it. Then the man left, mounted his camel and departed immediately.

This report is in the *Book of the Tamhid* by Imam Abu Bakr al-Baqillani.[222] More extraordinary than that was what at-Tabari related[223] – 'Umayr ibn Dabi al-Barjimi and Kumayl ibn Ziyad an-Nakha'i came to Madina to assassinate 'Uthman. They had planned that in Kufa with the rest of their gang. When they reached Madina, 'Umayr held back while Kumayl lay in ambush for the Caliph until he passed by him. When they met, 'Uthman was suspicious about him. He stabbed at his face and 'Umayr fell on his bottom. He said to 'Uthman, "You have hurt me, Amir al-Mu'minin!" 'Uthman said, "Aren't you an assassin?" He replied, "No, by Allah! There is no god but Him!" People gathered and said, "We will investigate him, Amir al-Mu'minin." He said, "No, Allah has given me well-being. I do not want to know any more about him than what he said." Then he said to Kumayl, "If you are speaking the truth, then settle with me," and he knelt. "By Allah, I only thought that you were aiming for me." He said, "If you are speaking the truth, then may Allah repay you. If you lie, Allah is the Abaser." He sat on his heels for Kumayl and said, "Here you are."

Kumayl said, "I leave it." O noble reader! This position is not the position of a Caliph, let alone one less than him. It is the position of those who have the character of the Prophets since Allah grants respite and does not overlook. Al-Hajjaj came forty years later and Dabi and Kumayl were killed since they had intended to assassinate a man whose heart was moulded with the mercy of Allah. "Allah will let the unjust man enjoy until what he cannot escape seizes him"[224]

Ibn 'Umar came to him and 'Uthman said to him, "See what these men say! They say: Abdicate or we will kill you!" Ibn 'Umar said to him, "Will you be immortal in the earth?" He replied, "No." Ibn 'Umar asked, "Can they do more than kill you?" He said, "No." He asked, "Do they possess a Garden or a Fire for you?" He said, "No." Ibn 'Umar said, "Do not remove the shirt of Allah from yourself lest that become a *sunna*. Whenever a people dislike their caliph, they will depose or kill him."

> Al-Baladhuri quoted this report in the *Ansab al-Ashraf*[225] from Nafi' ibn 'Umar. Before Ibn 'Umar gave the Caliph that opinion and called him with this noble good counsel, 'Uthman had a clear sign of that and a light from Allah. Ibn Majah related in the preface of his *Sunan*[226] from the *hadith* of an-Nu'man ibn Bashir from the Umm al-Mu'minin 'A'isha that the Messenger of Allah ﷺ said to 'Uthman, "'Uthman, if Allah appoints you to this matter one day, the hypocrites will want to remove your shirt which Allah has put on you. Do not remove it." He said that three times. In the *Musnad* of Imam Ahmad ibn Hanbal,[227] there is the *hadith* of 'A'isha with different words which 'Urwa ibn az-Zubayr ibn an-Nu'man ibn Bishr and others related from her.

'Uthman looked down at them from the wall and offered his argument against them in the sound *hadith* regarding the foundation of the mosque, digging the well of Ruma and the words of the Prophet ﷺ

when Uhud shook when they were on it. They conceded the things that he mentioned to them.

> Look in the *Musnad* of Imam Ibn Hanbal[228] at the *hadith* of Abu Salama ibn 'Abd ar-Rahman. Also look at the *Sunan* of an-Nasa'i,[229] the *Jami'* of at-Tirmidhi[230] and the *Musnad* of Ahmad[231] from the *hadith* of al-Ahnaf Qays at-Tamimi. The *Sunan* of an-Nasa'i[232] and the *History* of at-Tabari[233] has the *hadith* of Abu Sa'id, the client of Abu Asyad al-Ansari.

It is confirmed that 'Uthman looked down at them and said, "Are the sons of Mahduj among you? I ask you, by Allah, do you not know that 'Umar said, 'Rabi'a is corrupt or perfidious? By Allah, I will not allot them shares or shares to a people who have come from a month's distance. The *mahr* of one of them is with his doctor. I gave them five hundred more in one raid until I joined them together.'" They said, "Yes."

He said, "May Allah remind you! Don't you know that you came to me and said, 'Kinda is a bite of the head and Rabi'a is the head? Al-Ash'ath ibn Qays has eaten them.' So I removed him and appointed you." They said, "Yes."

He said, "O Allah, they have rejected my equity and they have bartered my favour. Do not give them pleasure from their Imam and do not be pleased with an Imam from them."

'Abdullah ibn 'Amr ibn Rabi'a said, "I was with 'Uthman in his house. He said, 'I ask those who believe that they owe me obedience to hold back their hands and their weapons.'

> The collection of reports about the position of 'Uthman in respect of defending himself or submitting to fate indicates that he disliked sedition and feared Allah regarding the blood of the Muslims. However, at the end of the business, he did wish that he had had a dominant force with him to frighten the attackers and one which would prevent them from

attacking without there being any need for using arms to obtain this result. Before matters came to a head, Mu'awiya offered to send him a force from the army of Syria which would be subject to his directions. He refused to oppress the people of the Abode of the Hijra with an army that would have to be billeted with them.[234] He did not think that the audacity of these men would lead a group of his brother Muslims to assail the blood of the first man to do *hijra* for Allah in the way of His *deen*. When the attackers acted like wolves towards him and he believed that defending himself would cause blood to be shed, he begged all of those who obeyed him to keep their hands and weapons from the perils of force. There are many reports about that in sources both from his friends and his enemies. However, if an ordered military force had appeared in the arena to face the rebels and to put a limit on their insolence and their rashness, 'Uthman would have been spared that and would have rejoiced at it, even though he was content to die as a martyr.

Then he said, "Get up, Ibn 'Umar." Ibn 'Umar was wearing a sword. 'Uthman said, "Inform the people."

> In *al-Bidaya wa an-Nihaya*[235] about the raids of Ibn 'Uqba, it says that Ibn 'Umar did not wear any weapons except on the Day of the House during the caliphate of 'Uthman and on the day when Najda, the Haruri Kharijite wanted to enter Madina with those who rebelled in the time of 'Abdullah ibn az-Zubayr.

Ibn 'Umar and al-Hasan ibn 'Ali left. Then the men came in and murdered him.

> In the *History* of at-Tabari[236] it says that the last to leave was 'Abdullah ibn az-Zubayr. 'Uthman told him to take his will, which he had written in preparation for his death, to az-Zubayr. He told him to go to the people in the house (i.e. those who were defending him in the courtyard) and

tell them to go home. 'Abdullah ibn az-Zubayr was the last of them to leave. He continued to call people and speak to them about 'Uthman until he died. 'Uthman appointed az-Zubayr because az-Zubayr was his confidant among the great Companions. Ibn 'Asakir[237] related that six of the Companions made him a trustee: 'Uthman, 'Abd ar-Rahman ibn 'Awf, Ibn Mas'ud, al-Miqdad, Muti' ibn al-Aswad and Abu al-'As ibn ar-Rabi'. He used to give some of his property to their orphans and guard their property for them.

Zayd ibn Thabit came and said to him, "Those Ansar at the door are saying, 'If you wish, we are the Ansar of Allah' twice." 'Uthman said, "I have no need of defence of that kind."

Al-Baladhuri quotes it in the *Ansab al-Ashraf*[238] from the hadith of Ibn Sirin. Ibn 'Asakir transmitted from the historian of the first generation, Musa ibn 'Uqba al-Asadi (about whom Malik said, "You must have the *Raids* of Ibn 'Uqba. He is reliable. They are the soundest *Raids*.") that Abu Hubayba at-Ta'i (who is one of those from whom Abu Dawud, an-Nasa'i and at-Tirmidhi related), said, "When 'Uthman was under siege, the Banu 'Amr ibn 'Awf came to az-Zubayr and said, 'Abu 'Abdullah, we have come to you and we will do what you command us to do (i.e. to defend the Amir al-Mu'minin)'." Abu Hubayba said, "Az-Zubayr sent me to 'Uthman and instructed me, 'Give him my greetings and say to him, "Your brother tells you that the Banu 'Amr ibn 'Awf have come to me and they have promised me that they will come to me and do what I command. If you wish, I will come to you and be one of the people of the house and I will endure whatever happens to them, and I am willing to do that. If you wish, I will wait for the meeting with the Banu 'Amr and I will defend you with them. I can do that.'" Abu Hubayba said, "I came to 'Uthman and found him on a chair with a back. I found some clothes thrown down and some boiling tubs. I found al-Hasan ibn 'Ali, Ibn 'Umar, Abu Hurayra,

Sa'id ibn al-'As, Marwan ibn al-Hakam and 'Abdullah ibn az-Zubayr in the house. I conveyed the letter of az-Zubayr to 'Uthman. He said, 'Allah is greater! Praise be to Allah who has protected my brother! Tell him that if he comes to the house, he will be one of the men of the Muhajirun. His honour will be the honour of a man and his wealth will be the wealth of a man. Rather he should wait for the meeting with the Banu 'Amr ibn 'Awf. Perhaps Allah will protect me by you.' Abu Hurayra got up and said, 'People! My ears heard the Messenger of Allah ﷺ say, "There will be seditions and calamities after me." and I said, '"Where will a person be safe from them, Messenger of Allah?" He told me, "With the ruler and his party."' Then he indicated 'Uthman. The people said, 'Give us permission and we will fight. Our insight has enabled us to do so.' 'Uthman said, 'No, I beg you! No-one who obeys me should fight!'" Abu Hubayba said, "Those who murdered 'Uthman did so before the meeting with the Banu 'Amr ibn 'Awf. They killed him."[239]

The Banu 'Amr ibn 'Awf were a large clan from al-Khazraj, one of the branches of the Ansar. When the Prophet ﷺ arrived in Madina in his *hijra* from Makka, he stayed as their guest for three days. Then he moved to the Banu an-Najjar.

Abu Hurayra said to him, "Today, it is good to fight on your behalf." 'Uthman said, "I beg you to leave."

This report is in the *History* of at-Tabari.

Al-Hasan ibn 'Ali was another who left him. Al-Hasan and al-Husayn, Ibn 'Umar, Ibn az-Zubayr and Marwan had come. He begged them to put down their arms and leave and stay in their homes.

Ibn az-Zubayr and Marwan said to him, "We have resolved that we will not leave." 'Uthman opened the door and the men came in against him according to the soundest of statements.

The Defamation of 'Uthman

The basis of this report is in the *History* of at-Tabari[240] from Sayf ibn 'Umar at-Tamimi from his shaykhs.

The black man killed him.

It is like that in the Algerian edition. The *History* of at-Tabari[241] has "Black death." The sources from which the *History* of at-Tabari is published are sounder than the sources for the book in Algeria. It is well established that Ibn Saba' was with the rebels in Egypt when they came from Fustat to Madina.[242] In all the roles that he played, he was very eager to act undercover. Perhaps the "black death" is metaphorical for what he alludes to not wanting to communicate their intrigues for the destruction of Islam.

It is said that [Muhammad] ibn Abi Bakr grabbed hold of his beard and Kinana killed him.

He is Kinana ibn Bishr ibn 'Attab at-Tujibi, the general of one of the four Egyptian groups. Before that, he was one of those who embraced 'Ammar ibn Yasir in Fustat to try to make him become a Saba'ite. He was the first to enter 'Uthman's house with a naphtha torch for burning down the door. He is the one who unsheathed his sword to put it in the belly of the Amir al-Mu'minin. 'Uthman's wife, Na'ila, tried to shield him and Kinana cut off her hand and leaned with the sword on his chest. At-Tujibi's end was that he was killed in the battle that started in Egypt between Muhammad ibn Abi Bakr and 'Amr ibn al-'As in 38 AH.

"Kinana" is altered in the Algerian edition by the inscription "Ruman. The Algerian edition has many errors.

It is also said that it was a man from the people of Egypt called Himar...

I did not see the name among those who dared to commit the terrible crime. Perhaps the copyists altered the name of "Safwan ibn Humran" or the name of 'Amr ibn al-"Humq".

...and that a drop of 'Uthman's blood fell on the Qur'an at the words, *"Allah will be enough for you against them."* That contains elements that remain controversial right up until today.

It is related that 'A'isha, may Allah be pleased with her, said, "Would I defend you from flogging and not defend 'Uthman from the sword? You asked him for labours until you left him like a purified lump of boiled sugar. You washed him with the vessel and you left him like a garment cleaned of filth. Then you killed him."

> She said that the first time when she reached Madina on her return from the *hajj*. Some people gathered to her and she delivered an eloquent speech to them. This sentence comes at the end of it.[243] "*Maws*" is to wash with the fingers. "*Qand*" is sugar-cane syrup when it is hard.

Masruq said to her ...

> One of the Imams of the Tabi'un who are followed. He died in 63 AH. He is the one who said to 'Ammar in Kufa before the Battle of the Camel, "Abu al-Yaqathan, why did you kill 'Uthman?" He said, "For abusing our honour and for beating our skin." Masruq said to him, "By Allah, you did not punish him with the same punishment you received from him. If you had been patient, that would have been better for those who are patient."[244]

..."This is your doing. You wrote to people to command them to attack him." 'A'isha said, "By the One in whom the believers believe and the unbelievers reject, I never wrote anything at all to them." Al-A'mash said, "They related that it had been ascribed to her."

As letters had been written and ascribed to 'Ali and to 'Uthman.

It is related that he did not kill anyone except for some infidels from the people of Egypt.

Qadi Abu Bakr, may Allah be pleased with him, said, "This is the most likely of what is related in this subject, and the root of the question is the path of the truth. It is clear in it that none of the Companions acted against him nor held back from him. If he had asked for help, 1000 or 4000 outsiders could not defeat 20,000 or more of that land. However, he submitted to the affliction.

> Because he chose the lesser of two evils by that. He preferred to sacrifice himself to expanding the arena of the strife and shedding the blood of the Muslims. 'Uthman chose to sacrifice his own blood to ransom the blood of his community. How much better a reward he has then! Europe worships a man for the claim of ransom and self-sacrifice when he did not even have any choice in it.

Scholars disagree about someone who is in a similar situation. Should he submit or should he ask for help?

> Part of the policy of Islam is that in every case you should choose whatever has the least harm and least evil. If the good has a dominant force which will curb evil and restrict its spread, Islam guides us to curbing evil by the power of good without any hesitation. If the good does not have the strength to dominate and curb evil and restrict its spread as was the case in the situation of the Amir al-Mu'minin 'Uthman with those who attacked him, then the best interests of Islam lie in the like of what 'Uthman inclined to do. May Allah elevate his station in the everlasting Abode.

Some of them allow one to submit and surrender in imitation of what 'Uthman did and following the advice of the Prophet ﷺ to do that in civil war.

There are the words of the Prophet ﷺ according to what Imam al-Bukhari related in the Book of Virtues²⁴⁵ and in the Book of Seditions²⁴⁶ in his *Sahih* from Abu Hurayra that the Prophet ﷺ said, "There will be civil strife. The one who sits in it then will be better than the one who stands. The one who stands will be better than the one who runs. The one who contemplates them will be drawn by them. So the one who finds a shelter or a refuge should seek shelter in it." Abu Musa al-Ash'ari stated in Kufa before the Battle of the Camel that he had heard it from the Messenger of Allah ﷺ.²⁴⁷

Qadi Abu Bakr said, "I judged between people and obliged them to perform the prayer, I commanded the correct and forbade the objectionable so that no objectionable things would remain in the land. The situation was unbearable for the people of extortion. It was very distressing for the dissolute. Therefore they rallied together and plotted. They rose against me. I submitted to the command of Allah and I commanded all of those around me not to defend my house. I went out on the roof by myself and they wreaked havoc against me and proceeded to loot the house. If it had not been for a good decree, I would have been murdered in the house.

> We indicated the details of this event in the biography of the author at the beginning of this book.

"Three things moved me to do that. One of them was the previous advice of the Prophet ﷺ.

> We quoted it earlier from the *hadith* of Abu Hurayra in *Sahih Bukhari* and from the *hadith* of Abu Musa in Kufa before the Battle of the Camel.

"The second was to imitate 'Uthman. The third was the bad speech from which the Messenger of Allah ﷺ turned, supported by Revelation.

The Defamation of 'Uthman

That was when Ibn Salul spoke about the raid of Banu al-Mustaliq, "When we return to Madina, the mightier will drive out the weaker." 'Umar wanted to kill him, but the Prophet ﷺ stopped him. He said, "People will not say that Muhammad killed his Companions."

I feared that the one who was not there, the one who envies me, would say, 'The people went to ask him for help, and he shed their blood.'"

Everything 'Uthman's did was the *Sunna* and pleasing behaviour. It is confirmed that he was murdered because the truthful one [i.e. the Prophet ﷺ] told him he would be murdered and he gave him the good news of the Garden because of an affliction that would befall him. He said that he would be martyr.

The clarification of that was given earlier.

It is related that he said to him in a dream, "If you wish, I will help you. Otherwise you can break your fast with us tonight."

This transmission by Ibn Abi ad-Dunya is from the *hadith* of 'Abdullah ibn Salam in *al-Bidaya wa an-Nihaya* and in the *Musnad* of Ahmad ibn Hanbal[248] from the *hadith* of Muslim, Abu Sa'id, the client of 'Uthman. He said, "'Uthman freed twenty slaves. He called for trousers and put them on, although he had not worn them either in the *Jahiliyya* or in Islam. He said, 'I saw the Messenger of Allah ﷺ in a dream yesterday, and I saw Abu Bakr and 'Umar. They told me, "Be patient. You will break your fast with us tomorrow."' Then he called for a Qur'an and spread it open before him. He was killed while it was in front of him." Imam Ibn Hanbal said, "This *hadith* from Na'ila, 'Uthman's wife,[249] is similar to that." In *al-Bidaya wa an-Nihaya*[250] there is the *hadith* of Ayyub as-Sakhtiyani from Nafi' from 'Abdullah ibn 'Umar ibn al-Khattab and by various other paths.[251]

The apostates and the ignorant men were ready to say, "All the excellent Companions gathered and rebelled against him. They were satisfied with what happened to him." They contrived to write a letter full of eloquence and examples which 'Uthman had supposedly written to 'Ali asking for help. All of that was fabricated in order to fill the hearts of the Muslims with malice towards the past *Salaf* and **Rightly-guided Caliphs**.

> These forged letters and the information conveyed in them and the false letters fill up volumes on history and books of literature. There are two ways to distinguish the true from the false. One of them is the method of the people of *hadith*. They only accept reports with *isnads* going back to individuals with their names. Then they investigate the circumstances of those individuals and accept those they believe to be truthful and throw the lie back in the face of the liar.
>
> The second method is that of the historians. They present every report on the character of the one from whom they quote and they add his biography to it and whether it is something that you can expect to happen from the one to whom it is attributed and whether it agrees with what is known of his antecedents and his character or not. A thorough examination of our history requires both these methods together, which are used by the scholars who have firm knowledge of both of them.

Qadi Abu Bakr said: We can see in that that 'Uthman was wronged. He was defeated but without any proof.

> As is clear in this book with its definite *isnads*. Look at the *Book of the Tamhid* by Imam Abu Bakr al-Baqillani.[252]

The Companions were innocent of his blood because they did what he wanted and submitted to his opinion when he himself submitted.

Beyond that it was already stated that 'Abdullah ibn az-Zubayr said to 'Uthman, "We are with you in the house as an intelligent group of men who wish to help Allah. Give us permission to fight." He said, "I remind of Allah any man who sheds his blood for me (or blood for me)."

The Defamation of 'Uthman

When those going on *hajj* to the House of Allah began to return to Madina, the first of those who hurried among them was al-Mughira ibn al-Akhnas ibn Shariq ath-Thaqafi, the Companion. He reached 'Uthman before he was slain. He saw the skirmish at the door of 'Uthman's house and he sat at the door on the inside and said, "We have no excuse with Allah if we leave you while we have power. We will not leave you until we die." He was the first to go out against the attacking invaders. He fought until he was killed. Al-Hasan ibn 'Ali ibn Abi Talib went out with him to fight them, saying in criticism of what the attackers were doing:

> Their *deen* is not my *deen* nor am I one of them
> until I go to the proud mountains

i.e. the lofty mountains such that one who falls from them is not saved. Muhammad ibn Talha ibn 'Ubaydullah came out with them. He was known as as-Sajjad (the prostrater) because of his vast amount of worship. He was saying,

> I am the son of the one who defended [the Prophet] at Uhud.
> He repelled the confederates in spite of Ma'ad.[253]

Salit ibn Abi Salit said, "'Uthman forbade us to fight them. If he had given us permission, we would have fought them until we had expelled them from there."

Ibn 'Abd al-Barr related it in the *Isti'ab*[254] from the *hadith* of Ibn Sirin from Salit. Ibn Hajar quoted a summary of it in the *Isaba*.[255]

'Abdullah ibn 'Amir ibn Rabi'a said, "I was with 'Uthman in his house. He said, 'I beg all of those who think that they should obey me to restrain their hands and weapons. The best of you in ability is the one who restrains his hand and weapons.'"

In the *History* of at-Tabari,[256] it says that 'Uthman summoned 'Abdullah ibn 'Abbas and said to him, "Go, you are in charge of the Festival, i.e. in charge of the *Hajj*." Ibn 'Abbas said to him, "Amir al-Mu'minin, I prefer to fight these men than go on *hajj*." He begged him to go. Ibn 'Abbas was in charge of the *hajj* that year.

It is confirmed that al-Hasan, al-Husayn, Ibn az-Zubayr, Ibn 'Umar and Marwan were all armed to the teeth when they entered the house. 'Uthman said, "I beg you to return and put down your weapons and stay in your houses."

> Ibn Kathir said in *al-Bidaya wa an-Nihaya*,[257] "The siege continued from the end of Dhu al-Qa'da until Friday, the 18th of Dhu al-Hijja. The day before that, 'Uthman spoke to the Muhajirun and the Ansar who were with him in the house. They were about 700 and included 'Abdullah ibn 'Umar, 'Abdullah ibn az-Zubayr, al-Hasan and al-Husayn, Marwan, Abu Hurayra, and a group of his clients. If he had let them, they would have defended him. He said, 'I beg whoever owes me obedience to restrain his hands and go to his house.' He said to his slaves, 'Whoever sheathes his sword is free.' So the fighting from the inside cooled down while it was fierce on the outside until Shaytan completed what he had worked for and desired." The effect of the great atrocity on the people is clear enough. Look at what al-Baladhuri quoted in the *Ansab al-Ashraf*[258] from al-Mada'ini from Salama ibn 'Uthman from 'Ali ibn Zayd from al-Hasan. He said, "'Ali came in one day to his daughters and they were wiping their eyes. He asked, 'Why are you weeping?' They said, 'We are weeping for 'Uthman.' He wept and said, 'Weep then.'"

When Allah finished his business as it was finished and carried out His decree, it was known that the Truth would not leave the people in a fruitless situation and that people after him who needed a Caliph would have to look into his case. After the first three caliphs there were none like the fourth in merit, knowledge, *taqwa* and the *deen*, so allegiance was given to him. If it had not been for the speed of taking the oath of allegiance to 'Ali, the riff-raff would have started a disruption that would not have stopped. However, the Muhajirun and the Ansar decided on him and he thought that it was his duty. That is why he submitted to it.

In the *History* of at-Tabari,[259] Sayf ibn 'Umar at-Tamimi related from his shaykhs who said, "Madina remained for five days after 'Uthman's murder with al-Ghafiqi ibn Harb as its amir. They searched for someone who would respond to them and undertake to rule, but could not find anyone. The Egyptians went to 'Ali and he hid from them and sought refuge in the gardens of Madina. When they met him, he parted from them and repeatedly declared himself free of them and their position. The Kufans looked for az-Zubayr but could not find him. They sent to him when he was resting and he parted from them and declared himself free of them and their position. The Basrans sought out Talha. When he met them, he parted from them and declared himself free of their position. They sent to Sa'd ibn Abi Waqqas and said, "You were one of the people of the *Sunna*. We agree on you. Come forward and we will offer you allegiance." He sent to them, "I and Ibn 'Umar have left it. I have no need of it." They went to 'Abdullah ibn 'Umar and said, "You are the son of 'Umar. Take command." He said, "This command will entail revenge. By Allah, I will not offer myself for it. Seek someone else."

At-Tabari[260] transmitted that ash-Sha'bi said, "The people came to 'Ali while he was in the market of Madina. They said to him, 'Stretch out your hand. We will give you allegiance.' He said, 'Do not be hasty. 'Umar was a blessed man and he advised a council for it. Wait until the people gather and consult one another.' The people left 'Ali. Then one of them said, 'If people return to their cities with the murder of 'Uthman and no one has undertaken to rule after him, we will not be safe from the disagreement of people and the corruption of the community.' They returned to 'Ali. Al-Ashtar took his hand and 'Ali grasped it. He said, 'Is it after three? By Allah, if I were to leave it, you would have cast you eyes longingly on it for a time.' So the common people offered him their allegiance. The people of Kufa said, 'The first to offer him allegiance was al-Ashtar.'"

Sayf related from Abu Haritha Mihraz al-Abshami and from Abu 'Uthman Yazid ibn Asyad al-Ghassani, "On Thursday, five days after 'Uthman's murder, the people of Madina met. They found that Sa'd and az-Zubayr had left and they found Talha in one of his gardens. When the people of Madina gathered for them, the people of Egypt said to them, "You are the people of the *Shura*. You take the leadership and your command will be effective throughout the community. Look for a man and set him up. We will follow you." They all said, "We are pleased with 'Ali ibn Abi Talib." 'Ali said, "Leave me and seek someone else." They said, "We ask you by Allah, don't you see the turmoil? Don't you fear Allah?" He said, "If I answer you, I will pursue you by what I know. If you leave me, I will be like one of you, although I will listen and obey you in the one you appoint to rule over you." Then they parted on that note and arranged a meeting for the following day (i.e. Friday). On Friday morning, the people were in the mosque. 'Ali came and sat on the minbar. He said, "People, by an assembly and by permission if this is your command. No one has the right to it until you command it. We parted with something yesterday. If you wish, I will sit for you. If not, I will not be angry with anyone." They said, "We will have that on which we parted yesterday."

These events and their details indicate that the allegiance to 'Ali was like the allegiance given to his brothers before him. It came about as it happened in its time and proceeded from the pleasure of the Community at that moment, not from some alleged bequest or imaginary illusory signs.

Talha gave him the oath of allegiance. People said, "A paralysed hand has given allegiance to 'Ali. By Allah, this business is not over yet."

The Defamation of 'Uthman

The one who spoke these words was Habib ibn Dhu'ayb. At-Tabari related it[261] from Abu al-Mulayh al-Hudhali.

If it is said that they gave their allegiance…

i.e. Talha and az-Zubayr.

…under compulsion, we say, "Far be it that they should be forced, either them or the one to whom they offered allegiance. Even if they were compelled, that would have no effect because the oath of allegiance is effected by one or two, and it is binding for whoever gives allegiance after that. He is forced to do that by the Shari'a. If they had not given their allegiance, that would not have had any effect on them or on the allegiance offered to the ruler.

Qadi ibn al-'Arabi confirmed this judgment of the Shari'a in the oath of allegiance. That did not come from his opinion. Imam Abu Bakr al-Baqillani had some fitting words about it in his *Tamhid*.[262]

As for the one who said, "a paralysed hand: this business is not yet over," the opinion of the speaker was that Talha was the first to offer his allegiance, but that was not the case.

You know that the people of Kufa say that al-Ashtar was the first to offer allegiance. If Talha's hand had been the first to offer allegiance, it would have had greater blessing because that was a hand which had defended the Messenger of Allah ﷺ. Al-Ashtar's hand was one that was still wet with the blood of the martyr who had been given the good news of the Garden.

If it is said that Talha said, "I gave allegiance while the sword was on my neck,"…

i.e. "the sword was on my neck because of the state of fear which prevailed in Madina after the murder of 'Uthman."

...we say, "This *hadith* was fabricated by the one who uses *qafa* in the dialect as *qafi* as he made *hawa* into *hawi*. That is the dialect of Hudhayl, not the dialect of Quraysh.

> It is further from the dialect of Quraysh than the dialect of Hudhayl. Ibn al-Athir said in the *End* (the subject of dialects) that it is the Tayy' dialect. They double the *ya'* of the first person.

It is a lie that is not even to be considered.

As for their words, "a paralysed hand", if that is sound, one does not pay any attention to it. A hand paralysed by protecting the Messenger of Allah ﷺ has every matter completed for it. He is protected by it from every disliked thing.

> Talha was one of the group who pledged themselves to the Messenger of Allah ﷺ to the death on the Day of Uhud when the Muslims were routed. They were steadfast and stayed with him. Malik ibn Zuhayr al-Jushumi shot an arrow meant for the Messenger of Allah ﷺ, and he did not err in his shooting. Talha kept it from the Messenger of Allah ﷺ with his hand. That is why he was paralysed in his hand from his little finger. A man of the Banu 'Amr was dragging his spear while mounted on a bay horse with a blaze. He was armed to the teeth and shouted, "I am the one who has said farewell! Show me Muhammad!" Talha struck the hamstring of his horse and it put its tail between its legs. Then he took his spear and he did not err with it. The man made a noise like an ox. Talha kept his foot on his chest until he was dead. His two daughters, 'A'isha and Umm Ishaq said, "Our father was wounded twenty-four times over his entire body at Uhud. He fainted. In spite of that, he still carried the Messenger of Allah ﷺ when his teeth were broken and al-Qahqahri brought him back. Whenever any of the idol-worshippers met him, he fought to defend him until he got him back to the people." Abu Nu'aym al-Isbahani mentioned that.

Whenever Abu Bakr mentioned the Battle of Uhud, he would say, "That was the day of Talha." 'Ali ibn Abi Talib heard a man saying after the Battle of the Camel, "Where is Talha?" 'Ali scolded him. He said, "You were not present on the Day of Uhud. I saw him defending the Messenger of Allah ﷺ with his own body while the swords were covering him. He used himself as a shield for the Messenger of Allah ﷺ." Ibn 'Asakir related[263] by way of Mundah from Talha that he said, "The Messenger of Allah ﷺ called me Talha al-Khayr (the good) on the Day of Uhud. He called me Talha al-Fayyad (the Bountiful) in the Battle of Hardship. It was Talha al-Jud (the Generous) in the Battle of Hunayn."

The matter was completed as it should be and the decree was carried out after that according to it. The innovator is ignorant of that and fabricated evidence against it.

If it is said that they offered him allegiance provided that he kill the murderers of 'Uthman, we say that this is not a valid precondition of the allegiance. They should offer him allegiance provided that he rules by the truth. The person who seeks blood is summoned and the one from whom it is demanded is also summoned. The claim is then presented and an answer is given. If there is a clear proof, then judgment takes place. As for taking allegiance provided that he attacks a person by a general statement or by uninformed action or by hearing some words, that is not part of the *deen* of Islam.

> Look at the *Tamhid* by al-Baqillani.[264] The reality of the position of 'Ali with the murderers of 'Uthman was that when they gave him allegiance, they held the reins of power in Madina. The state of terror which was prevalent then did not allow 'Ali or anyone else the power to take a position with them in any way like the position the Companions had when 'Ubaydullah ibn 'Umar killed al-Hurmuzan, in spite of the great difference between the blood of the Amir al-Mu'minin, the Rightly-Guided Caliph, and the Zoroastrian prisoner of war who said that he had become Muslim

after he was captured. When 'Ali moved from Madina to Iraq in order to be near Syria, 'Uthman's murderers moved with him, especially the people of Kufa and Basra among them. When they went to Basra and Kufa, they were in the fortress of their might and the pride of their tribes. There is no doubt that 'Ali proclaimed himself free of them and that he wanted to reach an understanding with the people of the Camel with whatever agreement was permissible in the matter. 'Uthman's murderers started the battle between the army of 'Ali and the army of the people of the Camel. The people of the Camel were able to kill the Egyptians among the murderers of 'Uthman with the exception of one of the Banu Sa'id ibn Zayd Manah ibn Tamim. His tribe protected him.

When things got worse and blood was shed, 'Ali was put in a position where he needed the force of those men, although they were known to be 'Uthman's murderers. They were led by al-Ashtar and men like him. Most of them turned against 'Ali later and attacked him, claiming that he was an unbeliever. Scholars of the *Sunna* and the historians say that Allah lay in ambush for 'Uthman's murderers. He took revenge from them by killing them and punishing them one by one, even those who lived a long time until the days of al-Hajjaj. They ended by having their blood shed as a repayment for what their hands had done. Allah is the justest of judges.

The 'Uthmanis said, "A group of the Companions held back from him. They included Sa'd ibn Abi Waqqas, Muhammad ibn Maslama, Ibn 'Umar, Usama ibn Zayd and others like him."

He said, "As for offering him allegiance, they did not hold back from it. As for helping him, some people refrained from doing that. They included those you have mentioned because it was a question of *ijtihad*. Each one exercised *ijtihad* and acted by his opinion and reached his stand."

Look at the *Tamhid* by al-Baqillani.[265]

Disaster

The Battle of the Camel

SOME PEOPLE related that when the pledge of allegiance to 'Ali was completed, Talha and az-Zubayr asked 'Ali for permission to go to Makka.

> 'Abdullah ibn 'Umar ibn al-Khattab was one of those who asked him for permission to go to Makka. The reason for that was that when the oath of allegiance to 'Ali was finished, 'Ali decided to fight the people of Syria. He delegated the people of Madina to go with him. They refused to do that. He sought out 'Abdullah ibn 'Umar and urged him to go with him. He said, "I am a man of the people of Madina. If they go, I will go with them in full obedience. But I will not go out to fight this year." Then Ibn 'Umar made provisions and left for Makka.[266] Al-Hasan ibn 'Ali opposed his father about going out to fight the people of Syria. 'Ali left him in Madina as you will see later.

'Ali said, "Perhaps you mean to go to Basra and Syria?" They swore that they would not do that.

> 'Ali's words to them and their oath to him are part of what the perpetrators of the disaster and their transmitters added.

'A'isha was at Makka.

> She and the Mothers of the Believers went to Makka when the attackers

prevented water from reaching 'Uthman. He began to ask people for water. Umm Habiba brought him water and they treated her with contempt. They struck her mule's face and cut the mule's rope with the sword.[267] The Mothers of the Believers prepared to go on *hajj* to flee from the siege.[268]

'Abdullah ibn 'Amr, 'Uthman's governor over Basra, and Yahya ibn Umayya, his governor over the Yemen, fled to Makka.

All of them went to Makka. They included Marwan ibn al-Hakam. The Banu Umayya met and they wanted revenge for the murder of 'Uthman. Ya'la gave Talha, az-Zubayr and 'A'isha four hundred dirhams. He gave 'A'isha "Askar", a camel which he had purchased for two hundred dinars in the Yemen. They wanted to go to Syria. Ibn 'Amir stopped them and said, "You have no agreement to meet with Mu'awiya. I have hirelings in Basra. Go to them instead."

They came to Ma' al-Hawa'ib and the dogs barked.

> Al-Hawa'ib is one of the springs on the road to Basra. Abu al-Fath Nasr ibn 'Abd ar-Rahman al-Iskandari said that. Yaqut quoted him in the *Collection of the Lands*. Abu 'Ubayd al-Bakri said in his collection that it is some water near Basra on the Makkan road. It was named al-Hawa'ib bint Kalb ibn Wabara al-Quda'iyya.

'A'isha asked and was told, "This is the water of al-Hawa'ib." She took her halter from him. That was because she had heard the Prophet ﷺ say, "Which of you will be the one with the thick-haired camel when the dogs bark at her at al-Hawa'ib?"

> *Adib: adabb*. There is assimilation for the sake of the rhyme. *Al-Adabb* means much hair on the face. Ibn al-Athir said that in *an-Nihaya*.

Talha and az-Zubayr testified that it was not Ma' al-Hawa'ib and fifty men added their testimony.

The Battle of the Camel

They did not testify and 'A'isha did not say that nor did the Prophet ﷺ say that. We will make that clear in its place in the defence.

It was the first false testimony that had occurred in Islam.

The false testimony came from the rabble who did not fear Allah, men like Abu Zaynab and Abu al-Mawra' as was already stated. It came from those who claimed to have the power to create a personality which Allah did not create – like whoever fabricated the name of Thabit, the client of Umm Salama, as was already stated. As for Talha and az-Zubayr, they had been promised the Garden by the Prophet of Mercy who did not speak from passion. They had the highest character and were too noble to themselves and Allah to give false testimony. This lie against them came from men who hated the Companions of the Messenger of Allah ﷺ. It is not the first lie that they made in Islam nor was it the last of the lies that they forged against him and his people.

'Ali went to Kufa.

He left Madina at the end of the month of Rabi' al-Akhir in 36 AH in order to be near Syria. His son, al-Hasan, wanted his father to stay in Madina and take it as the abode of the caliphate as his three brothers had done before him.[269] 'Ali travelled from Madina to Iraq by way of ar-Rabadha, Fid, ath-Tha'labiya, al-Asawid and Dhu Qar. At ar-Rabadha, he sent Muhammad ibn Abi Bakr and Muhammad ibn Ja'far to Kufa. They came back to him while he was at Dhu Qar, saying that Abu Musa and the people of discernment among the Kufans wanted to refrain and not to go out. He sent al-Ashtar and Ibn 'Abbas. Then he sent his son, al-Hasan, and 'Ammar to win the people over to him. While he was on his way, 'Uthman ibn Hanif and Hukaym ibn Jabala started to fight with the people of the Camel. In al-Asawid, he received the news of the death of Hukaym ibn Jabala and 'Uthman's murderers. Then 'Uthman ibn Hunayf came to

'Ali while he was in ath-Tha'labiyya. He had had his beard plucked out and was helpless. 'Ali set up his army in Dhu Qar. Then he went with his men to Basra where the people of the Camel were located.

The two groups formed armies and met.

After 'Ali reached Dhu Qar, al-Qa'qa' ibn 'Amr undertook to attempt to reach an agreement. 'Ali came to Basra with his men. The murderers of 'Uthman were quick to scotch the attempts at peace by starting the battle.

When 'Ammar was near the howdah of 'A'isha, he asked, "What are you seeking?" They answered, "We are seeking revenge for 'Uthman's blood." He said, "On this day, Allah will kill the attacker and the one who seeks blood without a right."

The two groups were seeking an understanding and unity. The attackers were 'Uthman's murderers. Allah killed them all except for one. That will be made clear.

'Ali and az-Zubayr met. 'Ali asked him, "Do you remember the words of the Prophet ﷺ that you would fight me?" Az-Zubayr promptly left him and went back. His son tried to make him come back, but he would not do it. Al-Ahnaf followed az-Zubayr and then murdered him.

Az-Zubayr's murderers were 'Umayr ibn Jurmuz, Faddala ibn Habis and Nufay' at-Tamimi. Al-Ahnaf had too much fear of Allah to command them to kill him. He did hear them grumbling about the Muslims fighting one another. Then they caught up to az-Zubayr and murdered him.[270]

'Ali called to Talha from a distance and said, "What do you want?" He said, "Revenge for 'Uthman's blood." 'Ali said, "May Allah fight! We are entrusted with 'Uthman's blood. Have you not heard what the Prophet ﷺ said? He said, 'Be a friend to the one who is his friend and be an enemy to the one who is his enemy and help the one who helps him

The Battle of the Camel

and disappoint the one who disappoints him. You are the first to offer me allegiance and then break it'."

> Talha was too true in belief and high in character to give allegiance and then break it. He wanted to unify things by investigating the murderers of 'Uthman. 'Ali agreed to this as will come in the following study. However, those who had committed a crime against Islam the first time when they attacked 'Uthman were the enemies of Allah the next time by starting the fight between these two groups of Muslims.

DEFENCE

As for their going to Basra, that is correct without any doubt. But why did they go? There is no sound transmission regarding that and there is no one who is to be trusted in it because reliable individuals did not transmit anything. One does not listen to the words of a partisan, including a partisan who wants to attack Islam and find fault with the Companions.

It is possible that they went out to depose 'Ali because of something that seemed correct to them.

> This interpretation is very unlikely for such right-acting people, and they didn't do anything to indicate it, but all the events indicatd their being free of it. This was the position that Hafidh Ibn Hajar took in *Fath al-Bari*[271] and he transmitted from the book *Akhbar al-Basrah* by 'Umar ibn Shabbah the words of al-Muhallab, "Because no one had transmitted from 'A'ishah and those with her that they were contesting the khilafa with 'Ali nor did they call for anyone of them to appoint him to the khilafa."

That was because they had offered allegiance to him in order to still the rebellion, but they still sought what was right.

It is possible that they went out to get power over 'Uthman's murderers.

This is what they used to say. However, they meant that they would reach an agreement with 'Ali in any manner they could. This is what the striving Companion al-Qa'qa' ibn 'Amr attempted to do. Both parties accepted him as will be mentioned.

It is possible that they went to join the groups of the Muslims and to bring them together and refer them to the same law so that they would not be unsettled and fight. This is what is sound and nothing else. The sound reports show that.

As for the first possibilities, they are all false and weak.

As for their giving allegiance under coercion, that is false, as we already made clear.

As for their seeking to depose him, that is false because deposing a person is only by a universal opinion, although it is possible that one or two appoint. Deposing someone only occurs after evidence and clarification.

> Look at the *Tamhid* of al-Baqillani,[272] on the subject of deposing.

As for their going out for the murderers of 'Uthman, that is weak because the root before it was unity, and it was possible to reconcile both matters.

> The reconciliation of the two matters very nearly took place if it had not been that the Saba'ites foiled it. The people of the Camel came about 'Uthman's murderers. That was all that they sought. However, they wanted to reach an understanding about it with 'Ali because reaching an understanding with him was the first way to obtain that goal.

It is related that part of the riff-raff of the people had caused them to be absent.

> i.e. Talha and az-Zubayr and 'A'isha were absent from Madina.

The Battle of the Camel

Talha, az-Zubayr and 'A'isha, the Umm al-Mu'minin ﷺ, left hoping to return people to their source and to preserve the respect of their Prophet ﷺ. They used as argument against her...

When they induced her to go to Basra.

...the words of Allah who says: *"There is no good in much of their conspiring secretly except for the one who commands sadaqa or something correct or to put things rights between people."* (4:114) The Prophet ﷺ went out to make peace and he sent messengers for it. She hoped for the reward and sought to benefit from the opportunity. She went out so that things would reach their proper conclusions.

The people of Basra became aware of them, and those who had conspired against 'Uthman egged the people on and said, "Go out to them so that you can see what they have come to do." 'Uthman ibn Hunayf sent Hukaym ibn Jabala.

> 'Uthman ibn Hunayf was an Ansari from Aws. When the Prophet ﷺ emigrated to Madina, he was one of fifteen Awsi youths who joined Abu 'Amr ibn Sayfi when he went to Makka, since he was angry with the Prophet ﷺ. In the *Jahiliyya*, Abu 'Amr was called the Monk. The Prophet ﷺ called him al-Fasiq (the deviant).[273] It is clear that 'Uthman ibn Hunayf returned from Makka and became Muslim before Uhud, because it was the first of his battles.[274] The Shi'a claim that he rebelled against the Caliph of the Messenger of Allah ﷺ, Abu Bakr as-Siddiq, at the beginning of his caliphate.[275] He believed that he was one of those they lied about. He was in charge of the sector of the land of Iraq and collecting its *jizya* and *kharaj* taxes for 'Umar. If what they claim about his agitating against Abu Bakr is true, this would conflict with 'Umar's appointment of him unless he had repented of that.
>
> When allegiance was given to 'Ali at the end of 35 AH and he chose his governors at the beginning of 36 AH, he appointed 'Uthman ibn Hunayf

over Basra.[276] When the people of the Camel reached al-Hafir, about four miles from Basra, 'Uthman ibn Hunayf sent 'Imran ibn Husayn al-Khuza'i, the bearer of the banner of the Prophet ﷺ for Khuza'a on the Day of the Conquest of Makka, to them to investigate them for him. When he came back to him and mentioned his conversation with the people of the Camel. 'Uthman ibn Hunayf told him, "Advise me, 'Imran." He told him, "I am not going out, so you should not either." 'Uthman said, "I will stop them until the Amir al-Mu'minin 'Ali comes." Hisham ibn 'Amr al-Ansari, one of the people of *jihad* in the Conquest, indicated that he should make peace with them until 'Ali's command came. 'Uthman ibn Hunayf refused and summoned the people, "Take up your weapons!" 'Uthman occupied himself with deceit.[277] His end was unsuccessful and he lost power to the people of the Camel. Ibn Hunayf was captured by the mob and his beard was plucked out. Then the people of the Camel rescued him from them. He retreated to the army of 'Ali which was in ath-Tha'labiyya and then in Dhu Qar. This was 'Uthman ibn Hunayf and his position with the people of the Camel. As for Hukaym ibn Jabala, the reader already knows that he was one of those who murdered the Amir al-Mu'minin, 'Uthman. This was already stated earlier.

He met Talha and az-Zubayr at az-Zabuqa, and Hukaym was killed.

Az-Zabuqa is a place near Basra. The first stage of the Battle of the Camel took place there after Talha, az-Zubayr and 'A'isha had spoken in the *mirbad*. As for the death of Hukaym ibn Jabala, that was after the first battle that ended in the victory of the People of the Camel and they had power in Basra. Hukaym ibn Jabala was insolent in this new situation and he fought with 300 of his helpers until he was killed.

If he had gone out as a submitting Muslim and not as a resister, ...

i.e. fighting.

The Battle of the Camel

...nothing would have happened to him. What good did he have in defence? What was he defending? They did not come as fighters or rulers. They were working for peace and desired to bring things together. Whoever went out to them and opposed them and fought them, did so defending their own purposes and ends, as they were wont to do in any other situation or to any other end.

When they reached Basra, the people met them in a group at the upper part of the *mirbad*.

> The *mirbad* of Basra is the place where the camel-market was held, outside of the city. Then it was the place where the poets boasted and the assemblies of the orators were held. Then the buildings of Basra were expanded and the *mirbad* became part of its inhabited areas. It was one of its most glorious streets and its market was one of the greatest markets. It became an immense quarter, full of people. When the position of Basra declined and its buildings grew old, it dwindled. The *mirbad* became separate from it until there were three miles between it and Basra in the time of Yaqut. It is now a ruin. It is like a city isolated in the middle of the desert. The location of Basra at that time is near to the present suburb, az-Zubayr.

There were so many of them that if a stone had been thrown, it would have fallen on a man's head. Talha spoke, az-Zubayr spoke, and 'A'isha spoke, may Allah be pleased with all of them.

> The people of the Camel were on the right of the *mirbad* and 'Uthman ibn Hunayf and those with him were on the left of it. At-Tabari[278] gave a summary of the speeches of Talha, az-Zubayr and 'A'isha. He quoted that from Sayf ibn 'Umar at-Tamimi from his shaykhs. They are the historians who have the best knowledge of the events in Iraq.

There was a great uproar.

Because those who were on the left spoke while Talha and az-Zubayr were speaking. They said, "They have split! They are treacherous! They are speaking this and command what is false! They gave allegiance and now they come saying this!" Those who were on the right were saying, "They are truthful! They are dutiful! They speak the truth and command the truth!" People broke up and threw pebbles at each other and spoke sharply. However, when 'A'isha finished her speech, those with the Camel were firm in their constancy, but the people of 'Uthman ibn Hunayf split into two groups. One group said, "She spoke the truth, by Allah. She is pious and has brought what is correct." The others said, "You lie! We do not recognise what you say!" They broke up and threw pebbles at each other.

Talha said, "Be quiet." They began to pester him and would not be silent. He said, "Shame, shame. A bed of fire and flies of ambition." They turned back without having clarified things.

When 'A'isha saw what the helpers of 'Uthman ibn Hunayf did, she went down with the people of the right side. They left Ibn Hunayf and stood elsewhere. Some of those who had been with Ibn Hunayf went with 'A'isha. Others remained with 'Uthman ibn Hunayf.[279]

They went down to Banu Nahd, and people threw stones at them until they had descended the mountain.

At-Tabari[280] has a fine description which Sayf ibn 'Umar at-Tamimi transmitted from his two shaykhs, Muhammad ibn Suwad ibn Nuwayra and Talha ibn al-A'lam al-Hanafi about the sound position of the people of the Camel in this Battle and the excess of Hukaym ibn Jabala when he started the fight. They both said, "'A'isha commanded her companions and they went to the cemetery of the Banu Mazin. Then night separated the two groups. The following day, the people of the Camel moved to the side of Dar ar-Rizq. In the morning, 'Uthman ibn Hunayf and Hukaym

The Battle of the Camel

ibn Jabala renewed the fight. Hukaym continued to curse the Umm al-Mu'minin 'A'isha and he killed the men and women who censured him for that. 'A'isha's herald told people not to fight. They refused until when evil touched and then seized them. Then the Companions of 'A'isha called for peace.

Talha, az-Zubayr and 'Uthman ibn Hunayf, the governor of 'Ali over Basra, met. They agreed in writing between them not to fight, that 'Uthman would remain in possession of the governor's house, the mosque and the treasury, and that Talha and az-Zubayr could stay wherever they wished in Basra and the two parties would not turn against each other until 'Ali had come.

> The text of this peace treaty is in the *History* of at-Tabari.[281] When 'Ali heard what had happened, he wrote to 'Uthman ibn Hunayf, describing him as a failure. Talha and az-Zubayr gathered the people and went to the mosque. They waited for 'Uthman ibn Hunayf. He was late and did not attend. Turmoil grew in the mosque among the rabble of Basra, the followers of Hukaym ibn Jabala. That made some people react and they went to 'Uthman ibn Hunayf to summon him to attend. The people trampled on him and plucked out his beard. Mujashi' ibn Mas'ud as-Sulami, the leader of Hawazin, the Banu Sulayman and some members of the tribes of Basra, told them to do that.[282]

It is related that Hukaym ibn Jabala opposed them and he was killed after the truce.

> The clarification of that is in the *History* of at-Tabari.[283] Look at this book for confirmation.[284]

'Ali came to Basra...

> He camped in a place there called az-Zawiya. The people of the Camel

camped in a place called al-Furda.

...and they drew near enough to see each other.

In the place where the castle of 'Ubaydullah ibn Ziyad is located. That was Thursday in the middle of Jumada al-Akhira, 36 AH.[285] The lofty Companion, al-Qa'qa' ibn 'Amr at-Tamimi stood between the two groups attempting intelligent mediation. The People of the Camel answered him and 'Ali agreed to that. 'Ali sent to Talha and az-Zubayr saying, "If you still hold to what you told al-Qa'qa' ibn 'Amr, then hold back until we come and investigate this matter." They went to him, "We hold to what we told al-Qa'qa' ibn 'Amr regarding peace between the people."

Ibn Kathir said in *al-Bidaya wa an-Nihaya*,[286] "People were reassured and tranquil. Each group gathered with its own people. In the evening, 'Ali sent 'Abdullah ibn 'Abbas to them. They sent Muhammad ibn Talha as-Sajjad to 'Ali. They all decided on peace and spent the best night they had ever spent in well-being while those who had agitated in the business of 'Uthman spent the worst night they had ever spent. They were staring destruction in the face. They began to consult each other for the entire night until they agreed to start the war secretly. They concealed that, fearing that the evil they were attempting would be known. They went out in the dead of night so that their neighbours would not be aware of them. They slipped into that business. (As well as the *History* of Ibn Kathir, look at the *History* of at-Tabari[287] and the *Minhaj as-Sunna*[288]) That is how they started the war between 'Ali and his brothers, az-Zubayr and Talha. The People of the Camel thought that 'Ali had deceived them. 'Ali thought that his brothers had deceived him. Each of them had too much fear of Allah to do that even in the *Jahiliyya*. How then could they do such a thing after they had reached the highest rank of the qualities of the Qur'an?

The people of sects did not leave them alone. They hastened to shed blood and the battle started. There was clamour in the mob. All of that was done so that there would not be a clear proof and the true state would not be made clear and the murderers of 'Uthman would remain hidden. If one man in the army can pervert its direction, then how much more is that the case when there were a thousand perverting it?

It is related that when Marwan saw Talha in the ranks, he said, "We do not seek for tracks after finding the source!" and he shot his arrow and killed him.

> The bane of reports is their transmitters. In Islamic knowledge, there is a cure for the bane of false lies. Every person who relates a report is demanded by Islam to specify his source according to the rule, "From where did you get this?" No community knows such precision in seeking out the sources of reports as the Muslims do, especially the people of the *Sunna* among them. This report from Talha and Marwan is "a foundling" whose father is unknown as is the person responsible for it. Since no-one reliable transmitted it with a known *isnad* from reliable men, Qadi Ibn al-'Arabi can say with deep conviction, "Who knows this except the One who knows the unseen worlds?"

Who knows this except the One who knows the unseen worlds, since no reliable source transmitted it? It was related that an arrow at the command of Marwan struck him, not that Marwan himself shot the arrow.

> This claim is like the earlier claim regarding az-Zubayr that al-Ahnaf was the one who commanded his murder.

Ka'b ibn Suwar brought out a Qur'an which was in his hand, begging the people of Allah not to shed blood.

> Ka'b ibn Suwa al-Azdi was the first of the Qadis of the Muslims in Basra. 'Umar appointed him. Ibn 'Abd al-Barr said, "He was a Muslim in the time of the Prophet ﷺ although he did not actually see him."

An arrow struck and killed him.

Ibn 'Asakir[289] said in Talha's biography, "'A'isha said to Ka'b ibn Suwar al-Azdi, 'Leave the camel, Ka'b and bring the Book of Allah and call them to it.' She gave him a Qur'an and he went forward to the people. The Saba'ites were in front of him. They were afraid that there would be peace. Ka'b confronted them with the Qur'an while 'Ali was behind them, urging them to accept. They refused to do anything but advance. When Ka'b called them, they shot him once and killed him. Then they shot at the Umm al-Mu'minin. The first thing she did when they refused was to say, 'O people! Curse 'Uthman's murderers and their parties!' She began to supplicate and the people of Basra shouted out the curse. 'Ali heard the invocation and asked, 'What is this shouting?' They said, "A'isha is calling and the people of Basra are praying with her against 'Uthman's murderers and their parties.' 'Ali began to call, 'O Allah, curse 'Uthman's murderers and their parties!'"

The men of right action of both parties shared in cursing the murderers of the Amir al-Mu'minin, the wronged martyr, in the very hour in which these murderers started the battle between the Muslim men of right action.

Perhaps it was the same with Talha. It is known that in the strife and the slaughter of the battle, those who had feuds and rancour were able to undo bonds and break agreements. The terms were at hand and the promises were carried out.

Ibn 'Asakir[290] quoted the words of ash-Sha'bi, "'Ali ibn Abi Talib saw Talha fallen in one of the valleys. He dismounted and wiped the dust from his face. Then he said, 'Abu Muhammad, it pains me to see you in the dust in a valley under the stars of the sky. I complain to Allah of all my hidden faults.' (al-Asma'i said, "i.e. my secrets and my sorrows which are inside of me.") He said, 'Would that I had died twenty years before this day!'"

Abu Hubayba, Talha's client, said, "I and 'Imran ibn Talha came to 'Ali

The Battle of the Camel

after the Camel. 'Ali greeted 'Imran and brought him near. He said, 'I hope that Allah will put me and your father among those about whom it is said, *"We stripped away all rancour in their hearts as brothers, they are on couches face to face."'* Al-Harith al-A'war[1] was sitting in a corner and said, 'Allah is too just to let us kill them when they will be our brothers in the Garden.' 'Ali said to him, 'Go to the furthest and remotest land of Allah! Who will be there if Talha and I are not in the Garden?'"

Muhammad ibn 'Abdullah mentioned that 'Ali took an inkwell and threw it at al-A'war, but it missed him. Ibn al-Kiwa'[2] said to him, "Allah is too just for that." 'Ali went for him with a stick and beat him. He said to him, "You! You have no mother! Your companions deny this!?"

If it is said, why did 'A'isha go out when the Prophet ﷺ had told them in the *Hajj* of Farewell, "After this, then constriction (*husr*) will appear,"…

In the *Musnad* of Ahmad ibn Hanbal[291] from the *hadith* of Salih, the client of Tawa'ma from Abu Hurayra there is that when the Messenger of Allah went on *hajj* with his wives, he said, "It is this *hajj*. The time of the appearance of constriction comes after." In it,[292] there is the *hadith* of Waqid ibn Abi Waqid al-Laythi from his father that the Prophet ﷺ said to his wives on this *hajj*, "After this, constriction will appear." The *hadith* of Abu Waqid is in the Chapter of the obligation of the *Hajj* in the Book of Practices in the *Sunan* of Abu Dawud.[293] *Husur* is the plural of *hasir*, i.e. staying in the house. Ibn Kathir transmitted in *al-Bidaya wa an-Nihaya*[294] saying that it is an indication by the Prophet ﷺ that he himself announced

---

1 Abu Zuhayr, al-Harith ibn 'Abdullah al-Hamdani al-Kufi al-A'war, one of the great men of the Shi'a. Ash-Sha'bi and Ibn al-Madini said that he was a liar.

2 Ibn al-Kiwa': 'Abdullah ibn Abi Awfa al-Yashkuri, one of those who brought about the sedition against 'Uthman. After Siffin and the Arbitration, he was at the head of the Kharijites against 'Ali. When 'Ali and Ibn 'Abbas argued with them, he returned to 'Ali before the Battle of Nahrawan.

his death to them and that this would be his last *hajj*. In it, he did not command that they should not leave for *hajj* or a need or to make peace between people. The enemies of the Companions quoted this *hadith* as an absolute prohibition. Qadi Ibn al-'Arabi considered that to be a lie because it was quoted in order to be used in a manner other than that which was desired by the Prophet ﷺ.

...we say that he related two *hadith*s to a woman. If she rejects it, then it is four. O intellects of women! Did I not make an agreement with you not to relate false *hadith*s? We already gave you the proof about the soundness of 'A'isha's going out.

> In the research on "The Aspects of Excellence and Preference" from the Book of *The Imamate and Preference*, included in Part 4 of the *Fasl*,[295] Imam Ibn Hazm quoted his shaykh Ahmad ibn Muhammad al-Khawzi from Ahmad ibn al-Fadl ibn Dinawari from Muhammad ibn Jarir at-Tabari that 'Ali ibn Abi Talib sent 'Ammar ibn Yasir and al-Hasan ibn 'Ali to Kufa when the Umm al-Mu'minin went to Basra. When they came there, people gathered to both of them in the mosque. 'Ammar spoke to them and told them that 'A'isha had gone out to Basra. Then he said to them, "I tell you, by Allah, I know that she is the wife of the Messenger of Allah ﷺ in the Garden as she was his wife in this world. But Allah has tested you by her so that you either obey her or obey Him." Masruq (or Abu al-Aswad) said to him, "Abu al-Yaqathan, we are with those who are promised the Garden rather than those who were not promised it." 'Ammar was silent.

Why do you say what you do not know? You repeat something you should disassociate yourselves from as well as that of which you have no understanding. *"The worst of beasts with Allah are the deaf and dumb who do not understand."*

As for what you mentioned about the testimony regarding Ma' al-

The Battle of the Camel

Hawa'ib, you have committed the greatest sin in mentioning it. There is absolutely nothing in what you mentioned. The Prophet ﷺ did not utter that *hadith*. These words were not spoken nor did anyone testify to them. Your testimony with this falsehood has been recorded and you will be questioned.

The location of al-Hawa'ib was made clear earlier. The words which they ascribe to the Prophet ﷺ and which they claim that 'A'isha said when she reached that water do not have a place in the volumes of the *Sunna*. We saw that report in at-Tabari.[296] We saw that he related from Isma'il ibn Musa al-Fazari (who is a man about whom Ibn 'Adi said, "They objected to an excessive leaning in him towards the Shi'a."). This man related it from 'Ali ibn 'Abbas al-Azraq whom an-Nasa'i said was weak. He related it from Abu al-Khattab al-Hijri (Ibn Hajar said in the *Taqrib at-Tadhhib* that he is unknown.) This unknown al-Hijri related it from Safwan ibn Qabisa al-Ahmasi (adh-Dhahabi said in the *Balance of Harmony* that he is unknown). This then is the report about al-Hawa'ib.

It is based on a bedouin whom they claimed to have met on the desert road. He had a camel which they liked and they wanted it to be 'A'isha's camel, so they bought it from him. The man went along with them until they reached al-Hawa'ib. He heard these words and related them, although he (i.e. the bedouin who owned the camel) does not have a known name nor do we know whether he is one of the liars or one of the truthful because he is a fictional man who did not exist since we know that the name of 'A'isha's camel was 'Askar. Ya'la ibn Umayya had brought it from the Yemen and 'A'isha rode it from Makka to Iraq. She was not walking on her feet so that they should buy this camel for her from this bedouin whom they claim to have met in the desert. They ascribed this silly story to him so that they could say that Talha and az-Zubayr, who were promised the Garden by the one who did not speak out of whim, had given false testimony.

If we thought that it was permitted to transmit weak reports, opposite this report we would transmit a report which Yaqut quoted in the *Collection of the Lands* (Subject: al-Hawa'ib) from Sayf ibn 'Umar at-Tamimi. He said that the one at whom the dogs of al-Hawa'ib barked was Umm Zaml Salma bint Malik al-Fazariyya who led the apostates between Zafr and al-Hawa'ib. The Muslims captured her and she was given to 'A'isha who set her free. This statement was made about her. This report is weak and the report which they related about 'A'isha is weaker still. This lie continues to be goods bartered by those who do not fear Allah. We already stated that.

Disaster

The Battle of Siffin

WAR TOOK place between the people of Syria and the people of Iraq.

At a place called Siffin, near ar-Raqqa on the edge of the Euphrates at the end of Iraqi territory and the beginning of Syrian territory. 'Ali went there with his armies at the end of Dhu al-Qa'da, 36 AH.

One side called for allegiance to 'Ali and unity around the Imam, and the others called for power over 'Uthman's murderers. They said, "We will not offer allegiance to the one who gives refuge to murderers."

When 'Ali finished the Battle of the Camel and left Basra for Kufa, he entered Kufa on Monday, 12 Rajab. He sent Jarir ibn 'Abdullah al-Bajili to Mu'awiya in Damascus to call him to obey. Mu'awiya gathered the leading Companions, the generals of the armies and the aides of the people of Syria and consulted them about what 'Ali had demanded. They said, "We will not give him allegiance until he executes 'Uthman's murderers or surrenders them to us." Jarir took that response back to 'Ali. 'Ali appointed Abu Mas'ud 'Uqba ibn 'Amr over Kufa and left. The army was at an-Nukhayla, where the road to Syria from Iraq begins. Some people indicated that he should stay in Kufa and send someone else to Syria, but he refused.

Mu'awiya heard that 'Ali had prepared and come out himself to fight him. His men advised him to go in person. The Syrians made for the Euphrates in the direction of Siffin. 'Ali advanced with his army there. 'Ali's army had 220,000 men and Mu'awiya's army was 70,000. The Battle started in Dhu al-Hijja 36 AH with skirmishes and sorties. Then they made a truce in Muharram 37 AH and fighting resumed later. 70,000 men were killed in this war. There were 90 battles in 110 days. This war was distinguished by noble courage in the fighting and noble dealings and contact during the truce and rest periods. Then the document of arbitration was written on 13 Safar 37 AH. It provided that two arbiters would announce the result in Ramadan at Duma al-Jandal at a place called Adhruh.

'Ali said, "I will not give power to someone who seeks a right over a person to carry out what he wants from him without any judgment or judge." Mu'awiya said, "We will not pledge allegiance to someone suspected of killing him or who killed him. He is one of those who we seek, so how can we appoint him as judge or give him allegiance when he is a caliph who has overstepped himself and given himself power?"

In the details about that, they mentioned some words that resulted in the use of letters, ...

> i.e. their ascription is a lie and it has no basis. Most of what you find in what biased historians relate comes from unknown transmitters or liars. The least of them in vehemence was Abu Mikhnaf Lut ibn Yahya. Adh-Dhahabi said, "Abu Mikhnaf was a historian and a writer. He is unreliable. Abu Hatim and others abandoned him." Ibn 'Adi said about him, "A fanatic who is one of their historians." Then others after him came who were worse for the history of Islam than this Lut. They corrupted what the community knew of their past.

...copying statements, composing poetry, and making examples that deviate from the path of the Salaf. The unworthy successors (*khalf*) confirmed them and the worthy successors (*khalaf*) rejected them.

Khalf are the mischievous. We find in the Revelation: *"An evil generation has succeeded them, inheriting the Book, taking the goods of the lower world."*²⁹⁷ *Khalaf* are the right-acting. There is the *hadith* that says, "This knowledge is carried by every successor of its just ones. They remove the twisting of the fanatics, the plagiarism of the liars and the interpretation of the ignorant."

DEFENCE

As for the war between them, that definitely happened. It is also known that this was the cause. The one who was correct in it was 'Ali because a claimant for blood revenge cannot properly give judgment and a claimant's suspicion of the Qadi does not necessitate that he attack him. Rather he should demand his right in the presence of the Qadi. If the judgment is clear, he is given that judgment. If it is not, then he should be silent and patient. Allah has given judgment in many rights. If he does not have any *deen*, then he rises in revolt against him and he has an excuse in this world.

> 'Uthman's murderers were in 'Ali's army. That is true and no one disputes that. Al-Ashtar, one of the leaders of those who attacked 'Uthman, was one of those who did the most to kindle the war between the Companions of the Messenger of Allah ﷺ who were in the army of 'Ali and the army of Mu'awiya. When 'Ali called Mu'awiya, the Companions and the Tabi'un who were with him to give him allegiance, they appealed to him regarding 'Uthman's murderers and demanded that he carry out the *hadd* of Allah on them. We already excused the Amir al-Mu'minin 'Ali earlier. When the murderers of 'Uthman went with 'Ali to Iraq, they were in the stronghold of their strength and the pride of their tribes. 'Ali thought that if he killed them, that would open a door which he would not be able to close later. The lofty Companion, al-Qa'qa' ibn 'Amr at-Tamimi pointed out this fact and he mentioned it to the Umm al-Mu'minin 'A'isha and

the two Companions of the Messenger of Allah, Talha and az-Zubayr. They conceded his point and excused 'Ali. They agreed to come to an understanding with him which would lead them out of civil strife. The murderers of 'Uthman quickly started the war between the two groups. Those who sought to carry out the *hadd* of Allah on the murderers were excused because they were seeking a right, whether they were from the People of the Camel or the people of Syria. 'Ali was unable to carry out the *hadd* of Allah due to the well-known constraints in which he found himself. However, when 'Uthman's murderers started the war between the first two groups in Basra, it would have benefitted Islam if the war of Siffin had not started between the other two groups. The grandson of the Messenger of Allah ﷺ, al-Hasan ibn 'Ali, did not want his father to leave Madina for Iraq since he feared that a war would break out with the people of Syria. If 'Ali had not moved from Kufa to prepare for this fight, Mu'awiya would not have moved a single inhabitant to fight. Ibn Taymiyya said in the *Minhaj as-Sunna*,[298] "Mu'awiya was not one of those who chose to start the war." In spite of that, this exemplary war was the first human war in history in which the combatants all acted according to principles of virtue that western philosophers wish they could act by in their wars, even in the twenty-first century. Many of the rules of war in Islam would not have been written down and known if it had not been for this war. Allah has a wisdom in everything.

If 'Ali was suspected of the murder of 'Uthman, then every Companion of the Prophet ﷺ in Madina was suspected of it. There is little information that he killed him because a thousand men who came to kill 'Uthman could not defeat 40,000 men.

> Not a single man of the people of the *Sunna* suspected 'Ali of the murder of 'Uthman, not in our time nor in his time. That was already discussed in this book. The only fact is that the murderers of 'Uthman were with 'Ali.

The Battle of Siffin

'Ali had a position in relation to them, and he had his excuse between himself and Allah for that position. We all have the opinion of al-Qa'qa' ibn 'Amr that the position of 'Ali was one of constraint. However, some stupid and biased historians attributed reports to 'Ali which imparted other than what his heart contained of love, pleasure, friendship and support for 'Uthman during his trial. They behaved badly to 'Uthman. As for Mu'awiya and his group, they did not mention 'Ali at all in the attack on 'Uthman except by virtue of the connection of 'Uthman's murderers to him and his seeking their help. 'Uthman's murderers were the ones who behaved badly towards Islam, 'Uthman and 'Ali as well. Allah will call them to account. If all the Muslims had been like 'Abd ar-Rahman ibn Khalid ibn al-Walid in his resolution before the sedition got out of control and the reins had been taken from the hands of the men of intellect, then the business would not have gone as far as it did.

This would lead you to say that 'Ali, Talha and az-Zubayr helped each other in the murder of 'Uthman. What kept the Companions, both the Muhajirun and the Ansar and those who were counted among them and joined them, from helping him?

There is the possibility that they thought that these men sought a right and acted correctly. That would be a testimony against 'Uthman and so the people of Syria would have nothing to say. If they had refrained from helping in order to mock the *deen* and they did not have any opinion about the situation or any concern for Islam or the confusion that occurred, that would be apostasy and not rebellion because weakness in respect of the *hudud* of the *deen* and letting the sacred things of the Shari'a go to waste is disbelief. If they refrained, it was because they did not think that they should go beyond 'Uthman's limit and what he had indicated. What wrong action do they have in that? What proof do Marwan, 'Abdullah ibn az-Zubayr, al-Hasan and al-Husayn, Ibn 'Umar and those who helped 'Uthman in his house have since they came in and then left with weapons and arms while those who sought to kill him were outside watching? If they had had sufficient force or could have sought refuge in a strong pillar of support, they would not have allowed any of them to see him or attack him. They were onlookers. If al-Hasan and al-Husayn, 'Abdullah ibn 'Umar and 'Abdullah ibn az-Zubayr had stood in front of 'Uthman, they would not have dared to attack. If they had killed them, none of the attackers would have been left alive on the face of the earth.

However, 'Uthman surrendered himself. He was left to his opinion. It is a question of *ijtihad* as we already stated.

What could 'Ali say after the allegiance had been completed for him and the relatives of 'Uthman had come and told him, "The Caliph was faced by a thousand persons who killed him. They are known."? What could he say except, "I am firm. Take."? On that day he was firm unless they could bring proof that 'Uthman deserved to be killed.

> The author admitted that the proof rested with the one who had the means because the crime was known and the criminals were public in their outrage and made no attempt to conceal it. How could justice be carried out and who would undertake to see to it while the city of the Messenger was humbled under the force of the terror? Who would guarantee 'Ali's life for him when he gave this judgment? Aren't those the very ones who discussed killing him when they formed their plot in Dhu Qar after 'Ali's speech which he gave to the new men before they went to Basra?[299] Was not al-Ashtar with the Amir al-Mu'minin 'Ali after the Battle of the Camel when he appointed his nephew, 'Abdullah ibn 'Abbas, over Basra and did not appoint al-Ashtar? Then he left him in anger, but 'Ali caught up to him and corrected his evil?[300] Did not the Kharijites who came out against 'Ali grow from this kernel? When 'Ali was killed, was he not killed with a weapon similar to the one which killed 'Uthman?

The Battle of Siffin

By Allah, company of Muslims, you know that what they said about 'Uthman was nothing but injustice and that the moment gave the seeker power, was more useful for the seeker in that situation and made it easier for him to reach the one he sought.

> The moment gave the seeker power, even if there had been a force in Madina for which 'Uthman wished. It is said that a force of the army of Syria had left Damascus, making for Madina. When the news of the martyrdom of the Amir al-Mu'minin, 'Uthman, reached them, they returned and Madina remained in the power of the murderers of 'Uthman until the homage was given to 'Ali. If the murderers had yielded to the judgments of this homage which held no harm for them, there is no doubt that they would have turned into savage beasts if the judgment of Allah had been given against them and the *hudud* had been carried out for the atrocious crime that they had committed.

That which refutes the lie is that when the authority went to Mu'awiya, it was not possible for him to kill any of 'Uthman's murderers unless through a judgment, not counting those who were killed in a war (by interpretation), or who intrigued against him, as was said.

> The force of Allah and His lofty justice fell on most of 'Uthman's murderers. None of them was left during Mu'awiya's rule except for the fugitive who fearfully sought a stone that he could hide under. Their power vanished and their evil decreased. Mu'awiya had no need to pursue them.

This lasted until the time of al-Hajjaj. Then they were killed by mere suspicion, not by fact.

> The author alludes to the incident with 'Umayr ibn Dabi and Kumayl an-Nakha'i. That report was already given earlier.

It is clear to you that they became liable for that which they had done.

It will cool your hearts to know that the Prophet ﷺ had mentioned the seditions and indicated and clarified them. He warned about the Khawarij...

> The name Khawarij has come about a group who 'went out' against 'Ali ibn Abi Talib and his company because he had accepted arbitration. They said that the judgment of Allah was clear and that this arbitration was not necessary. Their slogan was "Judgment belongs to Allah alone." They were also called al-Haruriyya, from a village in Kufa called Harura'. They went out to this village. The Amir al-Mu'minin, 'Ali fought them in a famous battle called the Battle of an-Nahrawan. He defeated them and killed many of them. However, he was unable to eradicate them. They then worked out a ruse which killed him at the hand of 'Abd ar-Rahman ibn Muljam, may Allah give him what he deserves!
>
> The Kharijties fought the Umayyad government and they disturbed their peace through continual war, taking as an argument the claim that the Umayyads had usurped the caliphate. However, the Umayayds were able to destroy their forces, even though they too were unable to eradicate them completely.
>
> The Kharijites claimed that 'Uthman was a *kafir* by virtue of changes and alterations he had made and that 'Ali was a *kafir* when he accepted arbitration. They attacked the people of the Camel. All of that came from their ignorance and misguidance.
>
> Part of their theory was that the caliphate was by the free choice of the Muslims. In that, they opposed the Shi'a who said that the caliphate was confined to the House of the Prophet ﷺ. That was also opposed to the people of the *Sunna* who said that the caliphate was in Quraysh when they were present and proved to be worthy. That is the true position.
>
> The Kharijites, in spite of their misguidance and twisting, were not known to lie like the Rafidites who did not recognise sound *hadith* and who fabricated false *hadith* which they ascribed to the Messenger of Allah

The Battle of Siffin

☬. They also interpreted the *ayats* of the Noble Qur'an according to their own whims.

...and he said, "The group closest to the truth will kill them."

We find in *Sahih Muslim*[301] from Abu Sa'id al-Khudri: "Renegades will emerge when there is a division in the Muslims who will be killed by the group closer to the truth."

He made it clear that both groups could claim a connection to the truth. However, the party of 'Ali's claim was stronger.

The people of the Muhammadan *Sunna* owe it to Allah to believe that 'Ali and Mu'awiya and the Companions of the Messenger of Allah ☬ who were with them were all people of the truth. They were sincere in that. Their disagreement was based on *ijtihad* and *mujtahids* can disagree regarding any subject which is open to dispute. They are rewarded for being right and being wrong because of their sincerity in their *ijtihad*. The reward of the one who is right is many times greater than the reward of the one who is wrong. After the Messenger of Allah ☬ no human being is protected from error. Some of them err in some things and are right in others. It is like that with other people. Those who renounced the truth by provoking the first sedition against 'Uthman are not considered to be one of the two parties who had the truth, even if 'Ali fought alongside them and attached himself to them, because those who stained their hands, intentions and hearts with the unjust attack on the Amir al-Mu'minin 'Uthman, whoever they were, deserved to have the Islamic *hadd* carried out on them although it was in a situation where no-one was able to carry it out. Their presence enflamed the fighting between the righteous Muslims. Whenever these men saw the Muslims' resolve for peace and brotherhood, as they did in the Battle of the Camel, they decided to persist in criminality as long as they could. When we say that both parties were among the people of the truth, we mean the Companions of the Messenger of Allah ﷺ who were with the two parties and those Tabi'un who went with them, and who were based on the *Sunna* of the Messenger of Allah. We think that 'Ali, who was promised the Garden, had a higher station with Allah than Mu'awiya, the uncle of the believers and the Companion of the Messenger of the Lord of the worlds. Both of them were men of excellence. When the parties of the people of evil infiltrated them, the one who did an atom's worth of good will see it and the one who did an atom's weight of evil will see it.

Ibn Kathir said in *al-Bidaya wa an-Nihaya*[302] that 'Abd ar-Rahman ibn Ziyad ibn An'am ash-Sha'bani, the Qadi of North Africa (d. in 156 AH), who was a man of right action and one of those who commanded the correct, said when he mentioned the people of Siffin, "They were Arabs who knew each other in the *Jahiliyya*. They met with them in Islam with zeal and the *Sunna* of Islam. They strove to outdo each in steadfastness and they were ashamed to flee. When they stopped fighting, each of them went into the other's ranks to bring out their dead and bury them." Ash-Sha'bi said, "They are the people of the Garden. They met each other and none of them fled from the other."

Allah says: *"If two groups of the believers fight, make peace between them. But if one of them attacks the other unjustly, fight the attackers until they revert to Allah's command. If they revert, then make peace between them with justice and be even-handed. Allah loves the those who are even-handed."*[303] He did not bring them out of "belief" through rebellion or an interpretation, nor did He strip them of the name "brothers", since He says after it: *"The believers are brothers, so make peace between your brothers."*[304]

The Prophet ﷺ said about 'Ammar: "The rebellious party will kill him."

The Prophet ﷺ said that when they were building the mosque, and

The Battle of Siffin

people were moving one brick at a time while 'Ammar was moving two at a time. The Prophet ﷺ spoke these words about him according to what Abu Sa'id al-Khudri related to 'Ikrima, the client of Ibn 'Abbas and 'Ali ibn 'Abdullah ibn 'Abbas. It is in the Book of *Jihad* and Biography from *Sahih Bukhari*.[305] Mu'awiya knew that he himself would not attack in the war of Siffin because he did not bring it or start it. He only came to it after 'Ali had left Kufa and camped his army in an-Nukhayla in order to go to Syria as was already stated. That is when 'Ammar was killed. Mu'awiya said, "The one who brought him out killed him."

My personal belief is that the wrong action for all the Muslims who were killed at the hands of the Muslims since the time of 'Uthman's murder rests on 'Uthman's murderers because they opened the door of sedition and because they stirred up anger in the breasts of the Muslims against each other. As they were the murderers of 'Uthman, so they killed all those who were killed afterwards. Those killed included 'Ammar and those who were better than 'Ammar – like Talha and az-Zubayr – until the sedition reached the point where they murdered 'Ali himself. They were part of his army and were in the group on which he was based. The *hadith* is one of the signs of prophethood. The groups fighting at Siffin were all Companions of the Messenger of Allah and were among the pillars of the state of Islam. The wrong action that took place in the seditions rests upon the attacking group for whose sake every person killed in the Battle of the Camel and the Battle of Siffin and what developed from that were killed.

He said about al-Hasan: "This son of mine is a master. Perhaps Allah will use him to make peace between two great parties of Muslims." He recommended to him that he remove himself and make peace.

This will be discussed in the peace between al-Hasan and Mu'awiya.

Similarly, it is related that the Prophet ﷺ gave 'Uthman permission in the dream to submit and break the fast with him that night.

All of these are things which happened because of the conflict. They are not the result of any method of *fiqh* nor are they considered to be part of the path of *ijtihad* in which the one who is right is rewarded ten times and the one who errs once.

> Ibn Taymiyya said in the *Minhaj as-Sunna*,[306] "Mu'awiya was not one of those who chose to start the war. He was one of the people who most desired that there should be no fighting. Others were more eager to fight him."
>
> People say different things about the Battle of Siffin. Some of them say that both of them were correct *mujtahids* as is stated by many of the people of *kalam*, *fiqh* and *hadith* among those who say that every *mujtahid* is correct. They said that they were both *mujtahids*. This is the position of many of the Ash'arites, the Karramiyya, the *fuqaha'* and others. This is also the position of Abu Hanifa, ash-Shafi'i and others. The Karramiyya said that each was a correct Imam and that it is permitted that there be two Imams when there is a need for that. Some of them say that one of them was correct without specifying which one. This is the position of one group. Some of them say that 'Ali alone was correct and that Mu'awiya was a *mujtahid* who erred, as is stated by some groups of the people of *kalam* and the *fuqaha'* of the people of the four schools. These three positions are related by Abu 'Abdullah Hamid, one of the people of Imam Ahmad ibn Hanbal and other people. They include those who say that the correct position is that there should not have been any fighting and it would have better for both groups not to fight. Fighting was not correct. However, 'Ali was closer to the truth than Mu'awiya. The fighting was a civil war. It was neither obligatory nor recommended. Not fighting would have been better for both groups, even though 'Ali was more entitled to the truth. This is the position of Ibn Hanbal and most of the people of *hadith* and most of the Imams of the *fuqaha'*. It is the position of the great Companions and those who followed them. That is the position of 'Imran ibn Husayn. He forbade

The Battle of Siffin

the sale of weapons for that fight. He said, "It is selling arms in civil strife." That is the statement of Zayd, Usama ibn Zayd, Muhammad ibn Maslama, Ibn 'Umar, Sa'd ibn Abi Waqqas and most of the first predecessors among the Muhajirun and the Ansar ﷺ. This is why it is the school of the people of the *Sunna* not to discuss the quarrels between the Companions. Their virtues are confirmed and their love and friendship is obligatory.

Do not pay any attention to a single letter of any of the *riwayat*s in the history books except for what we mentioned. They are all lies.

Disaster

The Arbitration

PEOPLE HAVE made arbitrary statements regarding the arbitration and said what did not please Allah about it. When you look at it with the eye of virtue without belonging to any sect, you will see that it is lack of the *deen* which causes foolishness in the books of most people, and deeply rooted ignorance in a few of them.

That which is sound is what the Imams like Khalifa ibn Khayyat…

> He is Imam Abu 'Amr Khalifa ibn Khayyat al-'Usfuri al-Basri, one of the vessels of knowledge and one of the shaykhs of Imam al-Bukhari. Ibn 'Adi said about him, "He is honest in reports, truthful, one of the sure transmitters of the *Sunna*. He died in 240 AH.

…and ad-Daraqutni related.

> He is Imam Abu al-Hasan 'Ali ibn 'Umar ad-Daraqutni (306-385). In addition to his majesty in *hadith*, he was one of the Imams of the Shafi'i *fuqaha'*. He had eminence in literature and the transmission of poetry. He came from Baghdad to Egypt to help Ibn Hanzaba, Kafur's wazir, to compose his *Musnad*. The wazir went to great lengths to show him esteem. 'Abd al-Ghani ibn Sa'id said, "The best of people in discussion on the *hadith* of the Messenger of Allah ﷺ are three: 'Ali ibn al-Madini in his time, Musa ibn Harun in his time, and ad-Daraqutni in his time."

The Arbitration

When the Iraqi group went out with 100,000 troops, while the Syrians had 70,000 or 90,000, they camped by the Euphrates at Siffin. They fought at the beginning of the day, Tuesday, by the water. The people of Iraq gained possession of the water.

> The fighting over the water was not serious. 'Amr ibn al-'As said on that day, "It is not just that we should have water while they are thirsty." Those in the Syrian army who pretended to bar the Iraqis from the water wanted to remind them that they had barred the water from the Amir al-Mu'minin 'Uthman during the tragedy in his caliphate, even though he was the one who had purchased the well of Ruma with his own money so that his fellow Muslims would have water from it. After they shared in the water, they had some skirmishes in the month of Dhu al-Hijja, 36 AH. Then there was a truce in Muharram, 37 AH. The battles took place in the month of Safar as the author will show.

Then they met on Wednesday, 23 Safar, Thursday, Friday and Saturday night.

> It was called the Night of *Harir* (Spitting). People fought until morning that night.

The people of Syria raised up copies of the Qur'an and called for a truce. They all parted with the stipulation that each party would entrust its business to one man and then the two men would judge between the two groups who both claimed to be right. Abu Musa came from 'Ali...

> The last commission of Abu Musa was when he was governor of Kufa. 'Ali's herald came to encourage the Kufans to arm themselves and join 'Ali's army in preparation for the fight they were anticipating with the People of the Camel in Basra and then Mu'awiya's helpers in Syria. Abu Musa was apprehensive that the blood of Muslims would be shed at the instigation of fanatics. He reminded the community of Muhammad about

what the Prophet ﷺ had said regarding civil strife, "The one who sits in it is better than the one who stands." Al-Ashtar left him speaking to the people in the mosque about the *hadith* of the Prophet ﷺ. Then he hurried to the governor's house and took possession of it. When Abu Musa returned there, al-Ashtar prevented him from entering it. He told him, "Retire from your rule." Abu Musa left them and chose to stay in a village called 'Urd, far from the seditions and bloodshed. When the people had had their fill of bloodshed and were satisfied that Abu Musa had given the Muslims good counsel when he forbade them to fight, they asked 'Ali to make him the Iraqi representative in the arbitration because the state which he had called for was a state which contained well-being. They sent for Abu Musa and brought him out of his retirement.

Abu Musa was a man of *taqwa*, culture, *fiqh* and knowledge, as we made clear in the *Book of the Lamp of the Murids*. The Prophet ﷺ sent him to the Yemen with Mu'adh. 'Umar appointed him and praised him for his understanding.

He specified him in his famous letter on judgment, its *adab* and its rules.

...and 'Amr ibn al-'As from Mu'awiya.

The pitiful historical group claim that [Abu Musa] was dull-witted, weak in opinion and misled by words and that Ibn al-'As was shrewd and skilful. People said things about his shrewdness to support the corruption they intended. Certain ignorant people followed one another in that and wrote stories about it. Other Companions were cleverer and shrewder than he was. They based that on the fact that when 'Amr deceived Abu Musa in the story of the arbitration, he became known for shrewdness and cunning.

They said, "When they met at Adhruh at Duma al-Jandal and negotiated, …

The Arbitration

Adhruh is a village in the precincts of ash-Shara which lies in the area between the land of eastern Jordan and Saudi Arabia at the southern end of the Syrian desert.

...they agreed that both men would be deposed.

It is true that when the expression of something is not good and is mixed with the defects of distortion, this can lead to presuming something which is not true. Then dispute arises about its judgment. The incident of the arbitration and those who falsify is part of that. When they say that Abu Musa and 'Amr agreed to depose both men and that Abu Musa deposed both of them while 'Amr was content to depose 'Ali rather than Mu'awiya. The root of the distortion comes from the fact that the falsifiers ignored the fact that Mu'awiya was not caliph at that time nor did he claim to be Caliph so that 'Amr would need to depose him. Abu Musa and 'Amr agreed to entrust the business of the caliphate over the Muslims to those who were still alive among the notable Companions with whom the Messenger of Allah ﷺ was pleased when he died. The two arbiters agreed on that. That did not extend to Mu'awiya because he was not a Caliph nor was he fighting to obtain the caliphate. He was seeking to have the *hadd* punishment carried out on those who had participated in the murder of 'Uthman.

When there was arbitration regarding the Imamate of the Muslims and the two judges agreed to leave its investigation to the great Companions and their notable men, the arbitration discussed one thing: the Imamate. As for practical action in the administration of lands under his command which Mu'awiya administered by his authority, there was no arbitration regarding it with either deceit or cunning. Neither foolishness nor heedlessness disturbed it. There would have been a place for cunning or negligence if 'Amr had announced in the result of the arbitration that he had appointed Mu'awiya to rule over the believers and be the Caliph of the Muslims. This is not what 'Amr announced nor did Mu'awiya lay any claim to that. No one in the past thirteen centuries has said that. Mu'awiya's caliphate only began after he had made peace with al-Hasan ibn 'Ali. It was completed with al-Hasan giving homage to Mu'awiya. From that day Mu'awiya was called the Amir al-Mu'minin. 'Amr did not trick Abu Musa and did not deceive him because he did not give Mu'awiya anything new and he only confirmed what Abu Musa confirmed in the arbitration. He did not go beyond what they had both agreed on. Iraq and the Hijaz and what was near them remained under the authority of the one who had authority over them before. The Imamate was connected to what would arise from the agreement of the notable Companions. What wrong action did 'Amr have in any of that? If there was any foolishness, it did not come from Abu Musa. Whoever wants to understand events differently than how they occurred will understand them as he wishes. However, they are clear and evident for all who see them as they really are.

'Amr said to Abu Musa, "Make your statement first." He said, "I have looked and 'Ali is removed from the command. Let the Muslims look for themselves as I remove this sword from my neck (or my shoulder)." He took it from his neck and placed it on the ground. 'Amr went and placed his sword on the ground. He said, "I have looked and confirm Mu'awiya in command as I put this sword of mine firmly on my neck," and he girded it on.

What command? If it is continuation in the administration of the land which was already under his authority, the command was effective for Mu'awiya and 'Ali. Each of them remained in control of what he administered. If what was meant by the command was the general rulership of the believers, Mu'awiya was not an Imam (i.e. the Caliph) so that 'Amr could confirm him as such. We made this clear in this previous section. This is the point of the falsification that the historians of the forged lies mock. They mock all their readers and make them imagine that there

The Arbitration

were two Caliphs or two commanders over the believers and that the agreement between the two arbiters was to depose both of them and that Abu Musa deposed the two Caliphs according to the agreement and that 'Amr deposed one of them and let the other remain Caliph, contrary to the agreement. This is all a lie, a falsehood, and slander. That which 'Amr did what was the same that Abu Musa did. He did not differ from him in a single jot or iota. The command of the rulership and the caliphate or command of the believers remained subject to the investigation of the Companions so that they could investigate what they thought on it when and how they wanted.

If this second firm step was not completed, it was not the fault of Abu Musa or 'Amr. They both carried out their task according to their *ijtihad* and pleasure and what that led them to. The two groups had not demanded that they both carry out this task, which they would not have turned to nor shown any opinion about. If the position of Abu Musa in this great historical event was one of foolishness and failure, that would have been a disgrace for him in history. The generations after him understood his position to be one of his glories because of which Allah wrote success and correctness for him. Dhu ar-Rimma the poet said when he addressed his grandson Bilal ibn Abi Burda ibn Abi Musa:

> Your father repaired the *deen* and the people after
> they had become far apart, when the house of the *deen* was cut off.
> He strengthened the covenants of the *deen* in the days of Adhruh.
> He repelled wars which had returned to stillness.

Abu Musa objected. 'Amr said, "This is how we agreed." Everyone broke up in disagreement.

DEFENCE

Qadi Abu Bakr said, "All of these are clear lies. None of it took place. It is something about which the innovators and the historians wrote for the kings. That was inherited by the people of insolence and public acts of rebellion against Allah and by people of innovations.

Islamic history did not begin to be written down except after the Umayyads had gone and dynasties had been established whose men did not like to talk about the glories of that past and the good qualities of its people. The recording of Islamic history was undertaken by three groups: one group who sought ease of life and good fortune by drawing near to those who hated the Umayyads by what they wrote and compiled. Another group thought that devotions would only be obtained and one would only draw near to Allah by tarnishing the reputation of Abu Bakr, 'Umar, 'Uthman and all the Banu 'Abd Shams.

A third group of the people of justice and the *deen* like at-Tabari, Ibn 'Asakir, Ibn al-Athir and Ibn Kathir thought that part of justice was to compile the reports of the historians from all the schools and positions – like Lut ibn Yahya, the fervent Shi'ite and Sayf ibn 'Umar al-'Iraqi al-Mu'tazili. Perhaps some of them were compelled to do that when they tried to please all the areas whose power and position were felt. Most of them furnished the names of the transmitters of the reports that they quoted so that the researcher would have some insight into every report and would be able to investigate the state of its transmitter. This legacy reached us, not inasmuch as it is our history, but because that provides ample material for study and research from which our history could be derived. This is possible and easy when it is undertaken by someone who looks at the places of strength and weakness in these sources. The shrewd person can use it to find the reality of what really happened and separate it from what did not take place and content himself with the sound sources of reports without the later additions. Reference to the books of the *Sunna* and the observations of the Imams of the community will make this task easy. Now is the time for us to carry out this duty which we have been very slow to undertake. The first person to wake up in our time to the machinations foisted off onto the history of the Umayyads was the great Indian scholar, Shaykh Shibli an-Nu'mani in his criticism of the books of Jurji Zaydan. Then the shrewd people among the fair began to study the facts. The truth became evident to them and other people. It was luminous and clear. When this effort continued in the path of the truth, it was not long until the Muslims' understanding of their history changed and they perceived the secrets of the miracles which had taken place in their past.

The first reliable Imams related that when they met to look into this matter in a noble group of people which included Ibn 'Umar and his like, 'Amr dismissed Mu'awiya.

> i.e. by his confirmation with Abu Musa that the Imamate of the Muslims should be left for the notable Companions to investigate.

Ad-Daraqutni mentioned with his *isnad* to Husayn ibn al-Mundhir:

> Ad-Daraqutni said: Ibrahim ibn Humam related to us from Abu Yusuf al-Falusi, who is Ya'qub ibn 'Abd ar-Rahman ibn Jarir, from al-Aswad ibn Sha'ban from 'Abdullah ibn Mudarib from Husayn ibn al-Mundhir (and Husayn was one of 'Ali's close friends who fought with him.)

"When 'Amr retired Mu'awiya, Husayn ibn al-Mundhir came and struck his tent near Mu'awiya's tent. This news reached Mu'awiya. He sent to him and said, 'I have heard such-and-such about 'Amr.

> i.e. about removing 'Ali and Mu'awiya and his entrusting his matter to the great Companions.

"'Go and see what is the case about what I have heard.' I went to him and said, 'tell me about the business which you and Abu Musa undertook. How did you act in it?' He said, 'The people said what they said about but, by Allah, the business is not as they have stated.'

i.e. they were neither dismissed nor appointed. The business was left to the notable Companions.

"I said to Abu Musa, 'What do you think about in this business?' He said, 'I think that it rests with some people with whom the Messenger of Allah ﷺ was pleased when he died.' I asked, 'Where will you put me and Mu'awiya?' He said, 'If you are asked to help, then you can help. If there is no need for both of you, then the command of Allah has no use for you.' He said, 'It was that which Mu'awiya himself wove from it.' I came to him and told him,'" i.e. Husayn came to Mu'awiya and told him what he had heard was just as he had heard it. He sent for Abu al-A'war adh-Dhawkani.

> He is Abu al-A'war as-Sulami (Dhakwan is a tribe of Sulaym). His name is 'Amr ibn Sufyan. He was one of the great generals of Mu'awiya. In the Battle of Siffin, al-Ashtar tried to get him to come forth [to fight]. He refused to do that because he did not think that al-Ashtar was one of his peers.

He had sent him to his horses. He went out with his horse at a gallop, saying, "Where is the enemy of Allah? Where is this libertine?"

Abu Yusuf said, …

> i.e. al-Falusi, the transmitter of this report from al-Aswad to Shayban from 'Abdullah ibn Mudarib from Hudayn.

…"I think that he said, 'He meant his own life.'" 'Amr went out to a horse under his tent and jumped onto its back without a saddle. He went out at a gallop towards Mu'awiya's tent while he was saying, "The grumbling she-camel is sometimes milked in the bowl, Mu'awiya. The grumbling she-camel is sometimes milked in the bowl."

> *Ad-Dajur*: the camel which grumbles and is distressed when it is milked. "The grumbling she-camel is sometimes milked in the bowl"

The Arbitration

is a metaphor. It means that the camel which grumbles can be milked to fill the vessel. They used it for the person of ill temper from whom compassion and kindness can be obtained. The miser can have property gotten from him.

Mu'awiya said, "Yes, and sometimes she is skittish with the milker, smashes his nose and overturns the vessel."

Ad-Daraqutni mentioned (with a proper *isnad*)...

> He said, "Muhammad ibn 'Abdullah ibn Ibrahim and Da'laj ibn Ahmad related to us from Muhammad ibn Ahmad ibn an-Nadr from Mu'awiya ibn 'Amr from Za'ida from 'Abdullah ibn 'Umar from Rib'i, etc. Rib'i was the son of Harash al-'Abasi, Abu Maryam al-Kufi.

...from Rib'i from Abu Musa that 'Amr ibn al-'As said, "By Allah, if Abu Bakr and 'Umar left this property while anything of it was lawful for them, they would have been deceived and there would be a fault their opinion. By Allah, they were not deceived nor are they imperfect in opinion. If they are two men for whom this property which we got after them was forbidden, then we are destroyed. O Allah, the mistake has only come from us!"

> The author quoted this report to indicate 'Amr's scrupulousness, his self-examination and his calling attention to the path of the Salaf.

This was the beginning and end of the *hadith*. So they turned away from the seducers and restrained those who howled. They left the path of those who broke agreements and went to the *sunan* of the guided. They restrained the tongues from those who went first to the *deen*. Beware, lest you be one of those destroyed on the Day of Rising because of the arguments of the Companions of the Messenger of Allah ﷺ. Leave what has passed alone. Allah has carried out what He decreed. Be serious in whatever you cling to regarding belief and action. Do not let your tongue discuss what does not concern you with every dog that barks among those who take the *deen* lightly. Allah will not let the action of the one who does good go to waste. May Allah have mercy on ar-Rabi' ibn Khaytham!

> He was one of the students of 'Abdullah ibn Mas'ud, Abu Ayyub al-Ansari and 'Amr ibn Maymun, Imam ash-Sha'bi, Ibrahim an-Nakha'i and Abu Burda. Ibn Mas'ud said to him, "If the Prophet ﷺ had seen you, he would have loved you." He died in 64 AH.

When he was told, "Al-Husayn has been slain!" he said, "Did they kill him?" They replied that they had. He said, *"O Allah, Originator of the heavens and the earth, Knower of the Unseen and the Visible! You will judge between Your slaves regarding what they differed about!"* (39:46) He did not say anything more. This is intellect and the *deen*. It is to restrain oneself from the states of the Muslims and to submit to the Lord of the Worlds.

Disaster

Claims made about 'Ali ibn Abi Talib ﷺ

IF IT is said that that only refers to matters whose significations are obscure, while there is no confusion in all these matters because the Prophet ﷺ mentioned that 'Ali should be appointed after him. He said, "In relation to me, you are as Harun was to Musa, even though there is no Prophet after me."

> In the Book of Raids from *Sahih Bukhari*[307] and in the Virtues of the Companions from *Sahih Muslim*[308] it is reported from Sa'd ibn Abi Waqqas that the Messenger of Allah ﷺ went to Tabuk and delegated 'Ali over Madina for him. 'Ali asked, "Do you leave me with the women and children?" He replied, "Are you not content to be in relation to me as Harun was to Musa, even though there is no Prophet after me?" Look at the debate on this *hadith* in 1157 AH between Sayyid 'Abdullah ibn al-Husayn as-Suwaydi and al-Mala' Bashi 'Ali, the greatest shaykh among the Shi'ite scholars and their *mujtahids* in the time of Nadir Shah on the Book of the conference of an-Najaf.[309]

He said, "O Allah, be a friend to the one who is his friend and an enemy to the one who is his enemy and help the one who helps him and disappoint the one who disappoints him."

> It is in the *Musnad* of Ibn Hanbal.[310] Look at the *tafsir* of al-Hasan al-

Muthanna ibn al-Hasan as-Sibt ibn 'Ali ibn Abi Talib on this *hadith*.[311] The discussion of the author regarding the two *hadiths* will come later.

After this, the stubborn person cannot resist.

Abu Bakr took it unjustly and sat in other than his proper place.

Then 'Umar followed him in this encroachment.

Then he hoped that 'Umar would have the good fortune to return to the truth. He made the state obscure and made it a council in order to curtail opposition to what he had heard from the Prophet ﷺ.

Then Ibn 'Awf used a trick and took it from 'Ali and gave it to 'Uthman.

Then 'Uthman was killed since he had ascended like a thief to the caliphate and the judgments of the Shari'a, (They have said something terrible which is only a lie. This book establishes their lies.) and the command went to 'Ali by the divine prophetic truth. Those who had made a covenant with him seized it and those who had offered him allegiance disobeyed him and those who had pressed him broke the agreement.

The people of Syria turned to deviation in the *deen*, rather they turned to disbelief.

> All of these things are part of the ravings and bias of those who brought about this calamity. The author has answered them in the following "defence" and refuted their foolishness. However, the scope of discussion is large and consequently the discussion overlooks the position of the people of Syria in these seditions that took place in Islam. Earlier you saw what Ibn al-Kiwa', one of the leaders of the seditions, said when he was describing his likes in the largest cities, "As for the people of these events among the people of Syria, they are the people who most obey their guide and rebel against the one who makes them err." If the people of these events in Syria were like that, based on testimony of one of the leaders

Claims made about 'Ali ibn Abi Talib

of the sedition, then the Amir al-Mu'minin 'Ali also testified to the people of well-being and belief among them, as Ibn Kathir quoted in *al-Bidaya wa an-Nihaya*[312] from 'Abd ar-Rahman ibn Humam as-San'ani, one of the notable Imams and *huffaz*, from his shaykh, Ma'mar ibn Rashid al-Basri, a notable man, from az-Zuhri, the *Sunna* recorder and shaykh of the Imams, that 'Abdullah ibn Safwan al-Jumahi said that a man from Siffin said, "O Allah, curse the people of Syria!" 'Ali said to him, "Do not curse the people of Syria. The *Abdal* are there. The *Abdal* are there."[3]

Abu Idris al-Khawlani, one of the notable bearers of the *Sunna* and the Shari'a, and one of the shaykhs of al-Hasan al-Basri, Ibn Sirin, Makhul and their likes states that Abu ad-Darda' said, "The Messenger of Allah ﷺ said, 'While I was asleep, I saw the Book taken from under my head. I thought that it was being taken. My eye followed it and it went to Syria. When the sedition occurs, belief will remain in Syria.'" This *hadith* is related from Companions other than Abu ad-Darda': Abu Umama and 'Abdullah ibn 'Amr ibn al-'As.

There is a comparison between the people of Syria and those who fought them. We quoted the report of al-A'mash from Ibn Kathir[313] from 'Amr ibn Murra ibn 'Abdullah ibn al-Harith from Zuhayr ibn al-Arqam who said, "'Ali addressed us on that Friday and said, 'I was told that some people went to the Yemen. By Allah, I reckon that those people will overcome you and you will only be overcome because of your rebellion against your Imam and their obedience to their Imam, and by your deceit and their trustworthiness, by your corruption and their correctness. I sent so-and-so and he deceived me and was treacherous. I sent so-and-so and he deceived me and was treacherous and sent money to Mu'awiya. If one of you were to be entrusted with a glass, he would take its handle. O Allah, I am bored with them and they are bored with me. I dislike them and they

---

3   The *hadith* of the Abdal from 'Ali is weak since it is broken. Shurayh ibn 'Ubayd al-Humsi says that it does not reach 'Ali.

dislike me. O Allah, give me rest from them and give them rest from me!'"
This is how 'Ali described his army and his party. Its opposite in virtues was the description of the people of Syria who were forced to take a position of warfare against his group. After 'Ali had described the people of Syria with obedience, trustworthiness and correctness, this bomb only blows up in the faces of those who described them with disbelief and corruption in the *deen*.

This is their actual *madhhab*:...

> i.e. the reality of the school of the Rafidites and the enemies of the Companions.

...that all that were with them were unbelievers...

> After 'Ali and some of his family, they excepted among them: Salman al-Farisi, Abu Dharr, al-Miqdad ibn al-Aswad, 'Ammar ibn Yasir, Hudhayfa ibn al-Yaman, Abu al-Haytham ibn at-Tihan, Sahl ibn Hunayf, 'Ubada ibn as-Samit, Abu Ayyub al-Ansari, Khuzayma ibn Thabit and Abu Sa'id al-Khudri. Some of the Shi'a thought that the good ones among the Companions of the Messenger of Allah were even less in number than these men.

...because part of their position is to consider people to be unbelievers on account of their wrong actions.

> Part of their school is that 'Ali and eleven of his family were protected from error and that they are the source of the Shari'a. They accept the making of the Shari'a which the transmitters ascribe to them provided that these men have the precondition of partisanship and friendship (of the Imam), even if people recognised that they had things incompatible with truthfulness or what contradicts what is known to be necessarily part of the *deen*.

Similarly, this group, called Imamiyya, said that every rebel with a great wrong action is an unbeliever...

> Proven by the great wrong action in their opinion. The Muslims do not corroborate that.

...according to the Qadariyya.

> Ibn Taymiyya said in the *Minhaj as-Sunna*,[314] "The early Shi'a agreed to affirm the Decree and the attributes. The rejection of the Decree became known among them when they joined the Mu'tazilites in the Buwayyid government."

They said that there were none more rebellious than the above-mentioned rebels...

> They were Abu Bakr, 'Umar and 'Uthman.

...and those who assisted them in their business and that the Companions of the Messenger of Allah ﷺ were the people with the greatest eagerness for this world and those with the least defence of the *deen* and the most destructive of them for the principles and the Shari'a.

> In spite of that, you will find people among those who are affiliated to the al-Azhar and the *Sunna* who are friendly to the House of Bringing the Schools Together which was founded in Cairo after World War II and console themselves by devoting their lives to the disagreement between them and to the mutual exchange of *taqiyya* they are based on.

DEFENCE

Qadi Abu Bakr said: You are spared from the evil of hearing it, so how can anyone be disgruntled by it? For five hundred years, up until this very day when I am writing this (and I do not decrease or increase a single day of it, in Sha'ban 536 AH), what can one hope for after perfection except imperfection?

The Christians and the Jews were not content with the Companions of Musa and 'Isa just as the Rafidites were not content with the Companions of Muhammad ﷺ when they decided that they had agreed on disbelief and what was false.

> Ibn 'Asakir[315] transmitted that al-Hasan al-Muthanna ibn al-Hasan as-Sibt ibn 'Ali ibn Abi Talib said to a Rafidite, "By Allah, if Allah gives me power over you, I will cut off your hands and feet. Then we will not accept any repentance from you." A man said to him, "You will not accept repentance from them?" He said, "We know these men better than you do. They confirm you when they want and deny you when they want. They claim that that is correct for them by *taqiyya*. Woe to you! *Taqiyya* is a door of indulgence for the Muslims when they are forced to use it and they fear the one in power. They give him something other than what is within themselves transferring responsibility to Allah. It is not a door to excellence. Excellence lies in carrying out Allah's command and speaking the truth. By Allah, *taqiyya* does not reach the point where one of the slaves of Allah can use it to misguide the slaves of Allah."

What does anyone hope for from these men? What will remain of them? Allah says, *"Allah promised those of you who believe and do right actions that He will make them successors in the land as He made those before them successors, and will firmly establish for them their deen with which He is pleased and give them, in place of their fear, security."*[316] This is a true statement and a real promise. Then their time passed and they had no caliph or strength in them, nor was there security or tranquillity for them. Then there was nothing but injustice, aggression, usurpation, chaos, splintering and rebellious agitation.

Claims made about 'Ali ibn Abi Talib

The community agreed that the Prophet ﷺ did not stipulate regarding who was to follow him.

> Ibn 'Asakir[317] transmitted the *hadith* of Fudayl ibn Mazruq from al-Bayhaqi that al-Hasan al-Muthanna ibn al-Hasan as-Sibt ibn 'Ali ibn Abi Talib was asked, "Did not the Messenger of Allah ﷺ say, 'If I am the master of anyone, 'Ali is his master'?" He replied, "Yes, but by Allah, the Messenger of Allah ﷺ did not mean the amirate and the sultanate by that. If he had meant that, he would have stated it more clearly. The Messenger of Allah ﷺ was the most eager to give sincere good counsel to the Muslims. If the business had been as you have stated, he would have said, 'O people! This one is to rule you and be in charge over you after me, so hear and obey him.' By Allah, if Allah and His Messenger had chosen 'Ali for this command and put him in charge of the Muslims after him and then 'Ali had left the command of Allah and His Messenger, then 'Ali would have been the first to have left the command of Allah and His Messenger." Al-Bayhaqi related it by many paths, some with some additions and some with omissions, but the meaning remains the same.

Al-'Abbas spoke to 'Ali, according to what his son 'Abdullah related from him. 'Abdullah ibn al-'Abbas said, "'Ali ibn Abi Talib ﷺ left the Messenger of Allah ﷺ while he was in the illness from which he died. People said, 'Abu Hasan, how is the Messenger of Allah ﷺ this morning?' He said, 'He is recovering, by Allah's praise.' Al-'Abbas took his hand and said to him, 'By Allah, after three days you will be the slave of the staff. I think that the Messenger of Allah ﷺ will die from this illness. I see death in the faces of the 'Abd al-Muttalib. Let us go to the Messenger of Allah ﷺ and ask him about who will be in charge after him. If it is for us, then we will know it. If it is for others, we will know and he can make us guardians.' 'Ali said, 'By Allah, if we ask the Messenger of Allah ﷺ

about it and he denies it to us, then the people will never entrust it to us later. By Allah, I will not ask the Messenger of Allah ﷺ.'"

> Al-Bukhari related this in the Book of the Raids in his *Sahih*.[318] Ibn Kathir quoted it in *al-Bidaya wa an-Nihaya*[319] from the *hadith* of az-Zuhri from 'Abdullah ibn Malik from Ibn 'Abbas. Ibn Hanbal related it in his *Musnad*.[320]

Qadi Abu Bakr said: In my opinion, the opinion of al-'Abbas is sounder and nearer to the Next World and clearer in precision. This invalidates the claim of those who claim that there was any indication that 'Ali should be appointed, so how can it be claimed that there is a text to that effect?

As for Abu Bakr, a woman came to the Prophet ﷺ and he ordered her to come back to him. She asked him, "And if I do not find you?" It was as if she meant if he was dead. He said, "Then you will find Abu Bakr."

> In the Book of the Virtues of the Companions from *Sahih Bukhari*[321] from the *hadith* of Jubayr ibn Mut'im. He said, "A woman came to the Prophet ﷺ and he told her to return to him. She said, 'What do you think if I come and do not find you?' as if she meant his death. He said, 'Then if you do not find me, go to Abu Bakr.'"

The Prophet ﷺ spoke to 'Umar when some words had passed between 'Umar and Abu Bakr. The Prophet's face went dark...

> His face darkened: changed and the joy and shining colour in it left.

...until Abu Bakr felt sorry for 'Umar because of it. The Prophet ﷺ said, "Will you leave my companion alone? (twice) I was sent to you and you said, 'You have lied' while Abu Bakr said, 'You spoke the truth.' I free every friend of his friendship."

> In the Book of the Virtues of the Companions from *Sahih Bukhari*[322] from Abu ad-Darda' in full.

Claims made about 'Ali ibn Abi Talib

The Prophet ﷺ said, "If I were to take a bosom friend in Islam, I would have taken Abu Bakr as a bosom friend, but he is my brother and companion."

> In this chapter from the Book of Virtues of the Companions in *Sahih Bukhari*[323] from the *hadith* of 'Ikrima from Ibn 'Abbas.

"Allah took your companion as a close friend. All the gates of the mosque should be closed except the door of Abu Bakr."

> There is confusion and imperfection in this sentence. Look at this meaning in the *hadith* of Abu Sa'id al-Khudri in that place of *Sahih Bukhari*[324] and the *hadith* of Ibn 'Abbas in the *Musnad* of Ibn Hanbal[325] and *al-Bidaya wa an-Nihaya*.[326]

The Prophet ﷺ said, "While I was asleep, I dreamt that I was at a well in which there was a bucket. I took as much of it as Allah wished. Then Ibn Abi Quhafa took it and took one or two buckets of it, and there was some weakness in his drawing. May Allah forgive him.

> *Dhanub*: a great bucket when it is filled with water. Ibn Abi Quhafa is Abu Bakr.

Then it turned into a big bucket.

> i.e. then it became great. It became like a wide bucket made from the skin of an ox because of its great size.

"Ibn al-Khattab took it and I have never seen such a mighty one among the people as 'Umar doing such hard work. People drank to their fill and watered their kneeling camels there."

> ...until people around it had their camels kneel for abundant water. The *hadith* is in that place in *Sahih Bukhari*[327] from the *hadith* of Sa'id ibn al-Musayyab from Abu Hurayra.

It is confirmed that the Prophet ﷺ climbed up Uhud with Abu Bakr, 'Umar and 'Uthman, may Allah be pleased with all of them. It shook with them. He said, "Uhud, be still. There is only a Prophet, a *siddiq* and two martyrs on you."

> In the Book of the Virtues of the Companions in *Sahih Muslim*[328] from the *hadith* of Qatada from Anas ibn Malik.

The Prophet ﷺ said, "There were men among those before in the tribe of Israel who were inspired, although they were not Prophets. If any of them is in my community, it is 'Umar."

> In the Book of the Virtues of the Companions in *Sahih Muslim*[329] from the *hadith* of Abu Salama from Abu Hurayra.

The Prophet ﷺ said to 'A'isha when he was ill, "Call Abu Bakr and your brother for me so that I can write a document. I fear that people will have wrong opinions and say, 'I am more entitled.' Allah and the believers refuse anyone except Abu Bakr."

> In the *Musnad* of Ibn Hanbal[330] from the *hadith* of az-Zuhri from 'Urwa ibn az-Zubayr from 'A'isha. Look at the *Musnad*,[331] the *Tabaqat* of Ibn Sa'd[332] and the *Musnad* of Abu Dawud at-Tayyalisi.[333]

Ibn 'Abbas said, "A man came to the Prophet ﷺ and said, 'Messenger of Allah, last night I dreamt that a tent was oozing with fat and honey. I saw people begging with their hands, both those who were asking for a lot and those who were asking for a little. I saw a rope reaching from heaven to the earth. I saw you take it and you went up. Then another man took it and went up. Then another man took it and went up. Then another man took it and it broke. Then it reached him and he went up it.'" (and he mentioned the *hadith*). Then Abu Bakr interpreted it and said, "As for the rope which reached from the heaven to earth, it is the truth which you have. You took it and Allah will bring you up. Then another will take it after you and he will climb it. Then another man will take it and climb up. Then another man will take it and it will break with him and then it will reach him and he will climb it."

In the Book of Interpretation in *Sahih Bukhari*[334] from the *hadith* of 'Abdullah ibn 'Abbas and in the Book of Dreams in *Sahih Muslim*[335] from the *hadith* of Ibn 'Abbas. In the *Musnad* of Ibn Hanbal[336] from the *hadith* of Ibn 'Abbas.

It is confirmed that the Prophet ﷺ asked one day, "Who has had a dream?" A man said, "I dreamt that it was as if there was a balance which descended from heaven. You and Abu Bakr were weighed and you were the heavier. Abu Bakr and 'Umar were weighed and Abu Bakr was the heavier. 'Umar and 'Uthman were weighed and 'Umar was the heavier. Then the balance was taken away." Abu Bakra said, "We saw dislike in the face of the Messenger of Allah ﷺ."

In the Book of the *Sunna* from the *Sunan* of Abu Dawud[337] from the *hadith* of Abu Bakra. In the Book of Dreams from the *Jami'* of at-Tirmidhi[338] from the *hadith* of Abu Bakra. Look in the *Musnad* of Ibn Hanbal[339] at the *hadith* of Abu Umama about the scale of Abu Bakr weighing more than the scale of the entire community.

These *hadiths* are like mountains of clarity and mountains regarding the rope to the truth if Allah has given one success. O Sunnis, you only have the words of Allah: *"If you do not help him, Allah did held him when the unbelievers drove him out and there were two of them in the Cave."*[340] He put the community in one half and Abu Bakr in the other half, all the Companions standing with him.

When you look at these facts, the state of the qualities of the caliphs will not be hidden from you, nor will their rule and organisation, in particular and general. Allah says: *"Allah has promised those of you who believe and do right actions that He will make them successors in the land as He made those before them successors, and will firmly establish for them their deen with which He is pleased and will give them, in place of their fear, security. They worship Me, not associating anything with Me."*[341] If this promise was not realised for the caliphs, for whom then will it be realised? The proof of it is the consensus that no one has gone in advance of them in excellence until this very day although there is disagreement about those after them. Those men are definite and their Imamate is certain. It is confirmed that Allah's promise to them was carried out. They defended the territory of the Muslims and established the policy of the *deen*. Our scholars said, "Those after them follow them, the Imams who are the pillars of the religion and the supports of the Shari'a, those who advise the slaves of Allah and guide those who seek guidance to Allah. As for those who are unjust rulers, their harm is confined to this world and its judgments."

As for those who preserve the *deen*, they are the Imams, those who give good counsel for the *deen* of Allah. They are of four sorts:

The first rank preserved the reports of the Messenger of Allah ﷺ. They are in the position of those who guard the food of life.

The second rank are the scholars of the fundamentals (*usul*). They defend the *deen* of Allah from the people of stubbornness and innovations. They are the courageous ones of Islam and its heroes who defend it in the crisis of misguidance.

The third class are a people who were exact in the fundamentals of worship and the laws of behaviour and they distinguished *halal* things from *haram*, and they mastered injuries and blood-wits, and made the meanings of oaths and vows clear. They detailed the judgments in claims. In the *deen*, they are in the position of agents who deal with property.

The fourth group devoted themselves to service and they applied themselves to worship. They withdrew from people. In the Next World, they are like the elite of the men of this world.

In the *Book of the Lamp of the Murids*, in the fourth section on the Sciences of the Qur'an, we made it clear which of the positions are the best in those classes and how they are organised.

Qadi Abu Bakr said: All of these are allusions or statements or proofs or information. All of that indicates the soundness of what has passed and the confirmation of what the men of intellect have.

After this clarification, we will speak about another position. If there is a text about Abu Bakr or 'Ali, it would inevitably mean that that 'Ali would have used it as a proof, or another of the Muhajirun or Ansar would have used it as a proof. The *hadith* of Ghadir Khumm does not provide any proof because he appointed him over Madina during his lifetime as Musa had appointed Harun while he was alive when he went to speak with Allah for the tribe of Israel. All of the Jews agree that Musa died after Harun, so where then is his caliphate?

As for his words, "O Allah, be a friend to the one who is his friend..." these are sound words and are a supplication which was answered. None opposed him except the Rafidites. They put him in other than his proper place. They ascribed to him what was not appropriate to his degree. Adding to the limit is to diminish the one limited. If Abu Bakr had attacked him, he would not have been the only aggressor. It would have been all of the Companions as we have stated, because they would have been helping him in what was false.

Do not think that these words of theirs are strange, for they say that the Prophet ﷺ was being amiable to them and testing them in [their] hypocrisy and *taqiyya*.

> The *Sahih* of al-Bukhari[342] from the hadith of 'A'isha and Abu Musa al-Ash'ari.

Where are you in relation to the words of the Prophet ﷺ when he heard what 'A'isha said, "Tell 'Umar to pray with the people"? He said, "You are the women of Yusuf! Tell Abu Bakr to pray with the people."

We have already given these *hadith*s.

> In the Book of the Amirate from *Sahih Muslim* (Book 33, *hadith* 11 & 12, pt. 5, pp. 4-5) from the *hadith* of 'Urwa ibn az-Zubayr from Ibn 'Umar and from the *hadith* of Salim from Ibn 'Umar and in the *Musnad* of Ibn Hanbal (1:43, no. 299) from 'Urwa from Ibn 'Umar and (1:46, no. 322) from Hamid ibn 'Abd ar-Rahman from Ibn 'Abbas and (1:47, no. 332) from az-Zuhri from Salim from Ibn 'Umar.

They did something terrible. They have forged a great lie. 'Umar only made it a council to imitate the Prophet ﷺ and Abu Bakr when he said, "If I appoint, better than me appointed. If I do not appoint, the Messenger of Allah ﷺ did not appoint."

> From the long *hadith* of 'Amr ibn Maymun in the Book of the Virtues of the Companions from *Sahih Bukhari*.[343]

No one refuted these words. He said, "Make it a council between some people with whom the Messenger of Allah ﷺ was pleased when he died."

He was pleased with most of them, but there were those with whom he was the most pleased, and testified that they were worthy of the caliphate.

As for their statement that Ibn 'Awf used a device so that he could give it to 'Uthman, if that was a trick and was only that, it was because power was not his.

> Rather it belonged to Allah. Allah is the One who gave success to Ibn 'Awf and the rest of his brothers, the Companions, so that they were based on that position which Allah desired them to have – pure intention,

Claims made about 'Ali ibn Abi Talib

sincere goal, and action for Allah alone. The choice of the caliph 'Umar in choosing a council was a higher example for the human self when it is in the highest rank of nobility and stripped of all thoughts of passion.

If the action of the slaves is a stratagem or it is a judgment from strength, strength and power belong to Allah. Everyone knew that only one could take it on. 'Abd ar-Rahman ibn 'Awf had his own opinion in the business after he had removed himself, that he should strive on behalf of the Muslims to find the one who deserved that and no-one was better entitled to it than him, as we have made clear in the "Ranks of the Caliphate" from the *Lights of Dawn*[344] and in other books of *hadith*.

'Uthman was killed, and none remained on earth who was worthier of the caliphate than 'Ali. It came to him by worth and in its proper time and place. Allah made judgments and knowledge clear at his hands as Allah wished to make them clear. 'Umar said, "If it had not been for 'Ali, 'Umar would have been destroyed."

> This is along with the words of the Prophet ﷺ about it, "The first of those whom the truth touched was 'Umar," and his words, "Allah has placed truth on the tongue of 'Umar who spoke it." The Prophet ﷺ said, "If there had been a Prophet after me, it would have been 'Umar."

Part of his *fiqh* and knowledge appeared in the fight against the people of the *qibla* in summoning them and debating with them and not letting them go first and going to them before a war began with them. His call was: "We do not begin the war nor is a client pursued nor are the wounded finished off nor is a woman disturbed nor is property taken as booty from them." His command was to accept their testimony and to pray behind them, so that the people of knowledge said, "If it had not been for what happened, we would not know how to fight the people of rebellion."

As for Talha and az-Zubayr going out, that has already been made clear.

It was a war for mutual understanding and mutual help to establish the *hudud* of the Shari'a for the murder of the Amir al-Mu'minin.

As for some people declaring them to be unbelievers, it is those people who are the unbelievers. We explained the states of the people of wrong actions which there is no abuse directed towards without a book. We have explained it in every section.

If it is said, "Al-'Abbas spoke about 'Ali as the imams related, that al-'Abbas and 'Ali argued in the presence of 'Umar regarding the business of the *waqfs* of the Messenger of Allah 🕌. Al-'Abbas said to 'Umar, 'Amir al-Mu'minin, decide between me and this sinful despotic unjust one.'

> This mutual seeking of a judgment by al-'Abbas and 'Ali before the Amir al-Mu'minin 'Umar was already mentioned from the *hadith* of Malik ibn Aws ibn al-Hadathan al-Basri in *Sahih Bukhari*. Ibn Hajar said in the *Fath al- Bari*,³⁴⁵ "Shu'ayb and Yunus added that 'Ali and al-'Abbas called each other names. In the version of 'Uqayl from Ibn Shihab in the Shares of Inheritance, 'Decide between me and this unjust one.' They called each other names. In Juwayriyya's version, 'Between this perfidious, deceitful, wrongdoing liar.' Ibn Hajar said, 'I did not see anything in the paths of transmission that 'Ali said anything about al-'Abbas as opposed to what one understands from the words in 'Uqayl's version, 'They called each other names.' Al-Maziri approved of those who omitted these phrases from this *hadith*. He said, 'Perhaps one of the transmitters erred in it. If it is recorded, it is good to take it to mean that al-'Abbas said it, indicating 'Ali, because he was like a son to him. He wanted to make him retract what he thought was a mistake.'"

The group said to 'Umar, "Amir al-Mu'minin, decide between them and give them relief from each other." 'Umar said, "I ask you by Allah, by whose permission the heaven and the earth are established, do you know that the Messenger of Allah 🕌 said, 'We do not leave inheritance.

What we leave is *sadaqa*,' meaning himself when he said that?" They replied, "He said that." He turned to al-'Abbas and 'Ali and said, "I ask you by Allah, do you know that the Messenger of Allah ﷺ said that?" They answered, "Yes." 'Umar said, "Allah gave this booty to the Messenger of Allah ﷺ and it was something which He did not give to anyone else. The Messenger of Allah ﷺ acted that way in his lifetime. Then he died and Abu Bakr said, 'I am the inheritor of the Messenger of Allah ﷺ.' Then he died after two years in his rule. He acted in it as the Messenger of Allah ﷺ had acted. Then you both claim that Abu Bakr was a perfidious deceitful liar?

> Ibn Hajar[346] said, "Az-Zuhri used to relate it sometimes and he would be explicit. Then another time, he would allude to it. It is the same with Malik. He omitted that in the version of Bishr ibn 'Umar from him with al-Isma'ili and others. It is the same with what al-'Abbas said to 'Ali."

"Allah knows that he is truthful, dutiful, right-guided, following the truth." He mentioned the *hadith*.

We said: As for what al-'Abbas said to 'Ali, they are the words of a father to a son. That is possible at the very beginning. It is used by way of forgiveness and it is used between the old and young, so how is it with fathers and sons when the forgiven one is close to him? As for what 'Umar said about them believing Abu Bakr to be unjust, treacherous and perfidious, that is a report about the disagreement in an incident of judgments. He had this opinion regarding it and those men had another opinion regarding it. Abu Bakr and 'Umar gave judgment by what they thought was correct. Al-'Abbas and 'Ali did not hold that opinion. However, when judgment was given, they submitted to their judgment as one submits to the judgment of the Qadi although disagreeing with it. As for the one against whom judgment is given, he thinks that it is an error, but he remains silent and submits to it.

If it is said: that was the beginning of the business when the matter was not clear since the judgment in it was done by *ijtihad*. Later, the judgment led to Fatima and al-'Abbas being denied the inheritance by the words of the Prophet ﷺ, "We do not leave inheritance. What we leave is *sadaqa*." The wives of the Prophet ﷺ and his ten Companions knew it and testified to it. Therefore what you have said is not true.

We say that it is possible that that took place at the beginning of the business when the matter was not yet clear. They thought that you do not act by the single report when it contradicts the Qur'an, the principles, and the judgments known at the time unless the matter is confirmed. When it was confirmed, they submitted and obeyed, the evidence for which we already gave from the sound *hadith* and so on. So look into it. This is not a text in the question because his words, "We do not leave inheritance. What we leave is *sadaqa*" can mean that "our inheritance is not valid and we do not desire it since it is not my property and I am not involved in anything of this world such that it could be transferred from me to someone else." It is possible that "We do not leave inheritance" is one judgment and his words, "what we leave is *sadaqa*" is another specific judgment, which says that he paid the *sadaqa* which came to him from the share that Allah allowed him from that which was a special privilege for him in the booty for which the Muslims did not move their horses or camels, and also his share with the Muslims in what they took as booty by force. It is possible that "*sadaqa*" is adverbial qualifying the verb "leave" refers to the situation of what a person leaves when he dies. This is what the companions of Abu Hanifa indicated. It is weak and we will clarify that in its proper place. However, the course of the dispute will come to you in this question as well as the object of *ijtihad*. That is not by any text from the Prophet ﷺ. Therefore it is possible that both correctness and error can exist in the *mujtahid*. Allah knows best.

Defamation

of al-Hasan and Mu'awiya, al-Husayn and Yazid

Then 'Ali was killed. The Rafidites said that the caliphate was entrusted to al-Hasan and then al-Hasan surrendered it to Mu'awiya. Therefore he was called "the one who blackened the faces of the believers."

One of the elements of the creed of the Rafidites, indeed the first element of their belief was their belief that al-Hasan, his father and his brother were infallible as were nine of his brother's descendents. From this infallibility of theirs – and al-Hasan is at the front of it after his father – it follows that they do not err. All that comes from them is the truth, and the truth is not contradicted. The most important thing that al-Hasan ibn 'Ali did was to offer allegiance to Mu'awiya. Therefore they are obliged to enter into this allegiance and believe that it is the truth because it was done by someone considered to be infallible. However, we see that they rejected and opposed their infallible Imam in it. This must arise from one of two reasons: either they are lying when they claim infallibility for their twelve Imams and so their *deen* is demolished in its foundation, because belief in infallibility is their foundation and their only foundation, or they believe that al-Hasan was indeed infallible and that his offering allegiance to Mu'awiya came from the action of someone who is infallible. However, they attacked their *deen* and opposed the one whose opinion is infallible and opposed that with which he wanted to meet Allah. They advised each other to attack the *deen* generation after generation, class after class, so they persist in opposing the infallible Imam out of wilfulness, obstinacy, arrogance and disbelief. We do not know which of the two reasons was the most responsible for taking them into the abyss of destruction. There is no third reason.

Those of them who said that al-Hasan was the one who "blackened the faces of the believers" only have what they said applied as meaning "blackened the faces of those who believed in idols." As for those who believe in the prophethood of al-Hasan's grandfather ﷺ they thought that his making peace with Mu'awiya and offering him allegiance was one of the signs of prophethood because it carried out what the Prophet ﷺ had spoken about regarding his grandson, the master of the youths of the Garden. He said that Allah would use him to make peace between two large groups of Muslims, as will be made clear. All those who rejoiced in this prophecy and this peace consider al-Hasan to be the one "who brightened the faces of the believers."

One group of Rafidites declared that he was a deviant and another group that he was an unbeliever for that reason.

Defence

Qadi Abu Bakr said: As for the statement of the Rafidites about it being entrusted to al-Hasan, that is false. It was not entrusted to anyone.

Imam Ahmad ibn Hanbal related in his *Musnad*[347] from Waki' from al-A'mash from Salim ibn Abi al-Ja'd from 'Abdullah ibn Sabi' who said that he heard 'Ali say (and he mentioned that he would be killed) that they said, "Appoint someone over us." He said, "No, but I leave you what the Messenger of Allah ﷺ left you." They said, "What will you say to your Lord when you come to him?" He replied that he would say, "O Allah, you left me among them as long as seemed good to You. Then you took me to You

Al-Hasan and Mu'awiya, al-Husayn and Yazid

while You are still among them. If You wish, You will put them right. If You wish, You will corrupt them."

Ibn Hanbal related the like of it[348] from Aswad ibn 'Amir from al-A'mash from Salama ibn Kuhayl from 'Abdullah ibn Sabgh. Both traditions have *sahih isnad*s. Hafidh Ibn Kathir narrated in *al-Bidaya wa an-Nihaya*[349] from Imam al-Bayhaqi from the *hadith* of Husayn ibn 'Abd ar-Rahman from Imam ash-Sha'bi from Abu Wa'il, the brother of Ibn Salama al-Asadi, one of the masters of the Followers, that 'Ali was asked, "Will you not appoint someone over us?" He said, "The Messenger of Allah ﷺ did not appoint so should I appoint? But if Allah desires good for the people, He will unite them under the best of them after me, as He united them under the best of them after the Prophet. ﷺ" This *hadith* has an excellent *isnad*. Ibn Kathir also transmitted[350] from al-Bayhaqi the *hadith* of Habib ibn Abi Thabit al-Khalil al-Kufi from Tha'laba ibn Yazid al-Hamdani (who was one of the Shi'ites of Kufa and an-Nasa'i considered him to be reliable) that he said to 'Ali, "Will you not appoint someone?" He said, "No, I will leave you as the Messenger of Allah ﷺ left you." Look at the *Greater Sunan* of al-Bayhaqi.[351]

However, allegiance was offered to al-Hasan. He was worthier than Mu'awiya and many other people. He went out for the same thing that his father had gone out for – to call the attacking group to surrender to the truth and to enter into obedience. Mediation resulted in him abandoning authority in order to protect the community and avoid shedding their blood.

The story of the mediation between al-Hasan and Mu'awiya and their making peace is related by Imam al-Bukhari in the Book of Peace of the *Sahih*[352] from Imam al-Hasan al-Basri. He said, "By Allah, al-Hasan ibn 'Ali sent regiments like mountains against Mu'awiya." 'Amr ibn al-'As said, "I see regiments that will not be turned back until you kill their fellows." Mu'awiya (and by Allah, he was the better of the two men) said to him,

"'Amr! If these men kill these men, and these kill these, who will I have to be in charge of the affairs of the people? Who will I have for their women? Who will I have for their property?" He sent for two men of Quraysh from the Banu 'Abd Shams – 'Abd ar-Rahman ibn Samura and 'Abdullah ibn 'Amir ibn Kurayz – and he said, "Go to this man (i.e. to al-Hasan ibn 'Ali) and give him what he wants and tell him what pleases him and ask him (i.e. what you think has the best interests). You have full authorisation." They came to him and went in to see him. They spoke to him and questioned him. Al-Hasan ibn 'Ali told them, "We the Banu 'Abd al-Muttalib have been injured by this property and the blood of the community has been wasted (i.e. they must have satisfaction for their blood by a lot of blood-wit)." They said, "He offers you such-and-such, and asks and requests you." He said, "Who do I have as surety for this?" They said, "You have us for it." He did not ask them for anything but they said, "You have us for it." So he made peace with him

It confirmed the words that the Prophet of Fighting (*malhama*) uttered on the minbar, "This son of mine is a master. Perhaps Allah will use him to make peace between two large groups of Muslims."

> Al-Bukhari related with the previous *hadith* from al-Hasan al-Basri that he heard it from Abu Bakr and that Abu Bakr saw the Prophet ﷺ while he was on the minbar with al-Hasan ibn 'Ali at his side. He said that. Al-Bukhari also related it in the Virtues of al-Hasan and al-Husayn from the Book of Virtues of the Companions in his *Sahih*.[353] Look at *al-Bidaya wa an-Nihaya*[354] and Ibn 'Asakir.[355]

The promise was carried out. The allegiance offered to Mu'awiya was valid. That realised the hope of the Prophet ﷺ. Mu'awiya was a caliph. He was not a king.

If it is said that it is related from Sufayna that the Prophet ﷺ said, "The caliphate is thirty years. Then it will become a kingdom." When we count from the rule of Abu Bakr until the time when al-Hasan surrendered, that was thirty years, no more and no less, not even by a single day," we say:

> Take what you think and leave something you heard,
> When the full moon rises you can do without Saturn.

This *hadith* regarding al-Hasan...

> i.e. the *hadith*, "This son of mine is a master" which al-Bukhari related from al-Hasan al-Basri from Abu Bakra.

...and the good news for him and praise of him is due to his bringing about peace and surrendering authority to Mu'awiya.

> i.e. the Contract of the Allegiance given by al-Hasan to Mu'awiya. It took place in a place called Maskan at the rive, Dujayl, in Rabi' al-Awwal, 41 AH. That year was called the Year of the Community ('Am al-Jama'a) since the Muslims gathered together after having been separated and they then devoted themselves to external wars, conquests and the spread of the call of Islam after the murderers of 'Uthman had kept the swords of the Muslims from this task for about five years. The Muslims were able to record glories in it whose like no one has been capable of in five centuries. Allah has a wisdom in everything.

This is a *hadith* which is not sound.

> i.e. the *hadith* of Sufayna.
> Because the one who transmitted it from Sufayna was Sa'id ibn Juhman. They disagreed about him. Some of them said that there is no harm in him and others thought that he was reliable. Imam Abu Hatim said about him, "A shaykh who is not used as a proof." His *isnad* has Hashraj ibn Nabata al-Wasiti in it. An-Nasa'i said that he is not strong.
> 'Abdullah ibn Ahmad ibn Hanbal related this report from Suwayd at-

Tahan. Ibn Hajar said in the *Taqrib at-Tadhhib* that he is "soft in *hadith.*" This threadbare *hadith* is opposed by the sound clear explicit *hadith* in the Book of the Amirate in *Sahih Muslim*[356] from Jabir ibn Samura. He said, "I came with my father to the Prophet ﷺ and I heard him say, 'This business will not be finished until twelve caliphs have passed among you.'" He said, "Then he spoke some words which I could not hear. I asked my father, 'What did he say?' He replied, 'All of them are from Quraysh.'" Look at it in the Book of the Judgments from *Sahih Bukhari*,[357] in the *Fath al-Bari*,[358] in the *Sunan* of Abu Dawud,[359] the *Jami'* of at-Tirmidhi,[360] and in the *Musnad* of Imam Ibn Hanbal[361] from the *hadith* of ash-Sha'bi from Masruq ibn al-Adja' al-Hamdani, the model Imam. He said, "We were sitting with 'Abdullah ibn Mas'ud while he was reciting the Qur'an to us. A man said to him, 'Abu 'Abd ar-Rahman, did you ask the Messenger of Allah ﷺ how many caliphs would rule this community?' 'Abdullah ibn Mas'ud said, 'No one has asked me this question since the time I came to Iraq until now.' Then he said, 'Yes, we asked the Messenger of Allah ﷺ and he said, "Twelve like the number of the Chiefs of the tribe of Israel."'" The *hadith* is in the *Collection of az-Zawa'id*,[362] in the *Musnad* of Ibn Hanbal,[363] and in the *Musnad* of Abu Dawud at-Tayyalisi.[364]

If it had been sound, it would contradict this peace which they agreed on. So one must refer to that peace.

> Refer to the contract that al-Hasan gave Mu'awiya. They agreed on it. The good news from the Prophet ﷺ accorded it his praise and pleasure. Ibn Taymiyya said in the *Minhaj as-Sunna*,[365] "This *hadith* makes it clear that making peace between two groups is praiseworthy and that Allah and His Messenger love that. What al-Hasan did in that was one of the greatest virtues and excellent qualities for which the Prophet ﷺ praised him. If fighting had been obligatory or recommended, the Prophet ﷺ would not have praised him for not doing something which is obligatory or recommended, etc."

Al-Hasan and Mu'awiya, al-Husayn and Yazid

If it is said, "Was there not any Companion more entitled to rule than Mu'awiya?"

We say, "Many."

> Like Sa'd ibn Abi Waqqas, the conquering fighter, one of the ten who were promised, 'Abdullah ibn 'Umar ibn al-Khattab, the scholar of the Companions who was firm in the footsteps of the Chosen One ﷺ in great and small things, and other men of this class and those who were near to it. After the Battle of Siffin, they left the business of the Imamate to the arbiters – Abu Musa and 'Amr, who were to look into it. When they saw that all of the community had united around Mu'awiya, they offered him allegiance after they had withdrawn from the civil strife after 'Uthman's death. Look at the *Fath al-Bari*.[366] Mu'awiya himself recognised people's worth. In *al-Bidaya wa an-Nihaya*,[367] it has come from Ibn Durayd from Abu Hatim from al-'Utbi that Mu'awiya said, "O people! I am not the best of you. Those who are better than me include 'Abdullah ibn 'Umar, 'Abdullah ibn 'Amr and other excellent men. But it may be that I am the one who will be the most useful in ruling for you and the most harmful of you to your enemy and the one to give you the most abundance." Ibn Sa'd related it from Muhammad ibn Mus'ab from Abu Bakr ibn Abi Maryam from Thabit, the client of Mu'awiya, who heard Mu'awiya say that."

However, Mu'awiya did have certain qualities. They were that 'Umar had united all of Syria under him and singled him out for that, ...

> Under his leadership and by his good management, it became the strongest force in Islam. It was at the forefront of the armies of *jihad* and victorious conquest, calling to Allah with its qualities, behaviour, the wisdom of its leaders, and the sincerity of their Islam.

...when he saw his good conduct,...

> The *hadith* of al-Layth ibn Sa'd, the Imam of the people of Egypt,

was already given with his firm *isnad* up to Sa'd ibn Abi Waqqas, the conqueror of Iraq and Iran and the one who destroyed Khosrau's state, that after 'Uthman, he did not see anyone who judged by the truth more than Mu'awiya. There is the *hadith* of 'Abd ar-Razzaq as-Sa'ani with his *isnad* to the sage of the community, Ibn 'Abbas, that he did not see a man more suited to rule than Mu'awiya." There are the words of Ibn Taymiyya,[368] "The behaviour of Mu'awiya with the people was the best behaviour of any ruler. His people loved him." The words of the Prophet ﷺ in *Sahih Muslim*[369] were confirmed, "The best of your Imams is the one you love and who loves you, who gives to you and you to him." At-Tabari[370] had the variant of Mujalid from ash-Sha'bi that Qubaysa ibn Jabir al-Asadi said, "Shall I tell you whom I accompanied? I accompanied 'Umar ibn al-Khattab and I did not see a man with more *fiqh* or better study than him. Then I accompanied Talha ibn 'Ubaydullah and I did not see a man who gave more generously without being asked than him. Then I kept the company of Mu'awiya and I did not see a man who was a better comrade nor whose secret was more like his outward than him."

…his undertaking to guard the territory and barricading the ports,…

His *himma* and great concern for that was such that he issued a threat to the Byzantine ruler while he himself was in the midst of the fight with 'Ali at Siffin. He heard that the Byzantine Emperor was drawing near the border with a large army. He wrote to him saying, "By Allah, if you do not stop and return to your lands, my nephew and I will make peace and come against you, and oust you from all your lands and will make the land which was wide narrow for you." The Byzantine emperor was afraid and withdrew.[371]

…putting the army in order, attacking the enemy,…

Both on land and at sea. The banners of Islam went in all directions

Al-Hasan and Mu'awiya, al-Husayn and Yazid

in the hands of his exemplary army. They carried the might which Allah desired for His *deen*, the message of the Messenger and those who believed in it. Egypt was conquered and entered into Islam and into the Arab sphere by the action of 'Amr ibn al-'As alone. The foundations of the Islamic fleet and their first naval conquest came from Mu'awiya's action alone. The one occupied with the history of the Arabs and Islam must learn that Mu'awiya naturally possessed the character of mastery and leadership and knew how to rule. Ibn Kathir transmitted in the *History*[372] from Hushaym from al-'Awwam ibn Hawshab from Jabala ibn Suhaym that 'Abdullah ibn 'Amr ibn al-'As said, "I have not seen anyone with more mastery than Mu'awiya." Jabala ibn Suhaym said that he asked, "And 'Umar?" He replied, "'Umar was better than him, but Mu'awiya had more mastery than him." They related words like these regarding Mu'awiya from 'Abdullah ibn 'Umar ibn al-Khattab. The statement of 'Abdullah ibn 'Abbas was already given: "I have not seen a man more suited to rule than Mu'awiya."

...and managing the people.

Ibn Taymiyya said in the *Minhaj as-Sunna*,[373] "None of the kings of Islam was better than Mu'awiya nor were the people in the time of any of the kings better than they were in the time of Mu'awiya when his days are compared to any of the kings after him. When his days are compared to those of Abu Bakr and 'Umar, then there is some rivalry. Abu Bakr al-Athram related (and Ibn Batta related it by way of him) that Muhammad ibn 'Umar ibn Hanbal related from Muhammad ibn Marwan from Yunus from Qatada who said, "If you had come upon work like that of Mu'awiya, most of you would have said, 'This is the Mahdi.'"

Ibn Batta related with his firm *isnad* from two directions from al-A'mash that Mujahid said, "If you had met Mu'awiya, you would have said that this is the Mahdi." Al-Atham said, "Muhammad ibn Hawash related to us from Abu Hurayra the scribe who said, "We were with al-A'mash and we mentioned 'Umar ibn 'Abd al-'Aziz and his justice. Al-A'mash said, 'How would it have been if you had met Mu'awiya?' They asked, 'In his forbearance?' He said, 'No, by Allah, in his justice!'"

'Abdullah ibn Hanbal said, "Abu Sa'id al-Ashajj informed us from Abu Usama ath-Thaqafi from Abu Ishaq as-Subay'i that he mentioned Mu'awiya and said, 'If you had met him (or you had been alive in his time), you would have said that he is the Mahdi.'"

This testimony from these notable Imams for the Amir al-Mu'minin Mu'awiya is an echo of Allah's answer to the supplication of His Prophet ﷺ when he said, "O Allah, make him guiding and guided and guide by means of him." It is one of the signs of prophethood.

There is testimony in a *hadith* in the *Sahih* that he possessed *fiqh*.

In the Book of the Virtues of the Companions from *Sahih Bukhari*,[374] there is the *hadith* of Ibn Abi Mulayka that Ibn 'Abbas was asked, "Do you have something on the Amir al-Mu'minin Mu'awiya, for he performed the *witr* with a single [*rak'a*]?" He said, "He is a *faqih*." In the Book of the Virtues from the *Jami'* of at-Tirmidhi[375] there is the *hadith* of 'Abd ar-Rahman ibn Abi 'Umayra al-Muzani from the Prophet ﷺ that he said to Mu'awiya, "O Allah, make him guiding and guided, and guide by means of him." At-Tabarani related it by way of Sa'id ibn 'Abd al-'Aziz at-Tanukhi (and he was for the people of Syria as Imam Malik was for the people of Madina) from Rabi'a ibn Yazid al-Ayyadi, one of the notable Imams, from 'Abd ar-Rahman ibn Abi 'Umayra that the Prophet ﷺ said to Mu'awiya, "O Allah, teach him the Book and reckoning, and guard him from the punishment." Al-Bukhari related it in his *History*. He said, "Abu Mushir (and he mentioned with the *isnad* narrated "from so-and-so from so-and-so") told me the *hadith*. The *hadith* of 'Umayr ibn Sa'd al-Ansari was already given regarding his being removed from the governorship of Hums

Al-Hasan and Mu'awiya, al-Husayn and Yazid

during 'Umar's caliphate and the fact that he appointed Mu'awiya, and he testified that the Prophet had made a supplication that Allah would guide by means of him. Imam Ibn Hanbal related it from the *hadith* of 'Irbad ibn Sariya as-Sulami. Ibn Jarir related it from the *hadith* of Ibn Mahdi. Asad ibn Musa, Bishr ibn as-Sari and 'Abdullah ibn Salih related it from Mu'awiya ibn Salih with his *isnad*. He added in the version of Bishr ibn as-Sari, "And make him enter the Garden." Ibn 'Adi and others related it from Ibn 'Abbas. Muhammad ibn Sa'd related it with its *isnad* to Maslama ibn Mukhallad, one of the conquerors and governors of Egypt.

Those Companions who transmitted this Prophetic supplication for Mu'awiya are too many to be counted. Look at *al-Bidaya wa an-Nihaya*.[376] Look at the biography of Mu'awiya under the letter *mim* in the *History of Damascus* by Ibn 'Asakir. Whoever does not confirm this *hadith*, rejects all that is confirmed in the *Sunna* of the Shari'a of Islam. Among those biased people who hate Mu'awiya and curse him, there are some who claim that they are related to the Prophet ﷺ. So do you see them harbouring hatred for their ancestor ﷺ since he was pleased with Mu'awiya and asked for help for him and made supplication for him? "If you are not ashamed, do whatever you like." Hafidh Ibn 'Asakir narrated from Imam Abu Zur'ah ar-Razi that a man said to him, "I hate Mu'awiya!" He said to him, "Why?" He said, "Because he fought 'Ali." Abu Zur'ah said to him, "Woe to you! The Lord of Mu'awiya is merciful, and Mu'awiya's dispute was noble, so why would you try to intervene between ['Ali and Mu'awiya]? may Allah be pleased with both of them."

There is testimony to the fact that he was the caliph in the *hadith* of Umm Haram when she related that some people from the Prophet's community would ride the middle of the Green Sea like kings on thrones. That happened while he was caliph.

Umm Haram bint Milham was a woman companion of the Ansar from the people of Quba'. When the Prophet ﷺ went to Quba', he rested in her house. She was the maternal aunt of his servant, Anas ibn Malik. Al-Bukhari related in the Book of Jihad from his *Sahih*[377] and Muslim in the Book of the Emirate[378] from Anas that the Prophet ﷺ slept in her house at midday. Then he woke up laughing because he had dreamt of his community raiding in the way of Allah, riding the middle of the sea, i.e. its deepest part, like kings on thrones. Then he put his head down and slept. He awoke and he had seen the same dream. Umm Haram said to him, "Ask Allah to put me among them." He told her, "You are among the first." Ibn Kathir[379] said that he meant the army of Mu'awiya when it raided Cyprus and conquered it in 27 AH in the days of 'Uthman ibn 'Affan (under the leadership of Mu'awiya after he had established the first Islamic fleet in history). Umm Haram was with him. She was accompanying her husband 'Ubada ibn as-Samit, and Abu ad-Darda', Abu Dharr and other Companions were with them. Umm Haram died in the way of Allah and her grave is still in Cyprus. Ibn Kathir said, "The general of the second army[380] was Yazid ibn Mu'awiya in the raid on Constantinople. He said, 'This was one of the greatest signs of prophethood.'"

There can be different degrees in rule: caliphate and then kingdom. The rule of the caliphate belonged to four, and the rule of the kingdom began with Mu'awiya.

> Caliphate, kingdom and amirate are technical designations which are used in history according to their actual usage. Consideration is always given to the behaviour and action of man. Mu'awiya was appointed over Syria for the rightly-guided caliphs for a period of twenty years. Then he took on the task of all Islam for another twenty years in the greatest Islamic land, after al-Hasan ibn 'Ali offered him allegiance. In both cases, he safeguarded justice and was good to people of all classes. He honoured the people of talent and helped them to advance their talents. He had

great forbearance towards the rashness of ignorant men and so he cured their imperfections through that means. He made the judgments of the Muhammadan Shari'a binding on everyone with resolution, compassion, diligence and belief. He led them in their prayers and directed them in their gatherings and institutions. He led them in their wars.

In *Minhaj as-Sunna*[381] there is the statement which the lofty Companion, Abu ad-Darda', made to the people of Syria, "I have not seen anyone with a prayer more like the prayer of the Messenger of Allah ﷺ than this Imam of yours," meaning Mu'awiya. You already saw what al-A'mash said to those who mentioned 'Umar ibn 'Abd al-'Aziz and his justice, "How would it have been if you had met Mu'awiya?" They said, "In his forbearance?" He said, "No, by Allah, in his justice!"

His integrity in the path of Islam was so great that men like Qatada, Mujahid and Abu Ishaq as-Subay'i, all notable Imams, would say about him, "Mu'awiya was the Mahdi."[382] Anyone who studies the biography of Mu'awiya in his judgment will see that his government in Syria was an exemplary government in justice, mellowness, and indulgence. When he was given a choice between the good and the better, he chose the better over the good. If this is how he acted for forty years, then the Muslim Amir was suited to be caliph over the Muslims. They were content with him because of that and envied him, so he was the caliph. Whoever calls him a king cannot contradict the fact he was the most merciful and correct of all the kings of Islam.

We were studying in Constantinople in an assembly for students when they were arguing about the subject of the life of Mu'awiya and his caliphate. This was during the caliphate of Sultan 'Abd al-Hamid. My friend, the happy martyr, 'Abd al-Karim Qasim al-Khalid who was a Shi'ite, stood up and said, "You call our Sultan a caliph. I, your brother Shi'ite, announce that Yazid ibn Mu'awiya, was more entitled to the caliphate by his good behaviour and that he was truer in acting by the Muhammadan Shari'a than our caliph. What then, was his father Mu'awiya, like?" However Mu'awiya used to say about himself, according to what Khaythama related from Harun ibn Ma'ruf from Damra ibn Shawdhab, "I am the first of the kings and the last of the caliphs." We already gave the *hadith* of Ma'mar from az-Zuhri, "Mu'awiya acted for two years as 'Umar had acted and did not alter it." Here we indicated the difference in the environment and its effect on the organisation of government. Mu'awiya himself used the excuse to 'Umar when 'Umar came to Syria and Mu'awiya met him with a great retinue. 'Umar disliked that. Mu'awiya excused himself saying, "We are in a land where there are many enemy spies. We must display the might of power in which the might of Islam and its people lie. We will frighten them by that." 'Abd ar-Rahman ibn 'Awf said, "How excellent is what resulted from what you did in it, Amir al-Mu'minin!" 'Umar said, "Because of that, we endured what we endured of it."[383]

Mu'awiya tried to act according to what 'Umar had done for two years. That was the highest example in his house. Yazid himself spoke about keeping to it. Ibn Abi ad-Dunya related from Abu Kurayb Muhammad ibn al-'Ala' al-Hamdani from Rishdin al-Misri from 'Amr ibn al-Harith al-Ansari al-Misri from Bukayr ibn al-Ashajj al-Makzumi al-Madini, then al-Misri, that Mu'awiya said to Yazid, "How do you think that you should act if you are appointed?" He said, "By Allah, father, I would act in it as 'Umar ibn al-Khattab acted." Mu'awiya said, "Glory be to Allah, my son! By Allah, I have striven in the path of 'Uthman as far as I was able. How can you have the behaviour of 'Umar then?"[384]

Those who do not know the life of Mu'awiya think it strange when you tell them, "He was one of the people of *zuhd* and purity and one of the men of right action." Ibn Hanbal related in the Book of *Zuhd*[385] from Abu Shibl Muhammad ibn Harun from Hasan ibn Waqi' from Damra ibn Rabi'a al-Qurayshi from 'Ali ibn Abi Hamala from his father who said, "I saw Mu'awiya speaking to the people on the minbar of Damascus, wearing a patched garment." Ibn Kathir quoted[386] from Yunus ibn Maysar al-Himyari az-Zahid (who was one of the shaykhs of Imam al-Awza'i), "I saw Mu'awiya riding in the Damascus market with his servant behind him. He was wearing a shirt with a patched pocket, going along in the Damascus markets. Mu'awiya's generals and his great Companions used to ask for his clothes to seek blessing from them. When any of them came to Madina wearing one of these garments, they recognised it and went to great extremes to obtain it." Ad-Daraqutni related from Muhammad ibn Yahya ibn Ghassan that the famous general, ad-Dahhak ibn Qays al-Fihri came to Madina. He went to the mosque and prayed between the grave and the minbar wearing a patched cloak which he had gotten from Mu'awiya's general. Abu al-Hasan al-Barrad saw it and recognised that it was Mu'awiya's cloak. He haggled with him over it, thinking that he was a common bedouin until Abu al-Hasan al-Barrad was ready to pay him 300 dinars for it. Ad-Dahhak took him to the house of Huwaytib ibn 'Abd al-'Uzza and put on another cloak and gave him the cloak for nothing. He told him, "It is ugly for a man to sell his cloak. Take it and wear it." Abu al-Hasan took it and sold it. It the first money he ever got.[387]

We quoted these examples so that people will know that the true form of Mu'awiya is different from the false form which his enemies created. Whoever wishes to call Mu'awiya the caliph and the Amir al-Mu'minin, knows that Sulayman ibn Mahram al-A'mash, one of the notable Imams and *huffaz* who was called the *Mushaf* because of his truthfulness, used to prefer Mu'awiya to 'Umar ibn 'Abd al-'Aziz, even in his justice. Whoever fails to have a full look at Mu'awiya and wants to withhold this title from him, should know that Mu'awiya went to Allah with his justice, forbearance, *jihad* and correct action. While he was in this world, he did not care whether he was called a king or a caliph. In the Next world, he has greater *zuhd* because of the *zuhd* which he had this world.

Allah said about Dawud who was better than Mu'awiya,...

Dawud in his Prophethood, as the Muslims know in their *deen*, was better than Mu'awiya. As for the David of the Jews that people know from their Torah, Mu'awiya was better than him. Part of the wretchedness of the Jews is that they do not recognise the excellence which the Qur'an and Islam has over them by declaring the prophets of the tribe of Israel free of how they used to tarnish them in their books.

..."*Allah gave him kingship and wisdom.*"[388] So He made Prophethood a kingdom. Do not pay any attention to *hadiths* that have weak *isnads* and weak texts.

Indicating the *hadith* of Sufayna, which was already discussed.

If the situation demanded that certain things be investigated – and Allah knows best – most people had different opinions. However, allegiance was given to Mu'awiya in the way in which Allah desired in the form which the Messenger of Allah ﷺ promised, praising it and pleased with it, hoping that there would be peace through al-Hasan as he had said, "This son of mine is a master. Perhaps Allah will use him to make peace between two large groups of Muslims."

Scholars have spoken about someone less excellent being the ruler when some better than him is present. The question does not reach the point to which the common people take it. We have made that clear in its place.

...in his other books. This is one of the fortifying questions contained in Islamic *fiqh*. Its rules are based on the texts, the *sunan* and the roots of the Shari'a on which the *deen* is based in the area of finding the best interests, repelling corruption and determining the measure of necessities. Qadi Abu al-Hasan al-Mawardi did not mention any opponent in *al-Ahkam as-Sultaniyya*[389] to the permissibility of the Imam being one less excellent – except for al-Jahiz. What harm comes to the Imams of the *deen* if al-Jahiz opposes them? Were the Abbasids whom al-Jahiz knew, since he ingratiated himself with them while they were alive, better than their contemporaries? As for most of the *fuqaha'* and the *mutakallimun*, they said that it is permissible for someone less excellent to be the Imam as long as he does not lack the preconditions for the imamate. Similarly, when undertaking judgment, it is permitted to model oneself on the less excellent even if someone better exists, because greater excellence is preferable, but is not considered to be a precondition of worthiness. We refer the reader to the book, *The Imamate and Rivalry* by Abu Muhammad ibn Hazm.[390]

If it is said that he killed Hujr ibn 'Adi, although he was one of the Companions who is famous for his goodness, and put fetters on him as a prisoner because of what Ziyad said, and 'A'isha sent to him about Hujr and she found that he had already killed him, we answer, "We all know about the execution of Hujr, but we disagree. Some say that he was killed wrongly and some say that he killed him with a right."

> Hujr ibn 'Adi al-Kindi, al-Bukhari and others considered him to be one of the Tabi'un. Others considered him to have been a Companion. He was one of the party of 'Ali at the Battle of the Camel and Siffin. Ibn Sirin relates that Ziyad, the Amir of Kufa, gave a very long *khutba*. Hujr ibn 'Adi called out, "The prayer!" Ziyad continued to speak and Hujr and some others threw pebbles at him. Ziyad wrote to Mu'awiya to complain about Hujr's aggression against his Amir in the house of Allah. He considered that to be part of corruption in the earth. Mu'awiya wrote to Ziyad telling him to send Hujr to him. When he was brought to Mu'awiya, he ordered that he be executed. Those who think that Mu'awiya acted justly say, "There is no government in this world which could give a lesser punishment than that against the one who throws pebbles at his Amir, while he is giving the *khutba* on the minbar of the General Mosque, and who rushes

into the calamity of partisanship and bias." Those who oppose them mention Hujr's virtues and say that Mu'awiya should not have abandoned his quality of forbearance and patience towards his opponents. Others answered them saying that Mu'awiya had forbearance and patience when he himself was attacked. When the community was attacked in the person of their ruler while he was on the minbar of the mosque, Mu'awiya could not tolerate that, especially in a place like Kufa which had produced the greatest number of seditious people who had attacked 'Uthman for showing tolerance like this. They had inflicted losses on the community in their lives, their reputations, their peace of mind and the position of their *jihad*. These were expensive sacrifices that could only have been safely ignored if the awe of the state had been maintained through disciplining the small party of the people of rashness and levity at the appropriate time. Just as 'A'isha wished that Mu'awiya would include Hujr in his patience, 'Abdullah ibn 'Umar wanted the same thing. It is true that Mu'awiya possessed some of the forbearance and qualities of 'Uthman. However, in the political situation, he saw how 'Uthman had ended and what had come about through the persistence of those who were audacious towards him.

If it is said that his execution was basically unjust unless something has been proven against him that demanded his execution, we say that the fundamental position is that the ruler executes by a right. Whoever claims that it is done unjustly must have proof. If it was pure injustice, then there was no house in which Mu'awiya would not have been cursed. Written on the doors of the mosques in the City of Peace, the abode of the caliphate of the Abbasids – in spite of what existed (of ill feeling) between them and the Umayyads that was not hidden from people – was: "The best people after the Messenger of Allah ﷺ were Abu Bakr, then 'Umar, then 'Uthman, then 'Ali, then Mu'awiya, the uncle of the believers, may Allah be pleased with them."

Al-Hasan and Mu'awiya, al-Husayn and Yazid

The author lived in Baghdad at the time of the Abbasids as we already mentioned in his biography. He knew its mosques with his own eyes. Mu'awiya is the uncle of the believers because he is the brother of the Umm al-Mu'minin Ramla bint Abi Sufyan, famous by her *kunya*, Umm Habiba.

However, according to what is said, Hujr saw some objectionable things in Ziyad.

Ziyad was one of the governors of 'Ali when he was Caliph. Hujr ibn 'Adi was one of Ziyad's friends and helpers. He did not object to anything that he did. When Ziyad became one of Mu'awiya's governors, then he began to object to him and dashed into the calamity of partisanship and bias. Hujr had acted in the same way towards whoever had been appointed over Kufa for Mu'awiya before Ziyad. Mu'awiya had an excuse for thinking that Hujr was one of those who strove to work corruption in the earth.

He threw pebbles at him and acted without restraint. He wanted to lead the people to sedition. Therefore Mu'awiya considered him to be one of those who strove for corruption in the land.

'A'isha spoke to Mu'awiya about the business of Hujr when he went on the *hajj*. Mu'awiya told her, "Leave me and Hujr alone until we meet before Allah." Therefore you, company of Muslims, should leave them alone until they meet before Allah with their just firm Companion the Mustafa. How can you go on where you have no awareness? Why do you not listen?

It has been said that Mu'awiya intrigued against al-Hasan in order to poison him. We say that this is impossible for two reasons. One of them is that he did not fear any force from al-Hasan once he had surrendered authority. The second is that it was an unknown business which only Allah knows. How can you state it without proof and accuse any of His creatures in a distant time when we do not have any sound transmission about it? Moreover, this occurred in the presence of people of sects who were in a state of sedition and rebellion. Each of them ascribed what he should not ascribe to his companion. Only the pure is accepted in it. Only the resolute just man is listened to in it.

> In *Minhaj as-Sunna*[391] Ibn Taymiyya spoke about the Shi'a claim that Mu'awiya had poisoned al-Hasan, "That was not established by any clear proof in the Shari'a nor by a considered statement nor by a clear transmission. This is part of what it is not possible to know. That is a statement not based on knowledge." He further said, "In our time, we saw people among the Turks and others who said that he was poisoned and died of poison. People disagree about that and even the place where he died and the fortress in which he died. You will find each of them relating something different from what the other people related." After Ibn Taymiyya mentioned that al-Hasan died in Madina while Mu'awiya was in Syria, he mentioned the possibilities of the report, assuming it to be sound. One of them is that al-Hasan was divorced and did not remain with a wife.

If it is said that Mu'awiya gave the caliphate to Yazid, but Yazid was not worthy...

> If the gauge of worthiness for that is that he achieve the level of Abu Bakr and 'Umar in all their qualities, this will never be achieved in the history of Islam nor was it by 'Umar ibn 'Abd al-'Aziz. Even if we desire the impossible and suppose that it is conceivable that another Abu Bakr and another 'Umar will appear, we will never have a milieu like the milieu which Allah granted to Abu Bakr and 'Umar.
>
> If the gauge of worthiness is uprightness in behaviour and establishing respect for the Shari'a, acting by its judgments, being just to people, looking after their best interests, *jihad* against their enemies, expanding

the horizons of its call, and compassion for their individuals and groups, the reports on Yazid can be closely examined and people know his actual state as he was while he was alive. That will make it clear that he was not less than many of those whose praises have been sung by history and who have been abundantly praised.

...and something took place between him and 'Abdullah ibn 'Umar, Ibn az-Zubayr and al-Husayn which historians have related from Wahb ibn Jarir ibn Hazim from his father and from others. He said that when Mu'awiya decided that allegiance should be given to his son Yazid, he went on *hajj*. He came to Makka with about a thousand men. When they neared Madina, Ibn 'Umar, Ibn az-Zubayr and 'Abd ar-Rahman ibn Abi Bakr went out. When Mu'awiya arrived in Madina, he mounted the minbar and praised and glorified Allah. Then he mentioned his son Yazid and said, "Who is more entitled to rule than him?"

> There were many young men of Quraysh who were contemporary with Yazid who thought that they could undertake to rule by certain strong points that they knew that they possessed. Indeed, even Sa'id ibn 'Uthman ibn 'Affan and those who were less than Sa'id, wanted to undertake to rule after Mu'awiya. The principle of a council to elect the caliph was much better than the principle of rule by contract. However, Mu'awiya knew that opening the door of consultation to choose someone to succeed him would cause carnage in the Muslim community and that blood would not cease to flow until all the worthy men of Quraysh capable of taking charge of the affairs of this community were annihilated. Mu'awiya was too judicious not to have seen the virtues those young men of Quraysh possessed. When any of them was distinguished by something over his peers, there was another one among them who was distinguished by something else. However although Yazid shared with others in their accomplishments, he was distinguished over them by the greatest thing

that the state requires – military force to support him in the caliphate so that it would be a force for Islam, as it supports it when Shaytan sowed sedition among those who compete for this throne so that the situation becomes what every Muslim dislikes. If Yazid had only had his uncles of Quda'a and their allies in the tribes of the Yemen, he would have had that which would not allow the farsighted one to remove him out of the reckoning if he reflects on these matters. Add to this what Ibn Khaldun stated when he spoke about al-Husayn's journey to Iraq to attack Yazid when he said in the section, "The Rule of Contract" in the preface of his *History*, "As for effective military power, he erred in it, may Allah have mercy on him, because the partisanship ('*asabiyya*) of Mudar belonged to Quraysh and the partisanship of Quraysh belonged to 'Abd Manaf and the partisanship of 'Abd Manaf belonged to the Banu Umayya. Quraysh and all people remembered that they had that. They did not deny it. That was forgotten at the beginning of Islam when people were distracted by astonishment at the miracles of the revelation. When the business of Prophethood and the awesome miracles stopped, then judgment returned to normal after a short time. Partisanship became as it had been and went to those who had had it before. Mudar began to obey the Banu Umayya rather than others.

Then he left and went to Makka and finished his *tawaf*. He went into his house and sent for Ibn 'Umar. He said the *shahada* and said, "Ibn 'Umar, you used to tell me that you would not like to spend a dark night without a ruler over you. I am cautioning you lest you sow dissension among the Muslims and lest you try to corrupt what they have." When he was silent, Ibn 'Umar spoke after praising and glorifying Allah. Then he said, "There were caliphs before you who had sons. Your sons are not better than them. They did not want for their sons what you want for your son. They gave the choice to the Muslims since the Muslims know best. You caution me lest I sow dissension among the Muslims when I have not yet done so. I am a Muslim man. When the Muslims agree on a business, I am with them." Then Ibn 'Umar left.

> This report contradicts what is in the Book of Raids of *Sahih Bukhari*[392] from Ibn 'Umar that his sister, Umm al-Mu'minin Hafsa, advised him to go quickly and offer his allegiance. She said, "The truth is that they are waiting for you. I fear that there will be divisions if you hold back from them."

He sent for 'Abd ar-Rahman ibn Abi Bakr. He said the *shahada* and began to speak. He interrupted Mu'awiya and said, "By Allah, you want us to give you authority to give power to your son for Allah. By Allah, we will not do it. By Allah, you will refer this business to a council of Muslims or the business will be taken back to the beginning for you."

> i.e. it will bring about civil strife against you in its worst states. It should be noted that the people who spoke thus against Mu'awiya did not attack the adequacy and worthiness of Yazid because it was the last thing that they doubted in him during Mu'awiya's lifetime.

Then he leapt up. Mu'awiya said, "O Allah, restrain him as You like!" Then he said, "O man, take it easy! Do not look to the people of Syria. I fear that they will beat me to you until it is reported this evening that you have offered allegiance. After that, you can do whatever seems best to you in your affair."

Then he sent to Ibn az-Zubayr and said, "Ibn az-Zubayr, you are a wily fox, which whenever it leaves one hole goes to another. You have relied on these two men and I have blown up their noses." Ibn az-Zubayr said, "If you are tired of being ruler, then leave it and bring your son and we will offer him allegiance. If I give allegiance to your son along with you, then which of you two do you think we should listen to and which should we obey? The allegiance cannot ever be for both of you."

> Ibn az-Zubayr was too intelligent to miss the fact that the homage to Yazid was after Mu'awiya and that both homages were not effective while Mu'awiya was still alive. Those who fabricated these reports and ascribed them to Wahb ibn Jarir have made a disgraceful lie.

Then he got up. Mu'awiya went out and ascended the minbar. He said, "We found that people's conversations contain faults. They claim that Ibn 'Umar, Ibn az-Zubayr and Ibn Abi Bakr did not offer allegiance to Yazid. They heard and obeyed and offered allegiance."

The people of Syria said, "No, by Allah, we will not be content until they offer allegiance before witnesses. If not, we will cut off their heads!"

Mu'awiya said, "Shame! Glory be to Allah! How quick people are to treat Quraysh badly! I will not hear these words from anyone after today!" Then he descended.

People said, "They offered allegiance." They said, "We did not offer allegiance." People said, "You offered allegiance."

Wahb related by another means: "Mu'awiya spoke and mentioned Ibn 'Umar, saying, 'By Allah, he will give allegiance or I will kill him.'" 'Abdullah ibn 'Abdullah ibn 'Umar went to his father and he travelled to Makka in three days and told him about this.

> This report from Wahb ibn Jarir shows that Mu'awiya made his speech while he was in Madina, coming from Damascus, before he had reached Makka and that Ibn 'Umar was in Makka on that day. His son rode to meet him in Makka and tell him about the speech. In the report before this, which is also related by Wahb ibn Jarir ibn Hazim, he clearly states that Ibn 'Umar was in Madina when Mu'awiya arrived from Damascus and that he was one of the notable men who went out to meet him. The two reports contradict and refute each other, although they are from the same man. I do not know where the author got them. At-Tabari did not relate them even though he was concerned with the reports of Wahb

ibn Jarir because he was reliable. Wahb died in 206 AH and his father died in 180 AH after he had become confused. Between these two and these reports are other transmitters, and between the two of them and at-Tabari and other historians there are many transmitters. I believe that these reports are not sound since they contradict each other. If we knew their transmitters up to Wahb and after Wahb we would know where the lie came from.

Ibn 'Umar wept. This news reached 'Abdullah ibn Safwan who went to Ibn 'Umar and said, 'Did that man say that?' He said, 'Yes.' He asked, 'What do you want? Do you want to fight him?' He said, 'Ibn Safwan, patience is better than that,' Ibn Safwan said, 'By Allah, if he means to do that, I will fight him!'

'Abdullah ibn Safwan, the grandson of Umayya ibn Khalaf al-Jumahi. He was killed with Ibn az-Zubayr in 73.

Mu'awiya came to Makka and alighted where he would spend the night. 'Abdullah ibn Safwan went to him and said, 'Do you claim that you will kill Ibn 'Umar if he does not offer allegiance to your son?' Mu'awiya replied, 'Me kill Ibn 'Umar!? By Allah, I will not kill him!'"

Wahb related by a third path...

This report is not in at-Tabari. I think that it was fabricated in the book from which the two previous reports came.

...that he said, "When Mu'awiya left Batn Marr on his way to Makka, he said to the master of the guard, 'Do not let anyone go with me until I give him a mount.' He went out alone until he was in the middle of al-Arrak. Al-Husayn ibn 'Ali met him. He stopped and said, 'Welcome, son of the daughter of the Messenger of Allah ﷺ and master of the young Muslim men! A beast for Abu 'Abdullah to ride!' He was brought a mule and he used it. Then 'Abd ar-Rahman ibn Abi Bakr came.

We know from the first report from Wahb himself that 'Abd ar-Rahman ibn Abi Bakr was in Madina. He was one of those who met Mu'awiya when he came there from Damascus. What took him to Makka so that he was among those who met Mu'awiya when he arrived there? Truly those who fabricated lies against Mu'awiya are dullards who do not act well, even in the craft of lying.

He said, 'Welcome, son of the shaykh of the Quraysh and its master and the son of the Siddiq of this community. A beast for Abu Muhammad to ride!' He was brought a mule and rode it. Then Ibn 'Umar came. He said, 'Welcome to the companion of the Messenger of Allah and the son of the Faruq and the master of the Muslims!' He was brought an animal and rode it. Then Ibn az-Zubayr came and Mu'awiya said, 'Welcome to the son of the disciple of the Messenger of Allah and the son of the aunt of the Messenger of Allah ﷺ.' He called for a beast for him and he rode it. Then he began to go between them. He did not let any of them leave before he entered Makka. He was the first to enter and the last to leave. Every morning they received gifts and honour. He did not mention anything to them about Yazid until he had finished his *hajj* rites and loaded his baggage and was about to leave for Syria and his mounts were ready to go.

Then the people turned to one another and said, "People, do not be deceived! By Allah, he has not done this for your love and your honour. He only did it to gain what he wanted. Prepare an answer for him." Then they went to al-Husayn and said, "Abu 'Abdullah, you!" He said, "When the shaykh and master of Quraysh is among you? He is more entitled to speak." They said to 'Abd ar-Rahman ibn Abi Bakr, "You, Abu Muhammad!" He said, "I am not the one to speak when you have the companion of the Messenger of Allah ﷺ and the son of the master of the Muslims among you (i.e. Ibn 'Umar)." They said to Ibn 'Umar, " You!" He said, "I am not your man. Rather let Ibn az-Zubayr speak.

He will be enough for you." Then they said, "You, Ibn az-Zubayr." He said, "Yes, if you give me your contracts and your pledges that you will not oppose me, then I will deal with this man for you." They said, "You have that." Permission was sought and Mu'awiya gave them permission and they came in.

Mu'awiya spoke and praised and glorified Allah. Then he said, "You know how I behave with you, my connection to your kin, my indulgence to you and my enduring what you do. Yazid, the son of the Amir al-Mu'minin, is your brother and the son of your uncle, and people have the best opinion of you. I want you to give him the name of 'caliph', and you are those who depose and appoint, oblige and allot, and he enters into none of that in any way against you."

The people were silent. He said, "Won't you answer me?" The people remained silent. He said, "Won't you answer me?" They remained silent. He turned to Ibn az-Zubayr and said, "Come, Ibn az-Zubayr, by my life, speak for the people!" He said, "Yes, Amir al-Mu'minin. I will give you a choice between three qualities. Whichever you take, the choice is yours." He said, "Your father belongs to Allah, present them!" He said, "If you wish, you can do what the Messenger of Allah ﷺ did. If you wish, you can do what Abu Bakr did. He was the best of the community after the Messenger of Allah. If you like, you can do what 'Umar did, He was the best of the community after Abu Bakr." Mu'awiya said, "Your father belongs to Allah, what did they do?" He said, "The Messenger of Allah ﷺ died and did not appoint anyone. The Muslims were content with Abu Bakr. If you like, you can leave the business of this community until Allah decides what He decides in it. The Muslims will choose for themselves." Mu'awiya said, "Well, you do not have anyone among you today like Abu Bakr. I do not think that you will be safe from dispute." Ibn az-Zubayr said, "Then do as Abu Bakr did. He delegated a man from the far part of Quraysh who was not one of the children of his father and appointed him." Mu'awiya replied, "Your father belongs to Allah! And the third?" He said, "Do what 'Umar did. He made the business a council with six men of Quraysh none of whom was his relative." Mu'awiya asked, "Is there anything else?" He said, "No." Mu'awiya said, "And you all?" They said, "We as well." Mu'awiya said, "No, I wanted to meet you. Whoever is warned is excused. If any of you rises against me and rejects me in front of witnesses, I will take him for that. I have a statement. If I am truthful, I have my truthfulness. If I lie, the lie is mine. I swear by Allah, if any of you refutes me, his words will not come back to him before I have his head." Then he called for the Captain of the Guard and said, "Put two guards over each of these men. If any man begins to repeat something, true or false, then strike him with your swords."

> The author quoted these disgraceful reports that were falsified in order to expose them. Compare them with the hadith of al-Bukhari regarding the sound position of Ibn 'Umar in this event so that the people would know that the truth lay in one valley and those lying transmitters lay in another valley.

Then he left and they left with him. He went up the minbar and praised and glorified Allah. Then he said, "These are the party of the masters of the Muslims and the best of them. We do not act independently in anything without them nor do we decide any business without consulting them. They are satisfied and have given allegiance to Yazid, the son of the Amir al-Mu'minin, after him. They gave allegiance in the name of Allah. They have shaken his hand." Then he mounted his camel and departed.

The people met and said, "You made claims and you pretended. Then you were satisfied and presented yourselves and acted." They said, "By Allah, we did not do it." They said, "So what kept you from answering the man when he lied?" Then the people of Madina and the people in general offered their allegiance. Then Mu'awiya returned to Syria.

Qadi Abu Bakr said: We do not lack knowledge nor are we ignorant. We have not been moved by ignorant rashness nor do we have the rash zeal of the *jahiliyya* for the right. We do not bear any malice towards any of the Companions of Muhammad ﷺ. We say, *"Our Lord, forgive us and our brothers who preceded us in faith and do not put any rancour in our hearts towards those who believe. Our Lord, You are All-Gentle, Most-Merciful."*[393] However, we say that Mu'awiya abandoned the best course of action, to make it a matter for a council and not single out kin for it, let alone a son, and to follow what 'Abdullah ibn az-Zubayr suggested of non-action or action.

> Mu'awiya knew Ibn az-Zubayr better than Ibn az-Zubayr himself. Al-Baladhuri related in the *Ansab al-Ashraf*[394] from al-Mada'ini from Maslama ibn 'Alqama from Khalif from Abu Qilaba that Mu'awiya said to Ibn az-Zubayr, "Avarice and eagerness will make you enter a narrow entrance. I wish that I could be with you at that time so that I could rescue you." When Ibn az-Zubayr was near death, he said, "This is what Mu'awiya said to me. I wish that he had been alive."

He turned to appoint his son. He then contracted for him to receive allegiance and the people gave him allegiance and those who held back did so.

> He turned from the best course when he feared that seditions and slaughter would result if he were to make it a council.

Allegiance was effected in the Shari'a because it can be effected by one, or it is said that it can be effected by two people.

If it is said, "Only for the one possessing the preconditions of the Imamate," we say, "Age is not one of its preconditions nor is it confirmed that Yazid lacked any of them."

If it said, "Justice and knowledge are among its preconditions, but Yazid was neither just nor was he a man of knowledge," we said, "How do we know that he lacked either knowledge or justice?"

> As for justice, Muhammad ibn 'Ali ibn Abi Talib testified in his favour when he was arguing with Ibn Muti' when he rebelled against Yazid in Madina. He said about Yazid, "I do not see in him what you mentioned. I was present with him and I stayed with him. I saw him persevere in the prayer and I saw him eager for good. He asked about *fiqh* and kept to the *Sunna*."[395] As for knowledge, it was not necessary for someone like him in this sort of place. He was in a position of approval and beyond approval in it. Al-Mada'ini related that Ibn 'Abbas came to Mu'awiya after the death of al-Hasan ibn 'Ali. Yazid went to Ibn 'Abbas and sat with him to console him. When Yazid left him, Ibn 'Abbas said, "When the Banu Harb depart, then the scholars of the people will depart."[396]

"Does he lack them by the statement of the three excellent men who indicated that he should not do it? They alluded to a fault of judgment. They wanted it to be a council."

If it is said that there were men who were worthier than him and men with greater knowledge – there were some hundred men, even a thousand, then we say that the subject of the less excellent being Imam is a disputed topic among scholars as scholars have mentioned that topic as we already mentioned it.

Al-Bukhari completed the chapter and pursued an excellent course. In his *Sahih*, he related what will render all of this invalid. That is that Mu'awiya gave the *khutba* while Ibn 'Umar was present during that *khutba*. According to what al-Bukhari related[397] from 'Ikrima ibn Khalid, Ibn 'Umar said, "I came to Hafsa and her locks were dripping.

> i.e. her locks were dripping with water.

"I said, 'The matter is as you have seen. None of the matter has been given to me.' She said, 'True. They are waiting for you. I fear that there will be divisions if you hold back.'" She did not leave him alone until he went.

When the people parted, Mu'awiya spoke. He said, "Whoever wants to speak regarding this matter should raise his head. We are better for him than himself and his father." Habib ibn Maslama said, ...

> Habib ibn Maslama al-Fihri of Makka. He was a child at the death of the Prophet ﷺ. Then he went to Syria for *jihad*. He was famous for his might and he is considered to be the conqueror of Armenia. It is said that he was the general of the relief army which went from Syria to rescue 'Uthman from the hands of those who had attacked him. The news reached him that 'Uthman had been martyred while he was still on his way. Therefore he went back.

..."Will you not answer him?" 'Abdullah said, "I got up wanting to say, 'The one who fought you and your father for Islam has more right to this command,' but I was afraid that I would say something which would split up the community and cause bloodshed and other things would be interpreted about me, and I remembered what Allah has prepared in the Garden." Habib said, "You remembered and were protected."

Al-Bukhari related[398] that when the people of Madina threw off their allegiance to Yazid ibn Mu'awiya, Ibn 'Umar gathered together his servants and children. He said, "I heard the Messenger of Allah ﷺ say, 'A banner will be set up for every traitor on the Day of Rising.' We gave allegiance to this man according to the allegiance of Allah and His Messenger.

> This luminous report, which al-Bukhari relates in his *Sahih,* shames those who fabricated a lie and attributed it to Wahb ibn Jarir in those

contradictory reports, that Ibn 'Umar and others did not offer allegiance to Yazid and that Mu'awiya appointed people to cut off their heads if they refuted him when he lied against them, saying that they had given allegiance to his son. Now it is clear that he did not lie against them. Ibn 'Umar announced in the most critical situation – during the rebellion of the people of Madina against Yazid at the instigation of Ibn az-Zubayr and his agent, Ibn Muti' – that the allegiance by the Shari'a to their Imam is based on the allegiance to Allah and His Messenger and that that was on his neck as it was on their necks and that it was one of the greatest sorts of treachery that the community should give homage to an Imam and then fight him.

Ibn 'Umar did not limit himself to that in that rebellion against Yazid. Muslim related in the Book of the Amirate of his *Sahih*[399] that Ibn 'Umar came to Ibn Muti', Ibn az-Zubayr's agent and the instigator of this rebellion. Ibn Muti' said, "Give a cushion to Abu 'Abd ar-Rahman." Ibn 'Umar said, "I have not come to sit with you. I have come to you to relate a *hadith* to you which I heard from the Messenger of Allah ﷺ: 'Whoever takes a hand back from obedience will meet Allah with no proof on the Day of Rising. Whoever dies without homage on his neck has died a death of ignorance.'" Muhammad ibn 'Ali ibn Abi Talib (known as Ibn al-Hanafiyya) had a similar position with the agent of the rebellion, Ibn Muti', which the reader will see in another place when the life of Yazid is discussed.

"I do not know of any greater perfidy than to give allegiance to a man according to the allegiance of Allah and His Messenger and then to start fighting him. I do not know of any of you who would dismiss him nor give homage in this matter except that there will be a sharp sword between him and me."

Company of Muslims, look at what al-Bukhari related in the *Sahih* and at what we have already mentioned from him in the variant where 'Abdullah ibn 'Umar did not offer allegiance and Mu'awiya lied and said that he had given allegiance and then told his guards to cut off his head if he refuted him. But he said in al-Bukhari's version, "We gave [Yazid] allegiance according to the allegiance of Allah and the Messenger." There is conflict between the two of them. You yourselves can take the most likely stance in the pursuit of soundness and sincerity between the Companions and the Tabi'un. When you have not seen them – may Allah protect you from their sedition – do not be one of those who advanced against their blood with their tongues and who lick the rest of the blood on the earth like dogs after the horseman has removed his lance. The dog only gets the remainder of the blood that has fallen on the earth.

A reliable reputable person related from 'Abd ar-Rahman ibn Mahdi from Sufyan from Muhammad al-Munkadir. He said, "When he gave allegiance to Yazid, Ibn 'Umar said, 'If he is good, we are pleased. If he is evil, we will be patient.'"

It is confirmed that Humayd ibn 'Abd ar-Rahman said, "We went to one of the Companions of the Messenger of Allah ﷺ when Yazid ibn Mu'awiya was appointed. He said, 'You say that Yazid ibn Mu'awiya is not the best of the Community of Muhammad nor does he have the most *fiqh* among them nor he is the greatest of them in honour. I also say that. However, by Allah, I prefer that the Community of Muhammad be united rather than split. Do you think that a door which the Community of Muhammad may enter and which is wide enough for them will be unable to cope with a single man if he enters it?' They said, 'No.' He said, 'Do you think that if the Community of Muhammad said that no man among them should shed the blood of his brother nor take any of his property, would that be enough for them?' They said, 'Yes.' He said, 'That is what I say to you.' Then he said, 'The Messenger of Allah ﷺ said, 'Only good will come to you from modesty.'"

All of these sound reports show you that Ibn 'Umar submitted in the business of Yazid and that he gave allegiance to him, gave him a pledge, and held to what the people held to. He entered into what the Muslims entered. He forbade himself and those connected to him after that from leaving or breaking that contract.

It is clear to you that whoever says that Mu'awiya lied when he said, "Ibn 'Umar gave allegiance" when he did not give allegiance and that Ibn 'Umar and his companions were asked and said, "We did not give allegiance" has lied. In his *riwaya*, al-Bukhari supported Mu'awiya's words on the minbar, "'Umar gave allegiance' since Ibn 'Umar himself offered that...

> When Madina rebelled against Yazid.

...as well as affirming his submission to him. He kept that position.

Do you know which of the two groups is more entitled to be truthful? Is it the group among whom al-Bukhari spoke or that or another?

The Companion to whom Humayd ibn 'Abd ar-Rahman alluded was Ibn 'Umar. Allah knows best. If it was another, then there were two great men who agree on this statement. It supports what we established for you: the rule of the less excellent person is valid even if there is someone who is better than him when he assumes power. To remove him or to seek the more excellent man is to allow what is not permitted. That splits unity and divides the community.

If it is said that Yazid drank wine, we said, "That is only admissible by two witnesses. Who testified to that against him?"

> Mu'awiya, from his great love for Yazid because of his cleverness and perfect gifts, preferred that he grow up far from him in the midst of the natural state (*fitra*), the roughness and gallantry of desert life so that he would have the necessary qualities for the task which awaited those like him. He sent him to the tents of the desert with his uncles of Quda'a so that he would have the view of his mother, Maysun bint Bajdal when she said:

Al-Hasan and Mu'awiya, al-Husayn and Yazid

I prefer a house in which the winds tremble to a lofty castle.

Yazid spent his youth and the beginning of his manhood in that environment. It was not long after his father went to Allah's mercy that he undertook the position which Allah desired for him. When the things were opened up for Ibn az-Zubayr at Mu'awiya's death, his agents began to spread lies against Yazid in the Hijaz and they ascribed to Yazid what they were not allowed to ascribe.

Ibn Kathir states in *al-Bidaya wa an-Nihaya*[400] that 'Abdullah ibn Muti' (Ibn az-Zubayr's agent) went with his companions in Madina to Muhammad ibn 'Ali ibn Abi Talib, known as Ibn al-Hanafiyya. They wanted to depose Yazid, but he rejected them. Ibn Muti' said, "Yazid drinks wine and does not pray. He has exceeded the judgment of the Book." He answered them, "I have not seen him do what you mentioned, and I have been with him and I have stayed with him. I saw him constant in the prayer and desiring good. He asked about *fiqh* and kept to the *sunna*." They said, "That was pretence for you on his part." He said, "What could he fear or hope for from me so that he should display humility towards me? Would he tell you what you said about him drinking wine? If he let you know, then you must be his partners. If he did not tell you, it is not permitted for you to testify to what you do not know." They said, "He is caught in our opinion, even if we did not see him." Ibn al-Hanafiyya told them, "Allah refuses to accept that from the people of testimony. Allah says, *'except those who have testified to the truth with knowledge.'*[401] I do not have anything to do with you." They retorted, "Perhaps you dislike for anyone except yourself to assume power. We will entrust our business to you." He said, "Fighting is not permitted in what you want to do, either by a follower or one who is followed." They said, "You fought along with your father." He said, "Bring me the like of that for which my father fought and I will fight for the like of what he fought." They said, "Command your sons, Abu al-Qasim and al-Qasim, to fight with us." Ibn al-Hanafiyya replied, "If I would command them, I would myself fight." They went on, "Then take a position with us in which you encourage people to fight." He said, "Glory be to Allah! Command people to do what I would not do and that with which I am not happy? Then I would not be giving good counsel for Allah to His slaves!" They said, "Then we will force you." He said, "Then I would command people to have fearful awareness of Allah. The creatures do not like the wrath of the Creator." Then he went to Makka.

* Yazid was away from Syria when his father died. When he reached Damascus, the allegiance to him was renewed. Then the people gathered in the Mosque and he addressed them in a manner which indicates his *taqwa*. After praising and glorifying Allah, he said: "People! Mu'awiya was one of Allah's slaves whom He blessed and then took to Him. He was better than his successor and less than the one before him!

"I do not vindicate him before Allah for He has the best knowledge of him. If He pardons him, it is by His mercy. If he punishes Him, it is for his wrong action. I have taken command after him and I do not share in the request nor apologise for being put forward. If Allah wills something, it is.

"Mu'awiya let you make expeditions on the sea but I will not carry any of the Muslims on the sea. Mu'awiya let you spend the winter in Greek territory and I will not let anyone do so. Mu'awiya gave you gifts in thirds and I gather them all for you."

The transmitter said that the people left him and did not prefer anyone to him.[402]

Rather a just man testified to his integrity. Yahya ibn Bukayr related from al-Layth ibn Sa'd, "The Amir al-Mu'minin Yazid died on such-and-such a day." Al-Layth called him the "Amir al-Mu'minin" even after their kingdom had departed and their state had come to an end. If he had not been a "ruler" in his opinion, he would only have said, "Yazid died."

If it is said that even if Yazid had nothing more than killing al-Husayn ibn 'Ali, that would have been enough. We said: Alas for afflictions once, and alas for the calamity of al-Husayn a thousand times! His urine spilled on the breast of the Prophet ﷺ and his blood was shed in the dust and not spared. O Allah! O Muslims! The best model of what is related about him is that Yazid wrote al-Walid ibn 'Uqba to inform him about Mu'awiya's death and he ordered him to take the allegiance for him from the people of Madina even though it had already taken place. He summoned Marwan and told him about that. He told al-Walid, "Send to al-Husayn ibn 'Ali and Ibn az-Zubayr. See if they offer allegiance. If they do not, then we will smite their necks." He said, "Glory be to Allah! You will kill al-Husayn ibn 'Ali and Ibn az-Zubayr!" He said, "That is what I told you."

He sent for them. Ibn az-Zubayr came to him and he informed him about Mu'awiya's death and asked him for allegiance. Ibn az-Zubayr said, "Someone like me offer allegiance here! I will mount the minbar and give allegiance openly with the people!" Marwan leapt up and said, "Strike his neck! He is full of sedition and evil!" Ibn az-Zubayr said, "You there, Ibn az-Zurqa' (son of a blue-black woman)!" They cursed one another. Al-Walid said to both of them, "Leave me." He sent to al-Husayn and did not say a word to him about anything. They both left him. Then al-Walid set surveillance on the two of them. When morning was near, they left in haste for Makka and reached it. Ibn az-Zubayr said to him, "What keeps you from your party and the party of your father? By Allah, if I had the like of them, I would go to them." This is not sound.

The historians mention that the people of Kufa's letters reached al-Husayn....

> The first to write him from the shaykhs of the party, according to what their historian Lut ibn Yahya related, were: Salman ibn Surad, al-Musayyab ibn Najba, Rifa'a ibn Shaddad and Habib ibn Muzahir. They sent their

letter with 'Abdullah ibn Sab' al-Hamdani and 'Abdullah ibn Wali. They came to al-Husayn in Makka on the tenth of Ramadan, 60 AH. Two days later, Qays ibn Mushir as-Saydawi, 'Abd ar-Rahman ibn 'Abdullah ibn al-Kadn al-Arhaji and 'Umara as-Saluli went to him with 53 pages. After another two days, Hani' ibn Hani' as-Subay'i and Sa'id ibn 'Abdullah al-Hanafi hurried to him.[403] They are based on saying that they would not gather with their governor, an-Nu'man ibn Bashir, on Friday. They called al-Husayn to them. When he came they said that they would expel their Amir and send him to Syria. In one of their letters, they said, "The fruits will grow. If you so wish, you will find a large army for yourself." Al-Husayn sent them his nephew, Muslim ibn 'Aqil ibn Abi Talib, to see if they were loyal and united so then he could come to them later. Muslim ibn 'Aqil got lost on the way and those with him died of thirst. He wrote to al-Husayn asking him to relieve him of this task. He answered him, "I fear that cowardice has led you to ask to be excused." Muslim continued until he reached Kufa and 12,000 of them offered allegiance to him for al-Husayn.

The governor of Kufa, an-Nu'man ibn Bashir, became aware of their movements. He spoke to them and forbade sedition and division. He told them, "I only fight the one who fights me. I will not punish by supposition or suspicion. If you show me your page and you break your pledge of allegiance, then I will strike you with my sword as long as it is firm in my hand." Yazid knew that an-Nu'man was a forbearing man of piety not suited to opposing a movement like this. He therefore wrote to 'Ubaydullah ibn Ziyad, his governor over Basra, ordering him to take charge of Kufa as well. Then he commanded him to go to Kufa and seek out Ibn 'Aqil as one seeks out the pearl until it is found. He should bind him and kill or exile him. 'Ubaydullah left his brother in charge of Basra and went to Kufa. He met its leaders and put a stop to the immediate crisis. It was not long before Muslim ibn 'Aqil saw that the opinion of the 12,000 who had given

Al-Hasan and Mu'awiya, al-Husayn and Yazid

him allegiance was as thin as air. He found himself alone and cast out. He was taken and executed.

Al-Husayn had received the letters of Muslim ibn 'Aqil before that, saying that 12,000 had offered allegiance to him until death. At the end of the Hajj 'Id, he set out for Kufa. Ibn az-Zubayr was the only one to encourage him to go out because he knew that the people of the Hijaz would not offer allegiance to him as long as al-Husayn was with them. Al-Husayn was the heaviest of people for Ibn az-Zubayr.[404] Those who feared for al-Husayn in this ill-omened departure included all his friends, kin, those who gave good counsel and those who look after the *Sunna* of Islam in this sort of position. All of those men forbade him to go and warned him of its consequences. At the head of them was his brother, Muhammad ibn al-Hanafiyya,[405] his nephew and sage of the community, 'Abdullah ibn al-'Abbas[406] and his nephew, 'Abdullah ibn Ja'far ibn Abi Talib.[407]

'Abdullah ibn Ja'far asked the governor of Yazid over Makka, 'Amr ibn Sa'id ibn al-'As, to write a letter of safe conduct for al-Husayn to give him hopes of kindness and connection and to ask him to return. The Governor of Makka granted all of that. He told him, "Write whatever you wish and I will seal the letter." He wrote to the governor and sealed it. He sent it to al-Husayn with his brother, Yahya ibn Sa'id ibn al-'As. 'Abdullah ibn Ja'far, went with Yahya. They tried to dissuade al-Husayn from travelling. He refused. (The Governor's letter is in the *History* of at-Tabari[408]). No one was better than these counsellors in intellect, knowledge, position and sincerity. 'Abdullah ibn Muti', Ibn az-Zubayr's agent, was one of those advisers who had intellect and sincerity.[409] 'Umar ibn 'Abd ar-Rahman ibn al-Harith ibn Hisham al-Makhzumi held this opinion[410] and al-Harith ibn Khalid ibn al-'As ibn Hisham did not neglect to give him counsel.[411] Even al-Farazdaq the poet told him, "The hearts of the people are with you, but the swords of the people are with the Banu Umayya."[412]

None of this effort turned al-Husayn from this journey which was ill-omened for him, for Islam, and for the Muslim community until this very day and will be until the Last Day. All of this was due to the crime of his party who encouraged him to rashness, delusion and the desire for civil strife, division and evil. Then they disappointed him through their cowardice, baseness, treachery and perfidy. Their heirs were not content with what their ancestors did. They devoted themselves to clouding history and changing the truth and reversing things.

...and [al-Husayn] sent Muslim ibn 'Aqil, his nephew, to them to take allegiance from them and to investigate his followers. Ibn 'Abbas forbade him and told him that they had disappointed his father and his brother. Ibn az-Zubayr advised him to rise in insurrection, so he went out.

When he reached Kufa, Muslim ibn 'Aqil had already been slain and all of those who had invited him surrendered him. It is enough for you in this to have the warning of the one who is warned. He persisted and continued out of anger for the *deen* and to establish the truth. But he ﷺ did not accept the good advice of the man with the most knowledge among the people of his time – Ibn 'Abbas. He also turned away from the opinion of the shaykh of the Companions, Ibn 'Umar.

> He preferred well-being and encouraged the unity of the Muslims and their devotion to the spread of the call and conquest.

We will mention below some of the pleas the great Companions and thinkers made to al-Husayn that he should return:

At-Tabari related that when al-Husayn left Makka, the messengers of the governor, 'Umar ibn Sa'id under the leadership of his brother, Yahya, opposed him. They said to him, "Where are you going?" They asked him to turn aside but he refused, and the two parties pushed each other and hit each other with whips. Al-Husayn held back from them and then proceeded on his way. Yahya called to him, "Husayn! Fear Allah and do not leave the group (*jama'a*) and divide this community!"

Al-Hasan and Mu'awiya, al-Husayn and Yazid

Al-Husayn replied with the *ayat*, "*I have my actions and you have your actions. You are not responsible for what I do and I am not responsible for what you do.*"[413] Then he went on.

At-Tabari also related that when 'Abdullah ibn Ja'far heard that al-Husayn had left Makka, he sent a letter to him with his sons, 'Awn and Muhammad. In the letter he said, "I ask you by Allah, when you see my letter, do not go out. I fear that the direction that you are taking contains your destruction and the extermination of the people of your house. If you are killed today, the light of the earth will be extinguished. You are the banner of the guided and the man of the believers. Do not hasten to go out. I am coming after this letter."

Ibn Kathir related[414] that 'Abdullah ibn 'Umar heard that al-Husayn had set out for Iraq when he was in Makka. He joined al-Husayn three nights later and said to him, "Where are you going?" He replied, "Iraq. These are their letters and their allegiance" Ibn 'Umar said to him, "Let me tell you a *hadith*. Jibril came to the Prophet ﷺ and let him choose between this world and the Next. He chose the Next World and did not want this world. You are a bit of the Messenger of Allah ﷺ and no one will ever take that from you. Allah will only avert it from you to the one who is better than you." Al-Husayn refused to go back, so he embraced him and said, "I bid you farewell as a dead man."

It is also related that Abu Sa'id al-Khudri went to al-Husayn and said, "I am giving you good advice and I am fearful for you. I have heard that some people of your party in Kufa have written to you inviting you to go out to them. Do not go! I heard your father say in Kufa, 'By Allah, I am fed up with them and dislike them, and they are fed up with me and dislike me. They are never faithful. Whoever wins them, wins the most unfortunate portion. By Allah, they have neither intention nor resolution in any affair nor any steadfastness with the sword.'"[415]

Ibn Kathir said that Yazid ibn Mu'awiya wrote to 'Abdullah ibn 'Abbas, asking him to restrain al-Husayn. He told him, "I think that some men from the east have come to him and offered him the caliphate. You have information about them and experience of them. If he does that, he has severed firm relationship. You are the eldest of the people of your house and one who is looked up to, so turn him from being a faction." Ibn 'Abbas went to al-Husayn and spoke to him at length. He said, "I ask you by Allah lest you perish tomorrow in a constricted situation. Do not go to Iraq. If you must go, then wait until the Hajj festival is over and you meet people and see what they are about. Then you can make a decision." He refused.[416]

At-Tabari also related that one of the Banu 'Ikrima met him while he was going down into the valley of Qassaba. He asked him, "Where are you going?" and he told him. He said to him, "I ask you by Allah not to go! By Allah, you will only come against the spears and points of swords. If those who were sent to you can spare you the trouble of fighting and pave the way for you, then go to them if that is what you think." Al-Husayn said to him, "'Abdullah! What you think is not hidden from me! But Allah will not let it prevail!" Then he travelled. Al-Husayn continued his journey until he heard about the death of Muslim and the fact that the people had left him.

At-Tabari related that after Muslim ibn 'Aqil was weakened by the stones thrown at him, he surrendered and they took his sword. He said, "This is the beginning of treachery," and wept. 'Amr ibn 'Ubaydullah ibn 'Abbas was near him and said to him, "Whoever seeks the like of what you seek, should not weep when the like of what has happened to you happens to you."

He said to him, "By Allah, I do not weep for myself! Nor do I lament the fact that I will be slain. Rather, I weep for my family who are coming, and I weep for al-Husayn and his family!" Then he went before Muhammad ibn al-Ash'ath and said to him, "'Abdullah! By Allah, you will bring my hopes to naught. Do you have any information which you can send to a man on my tongue which will reach Husayn? I do not think that he and his family should

Al-Hasan and Mu'awiya, al-Husayn and Yazid

come to you. He can tell him that Muslim is a prisoner and will be killed and so he should go back with his family and not be deceived by the people of Kufa. They are your father's companions. I am the one who hopes to part from you only by death or killing. They have denied me and denied you. The liar has no opinion." He promised him that he would do so.

Then he sent someone to tell Husayn about the news of Muslim and his message. He met al-Husayn and told him. Al-Husayn said, "All that is decreed will occur, and we reckon our lives and the corruption of our community to be with Allah." Then he continued on his journey although it was possible to go back.[417]

At-Tabari related[418] that when al-Husayn was certain that Muslim had been killed and certain that the people of Iraq had disappointed him, he said to those who were with him and were not part of his family, and those who had joined him en route, "Our party has disappointed us! Whoever among you wants to depart should depart." Many people dispersed. Only his sons, some of his relatives and some sincere friends remained. The party was not more than a hundred.

Al-Mas'udi relates that 'Ubaydullah ibn Ziyad said to the one who killed al-Husayn, "He was the best of men in his mother and father, and the best of the slaves of Allah. Why did you kill him?" Then he commanded that the man be beheaded.[419]

At-Tabari related Yazid's letter to 'Ubaydullah ibn Ziyad advising him, "Do not overstep in what you do as I hope you will act in a resolute manner and attack firmly and bravely. I have heard that al-Husayn is making for Iraq, so set up watch-posts and armaments. Be on guard against supposition and punish suspicion and only kill the one who fights you!"[420]

Ibn Kathir related that Marwan ibn al-Hakam wrote to 'Ubaydullah ibn Ziyad when al-Husayn set out to Iraq, "Al-Husayn is heading for you. He is the son of Fatima and Fatima was the daughter of the Messenger of Allah ﷺ. By Allah, there is no Muslim I love more than al-Husayn. Beware of stirring yourself up in an uncontrollable manner. The common people will not forget him and he will be remembered until the end of time."

Mu'awiya advised himself, his governors and his son Yazid, to show concern for al-Husayn.

YAZID'S SORRROW OVER THE MARTYRDOM OF AL-HUSAYN AND HOW HE TREATED THE PEOPLE OF HIS HOUSE

It is related that Yazid wept when al-Husayn's head was brought to him. He said to the one who carried it, "I would have been pleased if you had obeyed without killing al-Husayn. May Allah curse Ibn 'Ubaydullah! By Allah, if I had been with him, I would have pardoned him! May Allah have mercy on al-Husayn. By Allah, Husayn, if I had been there, I would not have killed you."

Then he called for 'Ali the Younger, al-Husayn's son, and his wives, and they came to him when the nobles of Syria were with him. He said to 'Ali, "Your father cut off his relations with me and ignored my right. He contended for my authority and Allah has done to him what you saw."

Then he commanded that they be put up in his house and ordered that they have all they needed. 'Ali was at every lunch and supper with him. Then he commanded an-Nu'man ibn Bashir to give them all the provisions they required so they could travel to Madina with some righteous people. When they were about to leave, he called to 'Ali and bade him farewell, saying, "May Allah curse Ibn Marjana! By Allah, if I had been there, I would have offered him any favour he asked and tried to prevent his death as much as possible, even if I had to spend my own children. But Allah decreed what you saw. So write to me and I will give you all you need."

Ibn Qutayba related that when they brought Husayn's head and family to him, Yazid wept until he nearly fainted. The people of Syria wept loudly with him.

Al-Mas'udi related that Ibn Ziyad said to the one who had killed al-Husayn, "He was the best of people in mother and father, and the best of the slaves of Allah, so why did you kill him?" Then he commanded that the killer be beheaded.[421] At-Tabari also mentioned that when Husayn's family came to Ibn Ziyad, he ordered a house for them and sent them provisions and ordered that they be given maintenance and clothes. Then he sent them to Yazid.

Prof. Daruzah[422] said this. He gives the transmissions that are related about the excellent treatment accorded by 'Ubaydullah ibn Ziyad, and then the excellent treatment accorded by Yazid to the young son of al-Husayn, his daughters and wives, and how Yazid was overwhelmed by the fact that he had been killed and wept for him, and how his family, both men and women, did the same. Those transmissions are sounder than the ones which mention harshness and coarseness towards them, especially when there was not a fierce battle which provoked vengeance and reaction which would extend to the women and children. What took place was not what they wanted. Indeed, it was grievous to them and contrary to what they wanted.

Perhaps one of the indications of that is that at-Tabari and Ibn Qutayba both related that good prayers and letters continued to be exchanged between Yazid and 'Ali ibn al-Husayn. This is made clear in that they relate that neither 'Ali nor his relatives participated in the rebellion in Madina. Yazid also told his general to go to his assembly and tell him that he had received his letter and that those vile people had distracted him from replying. The general was to greet him and let him sit beside him and give him Yazid's letter.[423]

Where is this excellent treatment in the lies of the forgers who say that the People of the House were captured and taken by camel without ropes after Husayn's martyrdom? This is a clear lie. It is not lawful for the community of Muhammad to take captives from the Banu Hashim. They fought Husayn out of fear of him and because they thought that they might lose their authority. When he was martyred, that was the end of the business and his family was sent to Madina. However, the Rafidites were ignorant that the end had been reached. There is no doubt that the killing of al-Husayn was one of the greatest wrong actions, and that the one who did it and was pleased about it will have a punishment, but his killing was not more terrible than the killing of his father nor the killing of his sister's husband, 'Umar, and the killing of his aunt's husband, 'Uthman.

It is strange that the hypocrites and factious people among the people of Kufa who invited al-Husayn to take charge are the same people who disappointed him and failed to help him and then became the cause of his death and then went out to weep for him.

The People of the House attack the Shi'a

The author of the *Twelver Gifts* says that the Shi'a scholar of this age, Shaykh Hibat ad-din ash-Sharastani quotes what al-Jahiz related from Khuzayma al-Asadi, "I entered Kufa and happened upon the departure of 'Ali ibn al-Husayn with his family from Karbala' to 'Ubaydullah ibn Ziyad. I saw the women of Kufa standing there mourning, dishevelled. I heard 'Ali ibn al-Husayn say in a faint voice, 'People of Kufa! You weep for us but who except you killed us?' I saw Zaynab bint 'Ali, and by Allah, I did not hear any more eloquent than what she said: 'People of Kufa! People of treachery and disappointment! The grave is not still and friendship did not remain. You are like the woman *who spoils the thread she has spun by unravelling it after it is strong.*[424] You broke oaths after you took them. You are nothing but pomposity and flattery, and the creation of tears and slander of enemies. Evil is what you have advanced for yourselves! The wrath of Allah is upon you, and you will be in the punishment forever. Do you weep? Yes, by Allah, weep! By Allah, you should weep. Weep a lot and laugh little. You have won braggadocio and ignominy. If you were to try to wash it off, you will never do it!"

Was Yazid responsible for the killing of Husayn?

Al-Hasan and Mu'awiya, al-Husayn and Yazid

The historian, Daruzah, also said, "Part of what we used to know was that there was no justification for attributing the killing of al-Husayn to Yazid. He did not command that he be fought against, let alone killed. He only commanded that he be contained and should only be fought if he himself fought. This sort of statement can be validly ascribed to 'Ubaydullah ibn Ziyad. All he commanded was that al-Husayn should be contained and only be fought if he himself fought and that he should be brought to him so that he could place his hand in his or offer allegiance to Yazid, the one who had the *bay'a* in the Shari'a. It is correct to attribute his killing to the commanders of the forces who came between them and al-Husayn and his party. They are liable for what they commanded. Indeed, they have the worst expectations, for Allah will punish them with affliction for fighting him, let alone for killing him. They expended their efforts to give satisfaction by carrying out the judgment of Ibn Ziyad and the allegiance to Yazid. When al-Husayn refused to submit and enter into what the Muslims had entered into and opposed by force, to confront and fight him became the legal position and political direction.[425] The speaker says, "Was it not necessary for Yazid, and consequently for Ibn Ziyad, to accept one of the three just conditions of Husayn which he presented to him? It is that he be allowed to go back as he had come, or to go to Yazid or be sent to the frontiers." One scholar mentioned that these conditions and demands on the part of Husayn did not have a sound basis. At-Tabari related that Sam'an said, "I was with al-Husayn and I left Madina with him for Makka and from Makka for Iraq. I did not leave him until he was killed. There is nothing that he said to people in Madina, Makka, on the route, in Iraq or in the army until they day he was killed that I did not hear. By Allah, he did not give them what people mention nor what they claim about him putting his hand in Yazid's nor going to one of the Muslim frontiers. Instead he said, "Let me go in the wide earth so we can see what the situation among people is like."[426]

This demand on the part of al-Husayn could be not accepted by anyone who had the least amount of policy and reflection out of the fear that al-Husayn would begin to encourage his party in the cities and that would lead to rebellions and sedition.

We think that if 'Ubaydullah ibn Ziyad and his people had besieged al-Husayn and his army and surrounded them with all sorts of concern and solicitude and gave them what they wanted and left the business of a truce for some days hoping that al-Husayn's agitation would abate, that would have been better.

That would have been possible as long as they were few – no more than a hundred, even if they had fought to take their weapons from them by various means. However, the command of Allah was decreed and carried out. *"We belong to Allah and to Him we return."*

We ask Allah to guide those who recall this disaster from one year to another when they only destroy themselves in this world before the Next while they are not aware, especially after the end of the Umayyads.

In conclusion of this dangerous topic, we say as the careful investigative historian 'Izza Daruzah said[427] after transmitting some of what we have mentioned in this research:

"We call Allah to witness, that we did not write this book out of sectarianism or hatred for al-Husayn, may Allah be pleased with him and the People of his House. We testify that we have the greatest respect and love for them because of their noble connection to the Messenger of Allah ﷺ. We are historians who must write about history. We desire clarity, justice and truth because the self must have transmissions with which it feels secure."

We are not the only ones to deal with the results we found in the transmissions. There are many other people who have done that. Indeed, every author free of sectarianism among the Muslims, in all different parties, share with us in this.

Al-Hasan and Mu'awiya, al-Husayn and Yazid

Here we quote two statements regarding that. One of them is by Ibn Taymiyya, and the second is by the historian, Muhammad al-Khudri.

Imam Taymiyya quoted the report about all the numerous instances of advice which al-Husayn was given telling him not to go out and being warned about its consequences. Then he said, "There was no benefit in insurrection for the *deen* or for this world. His insurrection and being killed was part of the corruption that could have been avoided if he had stayed at home. He did not achieve any of the good and avoidance of harm which he had intended. Indeed, it increased the evil when he went out and was killed, and blessings decreased by it and it became a cause for immense evil. Al-Husayn's killing was more likely to occasion seditions."[428]

After mentioning the killing of al-Husayn, Shaykh al-Khudri said, "Generally speaking, al-Husayn made an immense error in going out which brought upon the community the misfortune of division, disagreement and shook the foundations which bind the community – which has continued right up until today.

"Many people who have written on this event only want to kindle fires in the hearts and to increase divisions between people. In the end, a man sought what he was not ready or prepared for, and he failed to obtain what he desired and was killed. His father had been killed before that and none of the writers found his murder quite as horrific. They increased the fire of enmity.

"Al-Husayn opposed Yazid whom people had pledged allegiance to, but he evinced nothing of injustice and tyranny upon his demonstrating his opposition until there was some benefit for the umma in going forth to battle."[429]

He sought the beginning in the end and the straight in the crooked and the greenness of youth in the white hair of old age. He had none around him equal to him, nor did he have any helpers who guarded his right or who expended themselves for him. We wanted to purify the earth of the wine of Yazid,...

> By the claim of those who provoked the sedition and testified to something which they did not know.

...so we shed al-Husayn's blood. A calamity befell us which the happiness of time cannot heal.

All who went against him had some form of justification for doing so, for they only fought him on the basis of what they heard from his grandfather, the overseer of the Messengers, who spoke of how bad the situation would become and warned people against becoming involved in matters of civil strife. There are many statements reported from him in this regard, including his words ﷺ, "There will [come a time when this community will be afflicted by] infighting and civil strife, Anyone who makes to break this community apart when it is united, regardless of who they are, should be struck down with the sword."[430] People went out because of this hadith and others like it. Would that the great one of this umma and the son of its great one, the noble one of this umma and the son of its noble man, al-Husayn, had made do with his house, holdings and camels. Even if the people, including Ibn 'Abbas and Ibn 'Umar, had come asking him to establish the truth, he should have paid them no regard. But that about which the Prophet ﷺ had warned and what he had said with respect to his brother befell him.

> "This son of mine is a master. Perhaps Allah will use him to make peace between two large groups of Muslims."

And given that he had seen the caliphate leave his brother despite him possessing the armies of the earth and the support of the great men of the Muslims, how could he then think that it would be brought back to him by the riffraff of Kufa, especially when the Companions were keeping themselves aloof and telling others to have no part of it?

I do not think that this is anything other than submission to the decree of Allah and sorrow for the grandson of the Messenger of Allah ﷺ for all time. If it had not been for the fact that the shaykhs and notable men of the community recognised that it was a matter which Allah had taken from the People of the House and a state of civil strife that no one should become involved in, they would never have surrendered it.

Ahmad ibn Hanbal, who was ascetic and had a great position in the *deen* and was very scrupulous, still included Yazid ibn Mu'awiya in the Book of *Zuhd* and mentioned what he used to say in his *khutba*, "When one of you falls ill, is treated, and recovers, he should look to the best action he has and cling to it. He should look to the worst thing he has done and abandon it." This indicates his immense position with Ibn Hanbal since he included him among the men of *zuhd* of the Companions and Tabi'un whose words were followed and because of whose admonition one repents. Indeed, he included him in the group of Companions before he mentioned the Tabi'un. Where is this in relation to what the historians say about him and wine and licentiousness? Are they not ashamed? When Allah strips them of virtue and modesty, why do you not desist and hold back, and follow the scholars and fearful ones of the people of excellence of this community, and reject the heretics and impudent men who are affiliated with this religion. *"This is a clear explanation for all mankind, and guidance and admonition for the godfearing."*[31] Praise be to Allah, the Lord of the worlds.

Look at Ibn az-Zubayr after that and what he did when allegiance was given to him in Makka and he had all of the land against him. Look there at Ibn 'Abbas and his intelligence and his concern for the matter itself. Look at Ibn 'Umar and his age and surrendering it to this world and casting it away. If there had been a reason for an uprising, the most entitled to it would have been Ibn 'Abbas. It is mentioned that the sons of his brother, 'Ubaydullah, were killed unjustly.

> That was in 40 AH in the Yemen at the end of the governorship of 'Ubaydullah ibn 'Abbas over Yemen for 'Ali. Mu'awiya sent Busr ibn Abi

Arta' to the Hijaz and the Yemen and he took allegiance on his behalf from the people of the Hijaz. Then Busr went to the Yemen. When 'Ubaydullah learned of his arrival, he fled to Kufa leaving his sons in the Yemen. Busr killed both of them according to what is said.

However, by his intelligence, he saw that 'Uthman's blood had not been spared, so how would the blood of the sons of 'Ubaydullah be saved? The business was a hasty one...

> i.e. its truth is was mixed up with what is false.

...and they had left it in order to preserve the basis which is the unity of the community, thus sparing the blood of the Muslims and unifying them. The command of the Master of the Shari'a ﷺ was to refrain from [contesting] command even if a mutilated person undertook it.[432]

Each of them had immense worth and strove. Each is correct and rewarded wherever he went. Allah has a judgment about it which He will carry out and He has judgment in the Next World which He has already decided and is finished with. Measure these matters by their proper measure. See how Ibn 'Abbas and Ibn 'Umar dealt with them and then deal with them in the same manner. Do not join the fools who have unleashed their tongues and pens with what is of no use to them. No one is independent of Allah nor can anything in this world dispense with Him.

Regard the best Imams and the *fuqaha'* in the cities. Did they turn to these fables and speak about stupidities like these? They knew that this was only ignorant partisanship and futile zeal. All it does is to sever the bonds between people, scatter unity and create different sects. What has happened has happened. The historians have said what they said. One should either be silent or follow the people of knowledge. Cast away the follies of the historians and the men of letters. May Allah perfect His blessings on us and you by His mercy.

NOTE

ON ZIYAD

It is a wonder that people consider the government of the Umayyads to be terrible when the first to appoint them to govern was the Messenger of Allah ﷺ. On the Day of the Conquest, he appointed 'Attab ibn Usayd ibn Abu al-'Is ibn Umayya over Makka while he was still a very young man, whether he had grown a beard or not. He made Mu'awiya ibn Abi Sufyan a custodian of his revelation. Then Abu Bakr appointed his brother, Yazid ibn Abi Sufyan, over Syria. After that, they continued to rise in the path of glory and ascend the levels of might and the positions of honour until time finished by bringing them to distinguished abodes.

People relate baseless *hadiths* regarding them. This includes the *hadith* of the dream that the Prophet ﷺ had about the Umayyads leaping on his minbar like monkeys. It grieved him, so he was given the Night of Power, better than the thousand months in which the Umayyads ruled. If this had been sound, he would not have initiated that state when he appointed them nor would he have established 'Attab in the best area of the earth: Makka. This is the root which one must grasp.

If it is said that Mu'awiya began to judge by what was not true in Islam and to decide what is not lawful when he attached Ziyad's paternity, we say, "We made it clear elsewhere that the ascription of Ziyad's paternity was based on sound things and correct action which we will explain after we have mentioned what they claim about him leaving the Straight Path, since there is no other way to arrive at their lies because the tear the lie makes cannot be mended and the one who uttered it is worse still. How is it then when the story goes on?

They said that Ziyad was ascribed to 'Ubayd ath-Thaqafi through Sumayya, the slave-girl of al-Harith ibn Kalda.

Ibn 'Asakir related in the biography of Ziyad in the *History of Damascus*[433] from 'Uwana ibn al-Hakam al-Kalbi (the oldest of the shaykhs of al-Mada'ini) that Sumayya, Ziyad's mother, belonged to a Persian landowner. He had a stomach-ache and feared that he was afflicted with dropsy. He summoned al-Harith ibn Kalda ath-Thaqafi, the Arab doctor, who used to attend Khosrau. He treated the landowner and cured him and he gave him Sumayya. She bore him Abu Bakra (his name was Masruh or Nufay'), but he did not acknowledge him. Then she bore Nafi' and he did not acknowledge him. When Abu Bakra went to the Prophet ﷺ, al-Harith ibn Kalda said to Nafi', "Your brother Masruh is a slave and you are my son." So he acknowledged him on that day. Al-Harith married her to a slave he owned called 'Ubayd and she bore Ziyad while she was married to him. Abu Sufyan went to Ta'if and stayed with a man called Abu Maryam as-Saluli. He said, "Abu Maryam brought Sumayya to him and he slept with her and she conceived Ziyad."

Ziyad purchased his father 'Ubayd for a thousand dirhams and set him free.

In Ziyad's biography in the *History* of Ibn 'Asakir[434] there is the report which Zuhra ibn Ma'bad and Muhammad ibn 'Amr related about Ziyad coming when he was a child to the Amir al-Mu'minin 'Umar from Abu Musa al-Ash'ari on the day of the Battle of Jalala'. They both said: "When 'Umar looked at him, he saw that he had a good form and fine white cotton clothes. He asked him, 'What is this garment?' He told him and 'Umar asked, 'How much did it cost?' He told him something small and he believed him. He asked him, 'What is your stipend?' He said, '2000.' He said, 'What did you do with the first stipend you were given?' He replied, 'I purchased my mother with it and then set her free. With the second, I purchased my foster father 'Ubayd and set him free." 'Umar said, 'You have been successful.' He asked him about the shares of inheritance, the *sunan* and the Qur'an, and he found that he had knowledge of the Qur'an and its rules and the shares of inheritance. So he sent him back to Abu Musa and commanded the amirs of Basra to follow his opinion."

Abu 'Uthman al-Hadi said, "We envied him." 'Umar put him in charge of part of the *zakat* of Basra. It is said that he was a scribe for Abu Musa.

> Ibn 'Asakir quoted from Abu Nu'aym that Ziyad wrote letters for Abu Musa al-Ash'ari and then for 'Abdullah ibn 'Amr ibn Kurayz, then for al-Mughira ibn Shu'ba, then for 'Abdullah ibn 'Abbas who were all in charge of Basra. The Amir al-Mu'minin 'Ali wanted him to take charge of Basra. Ziyad indicated to him that he should appoint 'Abdullah ibn 'Abbas, but he promised to help and advise him.

When he did not give testimony with the witnesses who testified against al-Mughira, …

> about his committing fornication.

…'Umar flogged them and dismissed him. He told him, "I did not dismiss you for any disgrace, but I dislike to impose your excess of intelligence on people." They related that 'Umar sent him to the Yemen to put corruption in order and he returned and made a speech whose like has never been heard. 'Amr ibn al-'As said, "By Allah, if this lad had been a Qurayshi, people would have held to his staff." Abu Sufyan said, "By Allah, I know who placed him in his mother's womb." 'Ali asked him, "Who?" He replied, "I did." He said, "Easy, Abu Sufyan." Abu Sufyan recited some verses:

By Allah, if it were not for fear of a person,
    i.e. 'Umar.
  'Ali, I should be seen among the enemies
To show Sakhr ibn Harb his business.

The statement is not from Ziyad.
My deceit by Thaqif was long
> and I left the fruit of the heart with them.

This is what affected Mu'awiya.

'Ali appointed him over Persia, Hama, Juba, Fath and Aslah.

Mu'awiya corresponded with him, intending to unsettle him. Ziyad sent his letter to 'Ali along with a poem. 'Ali wrote to him, "I have appointed you over what I have appointed you. You are worthy of that in my opinion. What you want will only be obtained by patience and certainty in what you have. It was only a slip on Abu Sufyan's part during the time of 'Umar. You do not deserve either lineage or inheritance by that. Mu'awiya will come to the believer from in front of him and behind him."

When Ziyad read the letter, he said, "Abu al-Hasan has testified for me, by the Lord of Ka'ba!" That was what emboldened Ziyad and Mu'awiya to do what they did. Then Mu'awiya laid claim to him in 44 AH and Mu'awiya married off his daughter to Ziyad's son, Muhammad. Abu Bakra, his brother by his mother, heard that and he swore that he would never speak to him again. He said, "This man committed adultery with his mother and he disowns his father. By Allah, Sumayya did not see Abu Sufyan at all. How should he behave with Umm Habiba?

Umm al-Mu'minin Umm Habiba bint Abi Sufyan the sister of Mu'awiya.

"Should he see her and then break the sanctity of the Messenger of Allah ﷺ? If she is veiled from him, then she would disgrace him." Ziyad said, "May Allah reward Abu Bakra! He did not leave good counsel in any situation!" The poets spoke about him. They related that Sa'id ibn al-Musayyab said, "The first false decision in Islam was the false ascription of Ziyad's paternity."

Qadi Abu Bakr said: We made this report clear in more than one place. We spoke about it and it does not need to be repeated. However, what is meant by it must be made clear. We say, "We neither affirm nor deny all you mentioned because there is no need of it. That which we know to be true and which we clearly state as knowledge is that Ziyad was one of the Companions by birth and sight,...

> Ibn Hajar gives his biography in the *Isaba* as does Abu 'Umar ibn 'Abd al-Barr in the *Isti'ab*. He stated that he was born in the year of the Conquest of Makka. It is said that it was the year of the *hijra* and it is said that it was the year of the Battle of Badr. Ibn Hajar said that Ibn 'Asakir stated that he lived in the time of the Prophet ﷺ, but did not see him.

...not by *fiqh* and knowledge. As for his father, properly speaking, we do not know that he had a father before the claim of Mu'awiya in attributing his paternity.

> It is confirmed that al-Harith ibn Kalda admitted to being the father of Nafi', Ziyad's brother by his mother. Therefore Nafi' was called Nafi' ibn al-Harith ibn Kalda. History does not say that either 'Ubayd ath-Thaqafi or al-Harith ibn Kalda acknowledged Ziyad.

There are jealous statements made by historians. As for buying him, that was because he had raised him. He was brought up by him when he came to him. He had lineage to him by virtue of upbringing if that is what the situation was.

As for their statement that Abu 'Uthman al-Hadi envied him for doing that, that was unlikely in Abu 'Uthman's case. There is no special virtue in anyone buying his foster father or his father and then setting him free such that Abu 'Uthman and his likes should envy him, because this is a rank which is obtained by rich and poor, noble and the low, and even if he were to spend an immense amount of money, that would protect his manliness in humbling the great men of wealth by his kinship to a dear friend. They used this tale in order to give him a father and to put him in the position of someone who denies his own father.

As for 'Umar appointing him, that is sound. That is enough for you as far as considering him to have integrity, honour and the *deen*.

As for their statement that 'Umar dismissed him because he did not bear false witness, on the contrary it is related that when his three companions testified,...

> The three companions who testified against al-Mughira were his two brothers by his mother: Nufay', and Nafi' who is ascribed to al-Harith ibn Kalda, and the third was Shibl ibn Ma'bad.

...'Umar said to al-Mughira, "Your fourth is gone, your half is gone, and three-quarters of your side have gone." When Ziyad came, he said to him, "I see that you have a handsome face and I hope that Allah will not disgrace a man who is one of the Companions of the Messenger of Allah ﷺ."

As for the oration that 'Amr is said to have admired, he did not have excellent knowledge nor eloquence greater than 'Amr had, or anyone below or above him. The falsifying shaykh included a speech which was not of this measure.

> Perhaps he meant al-Jahiz. The greatest of his speeches which he quoted is in the *Clarification and Making Clear*. That is his speech which is called al-Batra'. It is in the beginning of part 2.

As for their words that Abu Sufyan acknowledged him and spoke some poetry about him, someone who has studied does not doubt that if Abu Sufyan had acknowledged him during 'Umar's lifetime, he would not have concealed anything because the situation had to be one of two things: either 'Umar thought that he was indeed connected to him...

i.e. his connection and attachment.

...as others have related from him and that would have been carried out, or he would have rejected that. No punishment is required against Abu Sufyan for what he did in the *Jahiliyya*. They mentioned this stupid, broken and forged story that is outside the limits of the *deen* and proper learning. It is meaningless.

As for 'Ali appointing him, that shows his integrity.

As for Mu'awiya sending to him so that he would join him, that is sound in general. As for the details about what Mu'awiya wrote to Ziyad or Ziyad to 'Ali or what 'Ali replied to Ziyad, that is all fabrication.

As for 'Ali's words, "It was an error from Abu Sufyan in the time of 'Umar, so you do not deserve lineage by it," if that had been true, that is a testimony as is related from Ziyad. That does not invalidate what Mu'awiya did because it is a question of *ijtihad* between scholars. 'Ali had one opinion and Mu'awiya and others had another opinion.

As for the note in the discussion that is the statement about Mu'awiya giving Ziyad's paternity and people blaming him for that, what is he blamed for in it if he did hear that from his father? What fault rests with Abu Sufyan in laying claim to an illegitimate child when that came from something that happened in the time of the *Jahiliyya*? It is known that Sumayya did not belong to Abu Sufyan as Zam'a's son did not belong to 'Utba. However, 'Utba had someone who disputed with him and judgment was accorded to that person. No one disputed Mu'awiya concerning Ziyad.

O Allah! Here is a point on which scholars disagree. It is that when the brother claims to be connected to a brother saying, "He is the son of my father," and no one disputes him and he is alone, Malik says, "He inherits and the lineage is not confirmed." Ash-Shafi'i says in one of two statements that the lineage is confirmed and he receives property. This is when the one who is acknowledged does not have a known lineage.

Ash-Shafi'i used as a proof the words of the Prophet ﷺ, "He is yours, 'Abd ibn Zam'a. The child belongs to the bed (where he was born) and the adulterer is stoned." He decided that he belonged to the household and that the lineage was given. We said that this is great ignorance. That is because his statement that the Prophet ﷺ decided that he belongs to his household is true. As for the statement about the lineage being confirmed, that is false because 'Abd claimed him for two reasons: one of them was by virtue of his being born in the house and the second was by being his brother. If the Prophet ﷺ had said, "He is your brother and the child belongs to the household," that would have confirmed the principle and mentioned the cause. However, the Prophet ﷺ did not mention brotherhood nor go into it. He did not mention lineage nor make an explicit statement about it. It says in the *Sahih*, "He is your brother," and another version has, "He is yours," meaning you know him best. We made that clear in the questions under dispute.

Al-Harith ibn Kalda did not claim Ziyad nor did he have any lineage with him. The son of his slave-girl was the child in his household. He belongs to the one who claims him unless someone opposes him who is more entitled to him. There was no fault in Mu'awiya when he did that. He acted correctly in it according to the school of Malik.

If it is asked, "Why did the Companions reject it?" The answer is: because it is a question of *ijtihad*. Whoever thinks that lineage is not connected by the single heir, rejects it and thinks it a major matter.

If it is asked why they cursed him and use as a proof the words of the Prophet ﷺ, "Cursed is the one who is ascribed to other than his father or ascribed to other than his ex-masters," then we answer that the one who cursed him did so for two reasons: first, because he stated that his lineage was by this path. Whoever does not think that he is cursed for this, cursed him for another reason. In their opinion, Ziyad deserved to be cursed for what happened after Mu'awiya proclaimed his paternity.

The most important reason for that in their opinion lay in the execution of Hujr ibn 'Adi which was already discussed.

If it is said that the Prophet ﷺ held that fornication creates taboos created by kinship, he established that principle when he said, "Veil yourself from him, Sawda."

> In the Book of Judgments in the *Muwatta'* of Malik[435] from Ibn Shihab from 'Urwa ibn az-Zubayr from 'A'isha. She said, "'Utba ibn Abi Waqqas disclosed to his brother, Sa'd ibn Abi Waqqas, that he had fathered the son of the slave-girl of Zam'a and made him promise to look after him (after his death). In the Year of the Conquest, Sa'd took him and said, 'He is the son of my brother. He made a covenant with me about him.' 'Abd ibn Zam'a stood up and said, 'He is my brother and the son of my father's slave-girl. He was born on my father's bed.' The Messenger of Allah ﷺ said, 'He is yours, 'Abd ibn Zam'a.' Then the Messenger of Allah ﷺ said, 'A child belongs to the household (where he was born) and the adulterer is stoned.' Then he told Sawda bint Zam'a, 'Veil yourself from him' since he saw that he resembled 'Utba ibn Abi Waqqas.'" 'A'isha added, "He did not see her from then on until he met Allah, the Mighty the Majestic." Al-Bukhari related it[436] and Muslim.[437]

This indicates that adultery creates the same taboo-relationships as are created by intercourse in a valid marriage. That is similar to what the Kufans said. In Ibn al-Qasim's version, Malik aided them in the question, but did not help them in the proof in this way. We made it clear in the Book of Marriage. Ash-Shafi'i said, "The reason that the Prophet ﷺ told Sawda to veil herself in spite of the confirmation of Zam'a's lineage and the validity of him being her brother by the claim of 'Abd was in order to exalt respect for the wives of the Prophet ﷺ because they are not like any other women in their honour and excellence.

We said: "If he had been her brother by a firm lineage as you say and the words of the Prophet ﷺ, "The child belongs to the bed," confirms the lineage, then why did the Prophet forbid Sawda to be unveiled before him when 'A'isha was not kept from the man about whom she said, "This is my brother by suckling."? He said, "You can be seen by your brothers."

As for what is related from Sa'id ibn al-Musayyab, it is related that his position was that his claim to paternity is not sound. That is what some other Companions and Tabi'un thought. The question led to dispute in the community and the *fuqaha'* of the cities. It went beyond criticism to the level of belief. Malik clearly states his lineage in the Book of Islam in the *Muwatta'* when he refers to him. He stated, during the 'Abbasid period, "Ziyad ibn Abi Sufyan." He did not say, as did the failed person, "Ziyad ibn Abihi (son of his father)," This is based on what he thought about lineage being confirmed by a single statement. However, there is great *fiqh* in that which no one realises. It is that since it is a disputed question and judgment is possible by either aspect, it is not retracted. If the Qadi judged the disputed question by one of two statements, it is implemented and it lifts the dispute about it. Allah knows best.

As for the variant where 'Umar said, "I do not want to force your superior intellect on people," this is an unfounded addition made by someone with a defective intellect. What intellect did Ziyad have more than the people had in the time of 'Umar?

> Because when he went to see 'Umar he was seventeen years old, as al-Bukhari transmitted in his *Middle History* from Yunus ibn Habib from the family of Ziyad.

Every one of the Companions had more understanding and knowledge than Ziyad had. This is why everyone who has a fuller intellect than someone else is more suited to mix with people. They said, "He was an old fox." That is a weak statement. Cunning and shrewdness is knowledge of the meanings and judging ends by beginnings. Every single Companion and Tabi'i was above Ziyad (in this). Those narrations which the historians related – in their lying – are on the tricks of warfare and assaulting people. Anyone today can do the like or more than them. The stratagem is only amazing, and to be mentioned and related when it is in harmony with the *deen*. As for every story which is in opposition to the *deen*, there is neither good nor intellect in transmitting it. All people, the rulers of the Umayyads in particular, as we already mentioned, had more intellect and more eloquence than Ziyad. Do not pay any attention to the falsehoods that are quoted.

NOTE

Appointments and dismissals have meanings and realities which most people do not know. You know that the Messenger of Allah ﷺ died among 12,000 Companions who are known. They included about 2000 men famous for majesty. Among them Abu Bakr appointed Sa'd, Abu 'Ubayda, Yazid, Khalid ibn al-Walid, 'Ikrima ibn Abi Jahl and another group higher than them. He appointed Anas ibn Malik over Bahrayn when he was twenty years old, imitating what the Prophet ﷺ did with 'Attab. When were the shaykhs all used up so that he had to use young men? 'Umar also made appointments like that. He was quick to dismiss Khalid. All of that was due to great *fiqh* and wonderful knowledge which is made clear in its place in the books on the Imamate and Politics in the *Usul*. Study other things, for this topic is not part of that which good mannered and refined people discuss.

As for what is related from Mu'awiya that he summoned witnesses, and so as-Saluli and others testified, ...

> As-Saluli is Malik ibn Rabi'a ibn Maryam. That was in 44 AH. Those who testified with him were Ziyad ibn Asma' al-Hirmazi, al-Mundhir ibn

az-Zubayr (according to what al-Mada'ini mentioned with his *isnads*), Juwayriya bint Abi Sufyan, al-Miswar ibn Qudama al-Bahili, Ibn Abi Nasr ath-Thaqafi, Zayd ibn Nufayl al-Azdi, Shu'ba ibn al-'Alqama al-Mazini, a man from the Banu 'Amr ibn Shayban and a man from the Banu al-Mustaliq. They all testified that Ziyad was Abu Sufyan's son, except for al-Mundhir. He testified that he heard 'Ali say, "I testify that Abu Sufyan said that." Mu'awiya gave a speech and attached Ziyad. Ziyad spoke and said, "If what the witnesses have stated is true, then praise be to Allah. If it is false, I put them between me and Allah."

...those who appended to what was related from as-Saluli are ignoble, for it was not that at all. Be fortunate by dropping what Sa'd or Sa'id related in the story. As for the words of Abu Bakra, his maternal half-brother, about him, that does not injure him because that was the opinion of Abu Bakra and his *ijtihad*. As for their words narrating what Abu Bakra said, namely that he was the result of adultery with his mother, if that is true, what happened in the *Jahiliyya* does not harm her in the *deen*. Allah pardoned all the people of the *Jahiliyya* through Islam. He dropped wrong actions and shame from them. Only those who are ignorant of that mentioned this.

Qadi Abu Bakr said: If people did not find any fault in anyone, but envy of him and their enmity of him overcome them, they created faults for him. Accept the advice and only look at sound reports. As I already told you, avoid the people with histories. They mentioned sound simple reports from the Salaf in order to use that as a means to quote lies. As we already stated, they injected something into their hearts which is unpleasing to Allah. That was in order to demean the Salaf and to weaken the *deen*. The *deen* is too mighty for that and the Salaf are too noble for that. Allah is pleased with all of them.

Whoever looks at the actions of the Companions will clearly see the falseness of these disclosures on which the historians disagree and which they slipped into the hearts of those who are weak. This Ziyad had the good fortune to appoint Samura ibn Jundub, one of the great Companions. He accepted his appointment with his position. How could he think that he would accept the appointment of an unjust man who lacked right guidance? He had what the Companions had. That was without any compulsion or dissimulation. This is the clear proof. With whom would you like to be: with Samura ibn Jundub or with al-Mas'udi, al-Mubarrad, Ibn Qutayba and their likes?

> Qadi Abu Bakr gave this harsh judgment about Ibn Qutayba. He thought that the *Book of the Imamate and Politics* was one of his books as will come. The *Book of the Imamate and Politics* has some things in it which took place after Ibn Qutayba's death. That indicated that some foul person belonging to a sect foisted it off on him. If the author had known the truth, he would have put al-Jahiz in place of Ibn Qutayba.

This is the end of the clarification.

DISASTERS AND DEFAMATIONS

SUMMARY

THE *Jahiliyya* was based on partisanship and people acted with fervour in it. When Islam brought the truth and Allah showed His blessings to creation, Allah said: *"Remember Allah's blessings to you when you were enemies and He joined your hearts together so that you became brothers by His blessing."*[438] He said to His Prophet ﷺ: *"Even if you had spent everything in the earth, you could not have unified their hearts. But Allah has unified them."*[439] The blessing of the Prophet ﷺ joined them together and united them, made their hearts sound and wiped out their malice.

Allah took His Messenger to Himself. Then people became averse, but the outward form continued as long as the balance remained in place. Then the balance was removed, as was already mentioned in the *hadith*. Allah took the hearts away from harmony and spread out the wings of disunion until the wings were level at the time of 'Uthman's murder. It flew into the horizons and the bloodshed will continue until the Last Day. People became gangs…

> *'Izeen,* the plural of *'iza,* a party of people.

…wandering in every valley brimming with bigotry. Some of them were for Abu Bakr, some for 'Umar, some for 'Uthman and some for 'Ali and for 'Abbas. Each claimed that they were in the right and the one whom they supported was in the right and that the rest were

Summary

unjust miserly tyrants who lacked any good. That is not a *madhhab* nor is there any position to it. Those are stupidities and ignorance, or intrigues designed to lead people to misguidance so that the Shari'a will disappear and the heretics will be able to make fun of the religion while shaytan plays and jokes with them. He takes them outside of any path or *madhhab*.

The Bakrites said: "the Messenger of Allah ﷺ stipulated Abu Bakr for the prayer and the community was pleased with him for this world. He had the highest virtue and sincere love with the Prophet ﷺ. He was appointed and was just. He chose and did well. However, he erred about 'Umar, and his giving him command was a mistake. 'Umar's boorishness dominated," and they proceed to mention faults in 'Umar. "As for 'Uthman, what he did is not hidden. It is the same with 'Ali." They do not mention al-'Abbas.

The 'Umarites said: "Abu Bakr was an excellent weak man, while 'Umar was a strong just Imam, praised by the Prophet ﷺ in the *hadith* of the vision, the bucket, and the ingenious person," as was already stated. "As for 'Uthman, he left the path. He did not choose a ruler nor did he give anyone his due nor restrain his relatives. He did not follow the *sunan* of those before him. As for 'Ali, he dared to take blood." I heard in certain assemblies that Ibn Jurayj ...

> 'Abd al-Malik ibn 'Abd al-'Aziz al-Makki, one of the notable men, in 150 AH.

...used to put 'Umar ahead of Abu Bakr. I heard at-Tartushi say, ...

> At-Tartushi was one of the author's shaykhs. Look at his biography at the beginning of this book.

..."If anyone says that 'Umar should have been put forward, I will pursue him."

The 'Uthmanites said that 'Uthman had priority, virtues and excellent deeds both in himself and in his property. He was killed unjustly.

The 'Alids said, "'Ali was the son of his uncle and his in-law and the father of the grandson of the Prophet ﷺ and the foster son of the Prophet ﷺ."

The 'Abbasids said that 'Abbas was like the father of the Prophet ﷺ and the one who most deserved to be put forward after him. They spoke at length about that, saying things so vile it is not necessary to mention them.

> Most of that took place in the time of their dynasty.

They related *hadiths* which it is not lawful to mention because of the terrible forgery in them and the baseness of their transmitters.

Many heretics connected themselves to the People of the House and put 'Ali above all people.

> They used them as a means to their ends and attacked many of the best men. They made allusions to people like Imam Zayd. Then they opposed the clear Shari'a of the ancestor of the People of the House by the claim of infallibility and even actual deification which certain individuals among them articulated.

The Rafidites were divided into twenty groups. The worst of them were those who said that 'Ali was Allah. The Ghurabiyya said that 'Ali was the messenger of Allah, but that Jibril failed to give him the message and went instead to Muhammad due to his enthusiasm for him in cold disbelief that is only warmed by the sword. As far as the warmth of debate is concerned, it has no effect on it.

Defence

I have told you this so that you will be careful about people, especially the commentators, historians and people of letters. They are people

Summary

who are ignorant of the sacred things of the *deen* and who persist in their innovations. Do not pay any attention to what they relate nor accept their *riwaya* unless it comes from the Imams of *hadith*. Do not listen to the words of any historian except at-Tabari.

> Furthermore, at-Tabari mentioned the sources of his reports and named their transmitters, so that there would be a clear proof in the business. He said at the end of the preface of his book, "Whatever reports are found in my book which the reader does not like since he does not recognise that it is sound, should know that that has not come to you from me. It came from those who transmitted to me."

Anyone else is the Red Death and the Great Disease. They fabricated *hadith*s in order to disparage the Companions and the Salaf and to make light of them. They invented lengthy forgeries about words and actions which they then ascribed to them. Their goals lead them out of the *deen* to this world, and from the truth to sects. If you cut off the people of lies and content yourself with the transmissions of just men, you will be safe from these snares and will keep away from these spectres. One of the most terrible things for people is an ignorant man of intelligence or a cunning innovator. The ignorant man was Ibn Qutayba. He did not leave any trace of the Companions in the *Book of the Imamate and Politics* if all that that book contains is truly from him.

> Nothing in it is validly from him. If it had been sound to ascribe this book to the firm Imam, Abu Muhammad 'Abdullah ibn Muslim ibn Qutayba, he would have been as Ibn al-'Arabi states, because the *Book of the Imamate and Politics* is full of ignorance, stupidity, foolishness, lies and falsehoods. When I published the *Book of Gambling and Divining Arrows* by Ibn Qutayba more than twenty-five years ago and prefaced it with his full biography and enumerated his works, I mentioned[440] the source of scholars for the *Book of the Imamate and Politics*, and their proofs that

it was not by Ibn Qutayba. I now will add to that what I mentioned in *Gambling and Divining Arrows* that the author of the *Imamate and Politics* related a lot from two of the great scholars of Egypt. Ibn Qutayba did not go to Egypt and he did not take anything from these two scholars. All of that indicates that the book was foisted on him.

There was also al-Mubarrad in his literary book.

> Al-Mubarrad adopted some of the opinion of the Kharijites and he inclined towards them. The fact that he is an Imam in language and literature does not obscure his weakness in the science of *riwaya* and *isnad*. In the case of Abu Hamid al-Ghazali, in spite of his majesty in the sciences of the Shari'a and logic, scholars did not overlook his weakness in the sciences of *isnad*. So you should be even more careful not to overlook the like of that in al-Mubarrad. In any case, every report about the past or future in our community or in any other community can be considered either true or false until its truthfulness or falsity is established by the touchstone of experience and by scientific investigation.

Where is his intellect in respect of the intellect of Tha'lab, the Imam who preceded him in his *Amali*. He wrote it down in a literary manner, free of attack on the men of virtue in the community. As for the cunning innovator, that was al-Mas'udi. He brought something close to atheism in what he related concerning that. As for the innovation, there is no doubt about it.

> 'Ali ibn al-Husayn al-Mas'udi, whom the Shi'a consider to be one of their shaykhs and great men. In the *Tanqih al-Maqal*,[441] al-Mamqani mentioned the books about guardianship and the infallibility of the Imam and other things which show his bias and his keeping to a path which is not that of the people of the *Sunna* of Muhammad. Part of the nature of partisanship and fanaticism is that it takes a person far from equity and justice.

Summary

If you close your ears and eyes so that they do not read or listen to lies and do not listen to anything about a caliph from anyone who ascribes something unfitting to him and who mentions what it is impossible to quote, then you will travel the path of the Salaf and turn from the path of falsehood.

Malik, may Allah have mercy on him, used the judgment of 'Abd al-Malik ibn Marwan as a proof in his *Muwatta'* and put it among the rules of the Shari'a.

> An example of that is what is narrated in the Chapter about Raped Women in the Book of Judgments in the *Muwatta'*,[442] "Malik related to me from Ibn Shihab that 'Abd al-Malik ibn Marwan gave a judgment that the rapist had to pay the raped woman her bride-price." In the Book of the *Mukatab* in the *Muwatta'*[443] there is another judgment by 'Abd al-Malik. The Book of Blood-wits in the *Muwatta'* has another judgment by him. As for his father, Marwan ibn al-Hakam, there are many of his judgments and *fatwas* in the *Muwatta'* and other books of the *Sunna* which are in use by the Imams of the Muslims who act according to them. Look at the scrupulousness of Marwan and his son, 'Abd al-Malik, in the *hadith* of Malik from Ibn Abi 'Abla in the Book of Marriage in the *Muwatta'*.

He said in his *riwaya*, "From Ziyad ibn Abi Sufyan." He gave him that lineage and he knew his story. If he had considered what the common people believe to be the truth, he would not have been content to give him that lineage or to mention him in his book which he made a foundation for Islam.

> 'Amir ibn Sharahil ash-Sha'bi was one of the Imams of the Muslims as well. Malik thought of him as one of his Imams. Ibn 'Asakir related in the biography of Ziyad from the *History of Damascus*[444] that ash-Sha'bi said, "A case came to Ziyad regarding a man who died and left a maternal aunt and paternal aunt. He said, 'I will decide between you by a decision

which I heard from 'Umar ibn al-Khattab.' That was to put the paternal aunt in the position of the brother, and the maternal aunt in the position of the sister."

All of that was compiled in the days of the Abbasids and their dynasty when they were in power. They did not make him change it nor dislike that because of the excellence of their sciences and their recognition that the question of Ziyad was a question about which people disagreed. Some of them allow it and some forbid it. There is no way for them to object to it.

Similarly they were amazed to find that when the Caliph read the *Muwatta'* to Malik, he mentioned 'Abd al-Malik ibn Marwan in it and he mentioned his judgment because when scholars use someone's judgment as proof, he will also use his judgment as proof in a similar case. When he attacks it, he will attack it in a similar manner.

> Some of those who related from 'Abd al-Malik ibn Marwan included al-Bukhari in his book, *al-Adab al-Mufrad*, Imam az-Zuhri, 'Urwa ibn az-Zubayr and Khalid ibn Ma'dan from the *fuqaha'* and the worshippers among the Tabi'un, and Raja' ibn Haywa, one of the notable men. Nafi', the client of Ibn 'Umar, said, "I saw Madina, and there was no youth in it who worked harder nor with more *fiqh* nor who read the Book of Allah more than Sa'id ibn al-Musayyab, 'Urwa ibn az-Zubayr, Qabisa ibn Dhu'ayb and 'Abd al-Malik ibn Marwan before he became the Amir." Ash-Sha'bi said, "I did not sit with anyone but that I found that I was better than him except for 'Abd al-Malik ibn Marwan. I did not mention any *hadith* to him, but that he gave me more on it, nor any poem but that he gave me more of it."[445]

Al-Bukhari quoted[446] that 'Abdullah ibn Dinar said, "I saw Ibn 'Umar when the people gathered to 'Abd al-Malik ibn Marwan. He wrote, 'I confirm obedience to 'Abd al-Malik, the Amir al-Mu'minin, in the *sunna* of Allah and the *Sunna* of His Messenger as much as I can. My sons confirm the like of that.'"

Al-Ma'mun used to say that the Qur'an was created as did al-Wathiq. They proclaimed their innovation and the issue became known: when the Qadi or Imam innovates, is his government sound and are his judgments carried out or are they rejected? That is a well-known issue. This is worse than the indifference of the historians when they say that such-and-such a caliph drank wine or sang or was corrupt or committed adultery. This statement about the Qur'an is either innovation or disbelief – according to the disagreement of scholars regarding it, and these men were famous for it. But these acts of disobedience they did not do them publicly if in fact they did them, so how can one confirm the words of singers and indifferent historians regarding that when they used it to make acts of rebellion easy for people and to make people say, "If our caliphs do this, it is not difficult for us to do it." The leaders helped them to spread these books and read them because they wanted to act in this way so that what is correct would be considered disliked and what is disliked considered correct. They even allowed al-Jahiz to read his books in the mosques although they contain lies, falsehoods and disliked things and with respect to the Prophets that they were born illegitimately, as was said about Ishaq in the *Kitab as-Dalal wa at-Tadlil*. Reading the books of philosophy enables people to deny the Creator and invalidate the Shari'a due to the corrupt desires and false goals which their ministers and elite had. If a *faqih* errs or a scholar speaks badly:

The worst fire is at the top of Kabkab.

> Kabkab is a mountain behind Arafat which overlooks it. The poem is by al-A'mash. It ends:

> Whoever is in exile from his people continues to see the
> battlements of the wronged in course and flow.

Good actions are buried in it. If he is bad, the worst fire
is at the top of Kabkab.

If you understand these matters, your intentions will be excellent and your hearts will be free of alteration towards the earlier men.

I have made it clear to you that you should not devote yourselves to a dinar or even a dirham unless it is just and free of suspicion and free from appetite, so how can you accept anything about the circumstances of the Salaf and what happened among the first ones from those who have no rank in the *deen*, how can you accept when they have no rank in integrity?

May Allah show mercy to 'Umar ibn 'Abd al-'Aziz, When they were speaking about what had happened between the Companions, he said, *"That was a community which has long since passed away. It has what it earned. You have what you earned. You will not be questioned about what they did."*[147]

Praise be to Allah by whose favour right actions are perfected.

REFERENCES

1. pp. 98-193 of the Algerian edition, 1347
2. Surat al-Ma'ida (5:3)
3. al-Bidaya wa an-Nihaya (pp. 273-274)
4. al-Bidaya wa an-Nihaya (6:333)
5. al-Bidaya wa an-Nihaya (249:5)
6. Musnad of Ahmad ibn Hanbal (1:55, first edition, pt. 1, no. 391, second edition) in the hadith narrated by Ibn 'Abbas.
7. The Arab Race (7:14 et seq.)
8. History of at-Tabari (2:447)
9. Surat al-Baqara (2:51)
10. Surat al-A'raf (7:142)
11. Musnad of Ibn Hanbal (3:196, first edition)
12. 'Virtues of the Companions' in Sahih al-Bukhari (Book 62, Chap. 5)
13. al-Bidaya wa an-Nihaya (5:242)
14. al-Bidaya wa an-Nihaya (5:241)
15. Sahih al-Bukhari, the Book of Expeditions (Book 64, pt. 5, pp. 140-141). Ibn Kathir, al-Bidaya wa an-Nihaya (5:227 & 251) from the hadith of az-Zuhri from 'Abdullah ibn Ka'b ibn Malik from Ibn 'Abbas. Musnad of Ibn Hanbal (1:263 & 325, first edition, pt. 4, no. 2374 and pt. 5, no. 2999, second edition).
16. al-Bidaya wa an-Nihaya (6:394-305)
17. al-Bidaya wa an-Nihaya (5:244)
18. Sura Ali 'Imran (3:144)
19. Sahih al-Bukhari, (Book 62, Chap. 5, pt. 4, p. 194)
20. al-Bidaya wa an-Nihaya (5:242)
21. Musnad of at-Tayalasi, no. 926, from Abu Barza, no. 2133, from Anas
22. Sahih al-Bukhari, (Book 93, Chap. 2, pt. 8, pp. 104-105)
23. Musnad of Ibn Hanbal (3:129, first edition)
24. Musnad of Ibn Hanbal (3:183, first edition)
25. Musnad of Ibn Hanbal (4:421, first edition)
26. Sahih al-Bukhari (Book 63, Chap. 11)

27. Surat at-Tawbah (9:119)
28. *al-Bidaya wa an-Nihaya* (5:247)
29. *al-Bidaya wa an-Nihaya* (6:305)
30. *al-Bidaya wa an-Nihaya* (6:311)
31. Surat at-Tawba (9:103)
32. *Musnad* of Ibn Hanbal (1:11 & 19, and 35-36, first edition, pt. 1, no. 67, 117 & 239, second edition)
33. *Al-Bidaya wa an-Nihaya* (6:132)
34. Book of the Virtues of the Companions in *Sahih al-Bukhari* (Book 62, Chap. 22, pt. 4, pp. 209-210)
35. Book of Expeditions in the chapter on the raid on Khaybar in *Sahih al-Bukhari* (Book 64, Chap. 38, pt. 5, p. 82)
36. Book of Bequests from *Sahih al-Bukhari*, Book 55, Chap. 32, pt. 3, p. 197
37. Book of the Division of the *Khums* (Book 57, Chap. 3, pt. 4, p. 45)
38. *Minhaj as-Sunna* (2:157)
39. Book of the Division of the Khums in *Sahih al-Bukhari* (Book 57, Chap. 1, pt. 4, p. 42)
40. op cit *Sahih al-Bukhari* (pt. 4, pp. 42-44)
41. Al-Bukhari related this *hadith* of Malik ibn Aws in the Book of Expeditions in the *Sahih* (Book 64, Chap. 14, pt. 5, pp. 23-24) from the *hadith* of Shu'ayb from az-Zuhri from Malik ibn Aws in the Book of Maintenance from his *Sahih* (Book 69, Chap. 3, pt. 6, pp. 190-192) and in the Book of Holding Fast to the Book and the *Sunna* in his *Sahih* (Book 96, Chap. 5, pt. 8, pp. 146-147). Look at the Book of the Shares of Inheritance in *Sahih al-Bukhari* (Book 5, Chap. 3, pt. 8, pp, 3-5) and the *Musnad* of Ibn Hanbal (1:13, first edition, nos. 77 & 78, second edition).
42. *Minhaj as-Sunna* (3:230)
43. *Minhaj as-Sunna* (3:231)
44. *Muwatta'* of Malik (16:27)
45. *Jami'* at-Tirmidhi (Book 8, Chap. 33)
46. the Book of Funerals in the *Sunan* of Ibn Majah (Book 6, chap, 65)
47. Ibn Hisham (3:103)
48. *al-Bidaya wa an-Nihaya* (5:266-268)
49. Surat an-Nur (24:55)
50. *Sahih al-Bukhari* (Book 62, Chap. 8, pt. 4, pp. 204-207)
51. *Minhaj as-Sunna* (3:167-172)
52. *Minhaj as-Sunna* (3:233-234)

References

53. *Sahih Muslim* (Book 44, Chap. 26, pt. 4, p. 203)
54. Sura al-Ma'ida (5:93)
55. *Sahih al-Bukhari* (Book 62, Chap. 7, pt. 4, p. 202)
56. *Sahih al-Bukhari*, (Book 62, chaps. 5 & 6, pt. 4, pp. 195-197 and 201-202)
57. *Sahih Muslim* (Book 44, chaps. 28 & 29, pt. 7, pp. 117-119)
58. Ibn Majah in Chapter 11 of the preface of the *Sunan* (pt. 1, p. 28, Egyptian edition, 1313)
59. *Musnad* of Ibn Hanbal (1:582, in the first edition, no. 407, in the second edition)
60. *Jami'* at-Tirmidhi (4:324)
61. *Sunan* Ibn Majah (1:28)
62. *Mustadrak* on the two *Sahih* volumes (3:99)
63. *Musnad* of Ibn Hanbal (2:115, first edition, pt. 8, no. 5953, second edition)
64. *Jami'* at-Tirmidhi (4:323)
65. *al-Mustadrak* (3:102)
66. Surat al-Anfal (8:42)
67. *Minhaj as-Sunna* (3:164)
68. *Minhaj as-Sunna* (2:196)
69. Surat al-Baqara (2:14)
70. *Minhaj as-Sunna* by Ibn Taymiyya, (3:191:192).
71. *History* of at-Tabari (5:99)
72. Ibn 'Asakir in the *History of Damascus* (7:429)
73. *Minhaj as-Sunna* (3:192-193)
74. i.e. the books of Ibn al-'Arabi connected to the sciences of the Qur'an. We mentioned in his biography (pp. 27-28) that they included the *Lights of Dawn* (in 70 or 80 volumes), the *Law of Interpretation*, which is one of his great works, the *Judgments of the Qur'an* published in Egypt and the *Book of the Obscure* and the *Abrogating and Abrogated*.
75. In the preface of Ibn Hanbal to his *Musnad* (1:13, first edition, no. 76, second edition and 5:188-189, first edition), Imam al-Bukhari in his *Sahih* (Book of Tafsir, book 65, sura 9, Chap. 20, pt. 5, pp. 210-211, and the Book of the Virtues of the Qur'an, Book 66, Chap. 3 & 4, pt. 6, pp. 98-99, Book of the Judgments, Book 93, Chap. 37, pt. 8, pp. 118-119, and the Book of *Tawhid*, Book 97, Chap. 22, pt. 8, pp. 176-177).
76. *al-Bidaya wa an-Nihaya* (6:334-340)
77. *Sahih al-Bukhari* (Book 66, Chap. 3, pt. 6, p. 99)

78. Surat al-Hijr (15:9)
79. *History of the Qur'an* by Abu 'Abdullah az-Zanjani (p. 46)
80. the *Fasl* (4:181)
81. Surat at-Tawba (9:40)
82. the *Fasl* (2:78)
83. in what Imam al-Bukhari related from him in his *Sahih* (Book 56, Chap. 12, pt. 3, pp. 205-206, Book 64, chap, 17, pt. 5, p. 31, *sura* 9, Chap. 30 and *sura* 33, Chap. 3, Book 66, chaps. 3 & 4, book 93, Chap, 97 and Book 87, Chap. 22.
84. Surat al-Ahzab (33:23)
85. Sura Ali 'Imran (3:161)
86. see the *Musnad* of Ibn Hanbal, (1:25-26, first edition, no. 175, second edition)
87. Al-Bukhari related it from the *hadith* of as-Sa'b ibn Jaththama in the Book of Sharecropping (Book 42, Chap, 11) and the Book of *Jihad* (Book 56, Chap. 146) in his *Sahih*
88. *Musnad* of Ibn Hanbal (4:71 & 73, first edition)
89. *Musnad* of Ibn Hanbal (2:91, 155 & 157, first edition, no. 5655, 6438 & 6464, second edition)
90. In the Book of *Jihad* from *Sahih al-Bukhari* (Book 46, Chap. 180)
91. Surat at-Tawba (9:34)
92. *Minhaj as-Sunna* by Ibn Taymiyya (3:198-199)
93. *History* of at-Tabari (5:66)
94. the Book of Judgments in the *Principles of the Judgments* by Ibn Hazm (2:139)
95. Ibn Khaldun, *al-'Ibar* (the continuation of 2:139)
96. Ibn Kathir, *al-Bidaya wa an-Nihaya* (8:131)
97. Surat ar-Ra'd (13:1)
98. *Minhaj as-Sunna* (3:196)
99. Look also at *Minhaj as-Sunna* (3:235-236)
100. *al-Imama wa al-mufadala*, in part 4 of his book, *al-Fasl* (p. 154)
101. *The Smiling Meadows in the Defence of the Sunna of Abu al-Qasim* (1:141-142)
102. *History* of at-Tabari (5:57-58)
103. *Nayl al-Awtar*, ash-Shawkani (3:213).
104. *The Preface and the Clarification of the Murder of the Martyr 'Uthman*, a manuscript in Dar al-Kutub al-Misriyya (no. 23, *History*)
105. *Sahih al-Bukhari* (Book 18, Chap. 5, pt. 2, p. 36)
106. *Musnad* of Ibn Hanbal (94:4)
107. Here in the text, it has the word, "and determined" and

References

the clear text of another word. The meaning is not affected by dropping them.

108 *History* of at-Tabari (4:30)
109 *Futuh al-buldan* by al-Baladhuri (p. 48, published in Egypt in 1350)
110 *al-Bidaya wa an-Nihaya* (8:133)
111 *al-Bidaya wa an-Nihaya* (8:135)
112 *Hafidh* pl. *huffadh* in the language of hadith scholars denotes someone who has memorised one hundred thousand hadiths both in their texts and their *isnad*s
113 *Minhaj as-Sunna* (3:189)
114 *al-Bidaya wa an-Nihaya* (8:88)
115 *Minhaj as-Sunna* (3:189-190)
116 *History* of at-Tabari (4:7)
117 *History* of at-Tabari (4:22)
118 *History* of at-Tabari (4:155)
119 *Minhaj as-Sunna* (3:173-176)
120 See the *Minhaj as-Sunna*, (3:236-237)
121 *History* of at-Tabari (4:246 and before it)
122 *Minhaj as-Sunna* (2:123)
123 *Musnad* of Ibn Hanbal (first edition, 4:321, 323, 326, 328 and 5:179)
124 *Musnad* of Ibn Hanbal (4:328)
125 *Musnad* of Ibn Hanbal (6:317 & 323)
126 *Musnad* of Ibn Hanbal (6:312)
127 *Musnad* of Ibn Hanbal (6:299)
128 *Musnad* of Ibn Hanbal (4:32, first edition)
129 Surat al-Hujurat (49:6)
130 *Sahih Muslim* (Book of *Hudud*, Chap. 8, pt. 5, p. 126)
131 (pt. 1, p. 82 and 140, first edition, pt. 2, no. 264 & 1184, second edition)
132 *Musnad* of Ibn Hanbal (pt. 1, pp. 144-145, first edition, pt. 2, no. 1229)
133 *History* of at-Tabari (5:49, Egypt, 1:2814-2815, published in Europe)
134 *Book of Kharaj* (p. 61)
135 Book of Land Grants of the *Book of Kharaj* by Yahya ibn Adam al-Qurashi, published by as-Salafiyya, pp. 77-78.
136 (at-Tabari, 4:148)
137 *Book of Kharaj* (pp. 60-62, Salafiyya, pub. in 1352)
138 *History* of at-Tabari (5:103).
139 *Minhaj as-Sunna* (3:187-188)
140 *Minhaj as-Sunna* (3:237)
141 In the Book of the Virtues of the Companions in *Sahih al-Bukhari* (Book 62, Chap. 9, pt. 4, p. 108) from the *hadith* of Sa'd ibn 'Ubayda.

142 Perhaps the author is indicating the *hadith* of the book of the *tafsir* of *Sahih al-Bukhari* (Book 65, Chap. 2, *Tafsir* of *al-Baqara*, hadith 30, pt. 5, p. 157).

143 In the Book of the Virtues of the Companions in *Sahih al-Bukhari* (Book 26, Chap. 7, pt. 4, pp. 203-204).

144 *History* of at-Tabari (2:276)

145 Surat ar-Ra'd (13:11)

146 *History* of at-Tabari (5:43-44, Egypt and 1:2801, European edition)

147 *History* of at-Tabari (5:41)

148 *History* of at-Tabari (5:420)

149 *Minhaj as-Sunna* (3:200

150 Look at the book by the excellent professor, Sadiq 'Urjun about 'Uthman ibn 'Affan, (pp. 132-133)

151 *History* of at-Tabari, (5:122)

152 *Minhaj as-Sunna* (3:188)

153 *Futuh al-Buldan* (p. 448, pub. 1350)

154 *Isaba* (3:358, pub. in 1329)

155 *Minhaj as-Sunna* (3:189)

156 *History* of at-Tabari (5:194)

157 *History* of at-Tabari (4:86)

158 *History* of at-Tabari (5:107)

159 *History* of at-Tabari (5:130)

160 *History* of at-Tabari (5:155)

161 *History* of at-Tabari (5:99)

162 *History* of at-Tabari (5:103)

163 *History* of at-Tabari (5:123)

164 Surat al-Baqara (2:131)

165 *History* of at-Tabari (5:126)

166 *History* of at-Tabari (5:131)

167 *History* of at-Tabari (5:132)

168 *History* of at-Tabari (6:51-59 & 60)

169 *History* of at-Tabari (5:99)

170 *History* of at-Tabari (5:103)

171 *History* of at-Tabari (5:118)

172 *History* of at-Tabari (5:131)

173 *History* of at-Tabari (5:130)

174 *History* of at-Tabari (5:123)

175 *History* of at-Tabari (5:124-125)

176 *Isaba* (2:280)

177 *Isaba* (2:281)

178 *History* of at-Tabari (5:90)

179 *History* of at-Tabari (5:104)

180 *History* of at-Tabari (5:106)

181 *History* of at-Tabari (5:120)

182 *History* of at-Tabari (5:176 et seq.)

183 *History* of at-Tabari (5:179)

184 *History* of at-Tabari (5:180)

185 *History* of at-Tabari (5:182)

186 *History* of at-Tabari (5:63)

187 *History* of at-Tabari (5:56)

188 *History* of at-Tabari (5:85-86)

189 *History* of at-Tabari (5:87-88)

190 *History* of at-Tabari (5:101)

References

191	*History* of at-Tabari (5:93-94)	216	*History* of at-Tabari (5:122)
192	*History* of at-Tabari (5:104)	217	*History* of at-Tabari (5:105)
193	*History* of at-Tabari (5:120)	218	*History* of at-Tabari (5:108)
194	*History* of at-Tabari (5:194)	219	*History* of at-Tabari (5:117-118)
195	*History* of at-Tabari related (5:217)	220	*al-Bidaya wa an-Nihaya* (7:184)
196	*History* of at-Tabari (5:195)	221	*Ansab al-Ashraf* by al-Baladhuri (5:92)
197	*History* of at-Tabari (5:86)		
198	*History* of at-Tabari (5:86)	222	*Book of the Tamhid* by Imam Abu Bakr al-Baqillani (p. 216)
199	*History* of at-Tabari (3:379)		
200	*History* of at-Tabari (pp. 380-381)	223	*History* of at-Tabari (5:137-138)
201	*History of the Arab Race* (7:231)	224	al-Bukhari and Muslim
202	*The Arab Race* (7:232, quoting at-Tabari.)	225	*Ansab al-Ashraf* (76:5)
		226	*Sunan Ibn Majah* (Chap. 11, pt. 1, p. 271)
203	*The Caliph Lied against*, Prof. Muhammad Sadiq 'Urjun, (p. 64)		
		227	*Musnad* of Ibn Hanbal (pt. 6, first edition, p. 75, 86, 114 & 149)
204	*The Caliph Lied against*, Prof. Muhammad Sadiq 'Urjun, (p. 65)		
		228	*Musnad* of Ibn Hanbal (1:59, first edition, no. 420, second edition)
205	*History of Damascus* (7:299)		
206	*History* of at-Tabari (5:92)	229	*Sunan* of an-Nasa'i (2:124-125)
207	*History* of at-Tabari (5:87)	230	*Jami'* of at-Tirmidhi (4:319-320)
208	*History* of at-Tabari (5:87)	231	*Musnad* of Ibn Hanbal (1:70, first edition, no. 511, 2nd edition)
209	*History* of at-Tabari (5:87-88)		
210	*The Collection of the Land* by Yaqut (Hebron)	232	*Sunan* of an-Nasa'i (full and condensed, 2:65-66, 123-124)
211	*Al-'Awasim min al-Qawasim* (2:117)	233	*History* of at-Tabari (5:125)
212	*History* of at-Tabari (5:107)	234	*History* of at-Tabari (5:101)
213	*Fihrist* of Ibn an-Nadim (p. 39, published in Egypt.)	235	*al-Bidaya wa an-Nihaya* (7:172)
		236	*History* of at-Tabari (5:129)
214	*History* of at-Tabari (5:120)	237	*History* of Ibn 'Asakir (5:362)
215	*History* of at-Tabari (5:120)	238	*Ansab al-Ashraf* (5:73)

239 Look at the report summarised in *The Lineage of Quraysh* by az-Zubayri, (p. 108)
240 *History* of at-Tabari (5:128)
241 *History* of at-Tabari (5:125)
242 *History* of at-Tabari (5:103-104)
243 *History* of at-Tabari (5:165-166)
244 *History* of at-Tabari (5:187)
245 Imam al-Bukhari related in the Book of Virtues (Book 61, Chap. 25, pt. 4, p. 177)
246 Imam al-Bukhari (Book 92, Chap. 2, pt. 8, p. 92)
247 *History* of at-Tabari (5:188)
248 *Musnad* of Ahmad ibn Hanbal (1:72, first edition, no. 526, second)
249 Imam Ahmad (1:73, no. 536)
250 *al-Bidaya wa an-Nihaya* (7:172)
251 See the *History* of at-Tabari (5:125).
252 *Book of the Tamhid* by Imam Abu Bakr al-Baqillani (pp. 220-227)
253 The *History* of at-Tabari (5:128-129).
254 (2:11-119, in the margin of the *Isaba*)
255 *Isaba* (2:72)
256 *History* of at-Tabari (5:127)
257 *al-Bidaya wa an-Nihaya* (7:181)
258 *Ansab al-Ashraf* (5:103)
259 *History* of at-Tabari (5:155)
260 *History* of at-Tabari (5:156)
261 *History* of at-Tabari (5:153)
262 Imam Abu Bakr al-Baqillani in his *Tamhid*, p. 231
263 Ibn 'Asakir related it (7:78)
264 *Tamhid* of al-Baqillani (p. 231, 235 and 236)
265 *Tamhid* by al-Baqillani, pp. 233-234
266 (Ibn Kathir, 7:230)
267 *History* of at-Tabari (5:127)
268 (Ibn Kathir 7:229)
269 *History* of at-Tabari (5:171. Look at 5:163)
270 *History* of at-Tabari (5:197)
271 *Fath al-Bari* 13:41-42
272 *Tamhid* of al-Baqillani, pp. 211-212, and p. 232
273 *History* of at-Tabari (3:16)
274 (*Isaba* 2:249)
275 (*The Revision of the Article*, al-Mamqani 1:197)
276 *History* of at-Tabari (5:161)
277 *History* of at-Tabari (5:174-175)
278 *History* of at-Tabari (5:175)
279 *History* of at-Tabari (5:175)
280 *History* of at-Tabari (5:176-177)
281 *History* of at-Tabari (5:177)

References

282 *History* of at-Tabari (5:178)
283 *History* of at-Tabari (5:179-182)
284 p. 80
285 *History* of at-Tabari (5:199)
286 *al-Bidaya wa an-Nihaya* (7:239)
287 *History* of at-Tabari (5:202-203)
288 *Minhaj as-Sunna* (2:185 and 3:225 & 241)
289 *History* of Ibn 'Asakir (7:85)
290 *History* of Ibn 'Asakir (7:86-87)
291 *Musnad* of Ibn Hanbal (2:446, first edition)
292 *Musnad* of Ibn Hanbal (5:218, first edition)
293 *Sunan* of Abu Dawud (Book 11, Chap. 1)
294 *al-Bidaya wa an-Nihaya* (5:215)
295 the Book of *The Imamate and Preference*, (included in Part 4 of the *Fasl*, p. 134)
296 *History* of at-Tabari (5:170)
297 Surat al-A'raf (7:169)
298 *Minhaj as-Sunna* (2:219)
299 *History* of at-Tabari (5:165)
300 *History* of at-Tabari (5:194)
301 *Sahih Muslim* (Book 12, *hadith* 150, pt. 3, p. 113)
302 *al-Bidaya wa an-Nihaya* (7:277)
303 Surat al-Hujurat (49:9)
304 Surat al-Hujurat (49:10)
305 *Sahih al-Bukhari* (Book 56, Chap. 17, pt. 3, p. 207)
306 *Minhaj as-Sunna* (2:219-220)
307 *Sahih al-Bukhari* (Book 64, Chap. 78, pt. 5, p. 129)
308 *Sahih Muslim* (Book 44, Chap. 31, pt. 7, p. 120)
309 Book of the conference of an-Najaf (pp. 25-27) published by as-Salafiyya
310 *Musnad* of Ibn Hanbal (1:84,118,119,152, first edition, no. 641, 670,950, 131, 1310, and in 4:281, 368,370, 372, first edition and 5:347,366, 370, 419, first edition)
311 The *tafsir* of al-Hasan al-Muthanna ibn al-Hasan as-Sibt ibn 'Ali ibn Abi Talib on this *hadith*, pp. 185-186
312 *al-Bidaya wa an-Nihaya* (7:20)
313 *al-Bidaya wa an-Nihaya* (7:325)
314 *Minhaj as-Sunna* (2:24)
315 *History* of Ibn 'Asakir (4:165)
316 Surat an-Nur (24:55)
317 *History* of Ibn 'Asakir (4:166)
318 *Sahih al-Bukhari*, the Book of the Raids, (Book 64, Chap. 73, pt. 5, p. 140-141)
319 *al-Bidaya wa an-Nihaya* (5:227 & 251)

320 *Musnad* of Ibn Hanbal, (1:263 & 325, no. 2374 & 2999)

321 The Book of the Virtues of the Companions from *Sahih al-Bukhari* (Book 62, Chap. 5, pt. 4, p. 191)

322 The Book of the Virtues of the Companions from *Sahih al-Bukhari* (Book 62, Chap. 5, pt. 4, p. 152)

323 The Book of Virtues of the Companions from *Sahih al-Bukhari* (pt. 4, p. 197)

324 *Sahih al-Bukhari* (pt. 4, pp. 190-191)

325 *Musnad* of Ibn Hanbal (1:270, no. 2432)

326 *al-Bidaya wa an-Nihaya* (5:229 & 230)

327 *Sahih al-Bukhari* (pt. 4, p. 193)

328 the Book of the Virtues of the Companions in *Sahih Muslim* (Book 62, chap, 5, pt. 4, p. 197)

329 the Book of the Virtues of the Companions in *Sahih Muslim* (Book 62, chap, 5, pt. 4, p. 200)

330 *Musnad* of Ibn Hanbal (6:144, first edition)

331 *Musnad* of Ibn Hanbal (6:47 & 106)

332 *Tabaqat* of Ibn Sa'd (3 (1):127)

333 *Musnad* of Abu Dawud at-Tayyalisi (*hadith* no. 1508)

334 the Book of Interpretation in *Sahih al-Bukhari* (Book 91, Chap. 47, pt. 8, pp. 83-84)

335 the Book of Dreams in *Sahih Muslim* (Book 47, *hadith* 17, pt. 7, pp. 55-56)

336 *Musnad* of Ibn Hanbal (1:236, first edition, no. 2113)

337 *Sunan* of Abu Dawud (Book 39, Chap. 8, *hadith* 4634)

338 *Jami' at-Tirmidhi* (Chap. 1)

339 *Musnad* of Ibn Hanbal (5:259, first edition)

340 Surat at-Tawba (9:40)

341 Surat an-Nur (24:55)

342 *Sahih al-Bukhari* (Book 10, Chaps. 39, 46,47, 67, 68 & 70, pt. 1, pp. 161-162 & 165, 174-176)

343 the Book of the Virtues of the Companions from *Sahih al-Bukhari* (Book 62, Chap. 8, pt. 4, pp. 204-207)

344 The *Great Tafsir* by Ibn al-'Arabi in eighty volumes. We spoke about it earlier.

345 *Fath al- Bari* (Book 57, Chap. 1, pt. 6, p. 125)

346 Ibn Hajar (6:125)

347 *Musnad* of Ibn Hanbal (1:130, p. 1078)

References

348 *Musnad* of Ibn Hanbal (1:156, no. 1339)
349 *al-Bidaya wa an-Nihaya* (5:250-251)
350 *al-Bidaya wa an-Nihaya* (7:323)
351 *Greater Sunan* of al-Bayhaqi (8:149)
352 the Book of Peace in *Sahih al-Bukhari* (Book 53, Chap. 9, pt. 3, p. 169)
353 the Book of Virtues of the Companions in *Sahih al-Bukhari* (Book 62, Chap. 22, pt. 4, p. 26)
354 *al-Bidaya wa an-Nihaya* (8:17019)
355 *History* of Ibn 'Asakir (4:211-212)
356 the Book of the Amirate in *Sahih Muslim* (Book 33, hadith 5,6,7,8,9,10, pt. 6, pp. 3-4)
357 the Book of the Judgments from *Sahih al-Bukhari* (Book 93, Chap. 51, pt. 8, pp. 125-127)
358 *Fath al-Bari* (13:162 and afterwards)
359 *Sunan* of Abu Dawud (Book 35, hadith 1)
360 *Jami' at-Tirmidhi* (Book 31, Chap. 46)
361 *Musnad* of Ibn Hanbal (1:398 & 406, no. 3781 & 3859)
362 *Collection of az-Zawa'id* (5:190)
363 *Musnad* of Ibn Hanbal (5:86 & 87 2 with three variants, 88, 89, & 90 with three variants, 92 with two variants, 98 with four variants, 899 with three variants, an 100, 101 with two variants, 106 with two variants, 107 with two variants and 108)
364 *Musnad* of Abu Dawud at-Tayyalisi (*hadith* 967 & 1278)
365 *Minhaj as-Sunna* (2:242)
366 *Fath al-Bari* (13:50)
367 *al-Bidaya wa an-Nihaya* (8:134)
368 *Minhaj as-Sunna* (p. 68)
369 *Sahih Muslim* (Book 33, hadith 86 & 66)
370 *History* of at-Tabari (6:188)
371 *al-Bidaya wa an-Nihaya*, 8:119
372 *al-Bidaya wa an-Nihaya* (8:135)
373 *Minhaj as-Sunna* (3:185)
374 the Book of the Virtues of the Companions from *Sahih al-Bukhari* (Book 62, Chap. 28, pt. 4, p. 219)
375 the Book of the Virtues from the *Jami' at-Tirmidhi* (Book 46, Chap. 47)
376 *al-Bidaya wa an-Nihaya* (8:120-121)
377 the Book of Jihad from *Sahih al-Bukhari* (Book 56, Chap. 3, pt. 3, p. 201)
378 the Book of the Emirate in *Sahih Muslim* (Book 33, hadith 160)
379 *al-Bidaya wa an-Nihaya* (8:229)

380 Referring to the hadith of Umm Haram that al-Bukhari has in the chapter on what has been said about fighting the Byzantines, hadith number 2924, "The first army in my umma to embark on the ocean will have necessitated [the Garden], and the first army of my umma to raid Caesar's city are forgiven." Ed.

381 *Minhaj as-Sunna* (3:185)

382 Look at p, 207-8 in this book.

383 *al-Bidaya wa an-Nihaya* (8:124-125)

384 *al-Bidaya wa an-Nihaya* (8:229)

385 Ibn Hanbal related in the Book of *Zuhd* (p. 172, Makkan edition)

386 *al-Bidaya wa an-Nihaya* (8:134)

387 *History* of Ibn 'Asakir (7, p. 6)

388 Surat al-Baqara (2:251)

389 *al-Ahkam as-Sultaniyya* (p. 5)

390 *The Imamate and Rivalry* by Abu Muhammad ibn Hazm included in part 3 of his book, *al-Fasl*, especially the section in it devoted to the Imamate of the less excellent (pp. 163-167, published in Egypt, 1320).

391 *Minhaj as-Sunna* (2:225)

392 the Book of Raids of *Sahih al-Bukhari* (Book 64, chap, 29, pt. 4, p. 47)

393 Surat al-Hujurat (49:10)

394 *Ansab al-Ashraf* (4:2: 53-54)

395 *al-Bidaya wa an-Nihaya* (8:233)

396 *al-Bidaya wa an-Nihaya* (8:228)

397 *Sahih al-Bukhari* (Book 64, Chap. 29, pt. 5, p. 48)

398 In the Book of Seditions from *Sahih al-Bukhari* (Book 92, Chap. 21, pt. 8, p.99)

399 Muslim related in the Book of the Amirate of his *Sahih* (Book 33, hadith 58, pt. 6, p. 22)

400 *al-Bidaya wa an-Nihaya* (8:233)

401 Qur'an, (43:86)

402 *al-Bidaya wa an-Nihaya*, pt.8, p. 143)

403 *History* of at-Tabari (6:197 has the texts of some of their letters and the names of some of the people involved.)

404 *History* of at-Tabari (6:196-197 and see 6:216 & 217)

405 *History* of at-Tabari (6:190-191)

406 *History* of at-Tabari (6:216-217)

407 (2:219)

408 *History* of at-Tabari 6:219-220

409 *History* of at-Tabari (6:196)

410 *History* of at-Tabari (6:215-216)

411 *History* of at-Tabari (6:216)

412 *History* of at-Tabari (6:218)

413 Sura Yunus (10:41)

References

414 *History* of at-Tabari (pp 291-292)
415 *al-Bidaya wa an-Nihaya* (pt. 8, p. 160)
416 *al-Bidaya wa an-Nihaya* (pp. 161-163)
417 *History* of at-Tabari (pt. 4, pp. 278-281)
418 *History* of at-Tabari (pt. 4, pp. 292-294)
419 *Muruj adh-Dhahab* (pt. 3, p. 141)
420 *History* of at-Tabari (pt. 4, pp. 282-286)
421 *Muruj adh-Dhahab* (pt. 3, p. 141)
422 Prof. Daruzah (8:384)
423 *History* of at-Tabari (pt. 4, p. 379; *al-Imama wa's-Siyasa*, pt. 1, p. 200)
424 Surat an-Nahl (16:92)
425 Prof. Daruzah (8: 383-384).
426 Al-Mas'udi (p. 313)
427 'Izza Daruzah (8:386)
428 See *Minhaj as-Sunna* (pp. 287-288)
429 *Muhadarat al-Khudri, the History of the Islamic Nations* (2:235)
430 From the *hadith* of 'Arfaja in the Book of the Amirate in *Sahih Muslim*, in the Chapter of the Judgments on someone who divides the Muslims when they are united (Book 33, *hadith* 59, pt. 6, p. 22).
431 Sura Ali 'Imran (3:138)
432 In the Book of the Amirate in *Sahih Muslim* from the *hadith* of Abu Dharr (Book 33, *hadith* 36, pt. 6, p. 14)
433 *History* of Ibn 'Asakir (5:409)
434 *History* of Ibn 'Asakir (5:406-407)
435 the Book of Judgments in the *Muwatta'* of Malik (Chap. 21, p. 740)
436 *Sahih al-Bukhari* (Book 34, Chap. 3)
437 *Sahih Muslim* (Book 17, Chap. 10, *hadith* 36)
438 Sura Ali 'Imran (3:103)
439 Surat al-Anfal (8:63)
440 the *Book of Gambling and Divining Arrows* by Ibn Qutayba (pp, 26-37)
441 *Tanqih al-Maqal* (2:272-273)
442 Chapter about Raped Women in the Book of Judgments in the *Muwatta'* (36.16)
443 the Book of the *Mukatab* in the *Muwatta'* (39:3)
444 *History* of Ibn 'Asakir (5:406)
445 *al-Bidaya wa an-Nihaya* (9:62-63)
446 In the Book of the Judgments of *Sahih al-Bukhari* (Book 93, Chap. 43, pt. 8, p. 122). Look at the *Great Sunan* by al-Bayhaqi (8:147).
447 Surat al-Baqara (2:134)

www.ingramcontent.com/pod-product-compliance
Lightning Source LLC
Chambersburg PA
CBHW030230170426

43201CB00006B/164